Hold My Hand

Glenys Carl was born in Wales, but now lives in Santa Fe in New Mexico. She works as a hospice nurse and also runs hospice volunteer classes. She was awarded Santa Fe's annual Spirit of the Community Prize in 2003. Her dream is to produce a video to teach others how to nurse a patient at home.

Hold My Hand

A Mother's Journey

Glenys Carl
& Steve Rada

Pan Books

First published 2005 by Sidgwick & Jackson

This paperback edition published 2006 by Pan Books
an imprint of Pan Macmillan Ltd
Pan Macmillan, 20 New Wharf Road, London N1 9RR
Basingstoke and Oxford
Associated companies throughout the world
www.panmacmillan.com

ISBN-13: 978-0-330-43761-5
ISBN-10: 0-330-43761-5

1 3 5 7 9 8 6 4 2

A CIP catalogue record for this book is available from
the British Library.

Typeset by Intype London Ltd
Printed and bound in Great Britain by
Mackays of Chatham plc, Chatham, Kent

I dedicate this book to
Scott
Samuel and Jonathan
My Grandchildren
Meghan, Louise, and Oscar Scott

Acknowledgements

I wish to thank and acknowledge the following people who have assisted me on my journey: Nick Evans, my special friend with his wisdom and open heart, who always believed in me and in Scott's story. He also believed in whatever endeavour I chose to follow. He spent many hours listening and comforting me, he brought me in from the storm at a crucial time in my life when I faltered, made me laugh, encouraged and supported me for many years and taught me to never give up on myself. Sheila Crowley, my agent, who believed in the story as soon as she read it and took it to where it is now, giving me guidance all the way with her beautiful heart and spirit. Also everyone at A. P. Watt who helped me with this book, especially Caradoc who, throughout the years, listened and helped bring this book to fruition. Ingrid Connell, my publisher at Pan Macmillan, a very special lady who took the story in her quiet, gentle manner, out into the world. Also everyone else at Pan Macmillan who assisted. Thanks to Steve Rada who helped me shape and write this story. To Robin, Rollie, Julie, Richard, Johnny and all the people who helped Scott and myself through all our ups and downs, laughter and tears, on both sides of the ocean, Australia and England. There are too many of you to write all your names, you know who you are. Please forgive me for not keeping in touch.

To the many doctors, nurses and physiotherapists who never gave up on us. My friend Bob O'Connor, who brought me to Santa Fe where I healed and found myself and my wonderful life here. My friends Sue, Phil and David, their son and Scott's first friend in the Santa Cruz mountains. They grew up together with mutual respect and love. To Scott's and my friend Niall, Scott's best mate as they grew together into manhood, who was there until the end like a true Irish friend. A special, special thanks to Stephen Mishra Suloway who listened to the story from beginning to end whilst I dictated all my thoughts, which took many hours. Celia Owens who helped me put my thoughts together throughout the years. Randall Cherry, Daniel Johnson and Henry Shukman, who sat with me trying to organize my writings from a box of papers. To Charlotte who bought my designs and shared her music with me. To Pamela who throughout the years supported me by buying my clothing. My neighbours who sometimes cried with me, Susan, Mary, Alexana, Wendy, Kirby, Robert, Karen and Alexandra who brought endless cups of hot chocolate and goodies to me. My other friend Susan who became my confidante and inspirational healer; I thank you. Also all my nursing colleagues who taught me so much. To my overseas friends, Jane who encouraged me years ago to tell the story, Philip and Giovanna. To my dear friends who have tended Scott Scott's grave over the years while I have been living in America: Wendy, Sue and her daughters Claire and Holly, and Howard who planted the bush of red berries at the foot. Whenever I visit there are snowdrops or bluebells or summer flowers growing. To Robin and the boys from King's College. Sister Bendall and Dr Jenkins who provided contant, steady encouragement, even after Scott's death. Babies Isabel and Sophie, my charges, who wrapped their little loving arms around me, reminding me to look into the future. My special time with John Bishop who nurtured me through the last two and a half years when I needed comfort.

My gift of my sons Samuel, and Jonathan and his wife Ulla, giving me courage through my many crying days, and my three grandchildren, Meghan, Louise and Oscar Scott who have truly loved me through my journey of life and reminded me to laugh at myself. And of course Scott who taught me my joy and my strength and furthered my spiritual growth. I miss him. We must remember that we are nothing without love, and miracles happen every day.

I have written this book for all those mothers and fathers who have lost a child. I know the pain in their heart.

Foreword by Nicholas Evans

In the early spring of 1994 I went to New Mexico to see a man about a horse. At the time I was a struggling screenwriter with a drawer full of unsold scripts and a bank manager banging ever louder on the door. I hadn't told him – or anyone but my wife and kids – about the crazy idea for a novel that I was working on. Back then hardly anyone knew the term 'horse whisperer', not even those who are now known as such: men like Ray Hunt, who is one of the world's finest. It was Ray that I'd gone out there to see.

At that time he and his wife were working at the somewhat ominously named Dead Horse Ranch, some thirty miles out of Santa Fe. Ray likes horses a lot more than he likes people. There's no such thing as a man with a horse problem, he told me, only horses with man problems. He'd seen it again and again: gentle, beautiful animals turned dangerous and demented by the foolishness and cruelty of human beings. Nevertheless, he was courteous and patiently answered all my dumb questions. I watched him work some young colts and was greatly moved by their mutual love and understanding.

A friend of mine, a film producer called Bob O'Connor, had just built a fabulous new house in the desert just outside Santa Fe and he had kindly offered me a bed for the night. More than that, he laid on a dinner party to welcome me. The other guests were friends and neighbours, all of them pleasant and interesting. But there was someone else at the table, a little bird of a woman with a strange mid-Atlantic accent and the most luminous grey-blue eyes I'd ever seen. Her name was Glenys Carl and, from what I could gather, she was Bob's friend, lodger and temporary housekeeper. She had an aura of gentle wisdom and I couldn't stop staring at her.

I can't remember how the subject came up but she mentioned that she had spent some time in Sydney, a place that I love and had recently lived for a while, making a couple of films for TV. I asked her what had taken her there and for a moment she didn't answer. Instead she looked at Bob and I realized that she was asking his permission to tell me. He nodded and the whole table went quiet as Glenys told the story of what happened to her son Scott.

Looking back on it, I know I was in a rather heightened emotional state at that time. Frankly, I felt a failure. All my ambition and hard work to become a Hollywood screenwriter had come to nothing. I didn't know how I was to go on supporting my wife and children. Also, the story I was researching was affecting me profoundly. I had been travelling the American West, all on my own in this vast open country, and watching these astonishing horsemen save fearful, traumatized horses with love and gentle understanding. It had opened my heart and made me raw. I was probably having my mid-life crisis.

Anyway, whatever the reasons, as I listened to Glenys finish her story, I started to cry. It was so embarrassing. I tried not to, then did my best to disguise it, but to no avail. Pretty soon everyone was looking elsewhere, pretending not to notice. The dinner party never quite recovered. I felt like Banquo's ghost.

Hold My Hand

Looking back, I think what got me going was a combination of Glenys's clear blue eyes and the utter lack of self-pity in the way she told this extraordinary tale of courage, endurance, tragedy and love. It was as if what had happened had filled her with a sort of beneficent light. And talking more with her the following day, I realized that this wasn't simply a story about a mother and a son. It was also about the many lives the two of them had transformed. I never had the privilege of meeting Scott, but I believe my life was changed that night by meeting his mother. Glenys's spirit and some of the other things she told me found their way into *The Horse Whisperer*. In fact, there's even a character in the novel who is loosely based on her: Terri, Grace Maclean's physical therapist in Montana.

We became friends. And for several years afterwards we wrestled with how her story might best get told. She said she wasn't a writer. So should I try to write it? Should we hire someone else to? Should we see if we could get it going as a film?

Glenys is a woman of many talents. She designs and makes the most exquisite clothes from fabric that she weaves herself. This could easily have made her a fortune, were it not for the fact that she prefers to devote her life instead to helping others. She works, for next to nothing, as a hospice nurse, helping Aids patients and others who are terminally ill die in peace and dignity. She was recently voted 'Spirit of the Community', an annual award bestowed by the people of Santa Fe.

It soon became clear to us both that, despite all her modesty and reticence, this was a story that Glenys herself had to tell. Now, at last, with Steve's help, she has done so, and in a way that will move anyone who reads it, just as it moved me that night ten years ago.

Hold My Hand

In another era or culture, this astonishing person, so deceptively slight and fragile-looking but with the heart of a tiger, a woman who has moved so many mountains and enhanced so many lives, might have been called a saint or an angel. I've come to think of her as a kind of 'people whisperer'.

Nicholas Evans

One

On a snowy night, in a flat on the outskirts of Stuttgart, Germany, the harsh rasp of a phone shocks me from my dream with the subtlety of an air-raid siren. I manage to crack one eye open enough to see the glow of the clock: 1:00 A.M. Who would be calling at this hour? And on a Sunday morning. I give my German boyfriend Stefan a small shove with my bare heel that hardly rocks his six-foot frame. Surely he can't sleep through this clamour. I shove him again, harder.

'Hallo,' Stefan says groggily. 'Ja. Sie ist hier.' He rolls over and sticks the receiver to my ear. 'For you.'

Sitting up, I fumble to untangle the phone cord. Who would it be? After only seven months in Stuttgart I have made few friends. My boys wouldn't be calling at this hour. The oldest, Samuel, is working in Connecticut; Jonathan, my middle son, is at university in Denmark. My youngest, Scott, is away in Australia, finding himself and his strength as a young adult on a new adventure. Unless something dreadful has happened.

'Hello?' My voice is thin and scratchy.

'Is this Mrs Carl?' It's a man's voice, deep and resonant and very Australian.

Still trapped in the web of sleep, I hesitate before answering. 'Yes.'

'Do you have a son named Scott Carl?'

The question hits me like wind-blown hail. 'Yes,' I whisper.

'I'm with the Sydney Police Department. I'm sorry to be the one bearing this news, but there has been a serious accident. Your son was found unconscious, in a coma.'

'No, no!' My maternal denial kicks into gear. 'Not my baby. Are you sure?' The news is impossible to take in. Please, God, let this be a dream.

'Are you there, Mrs Carl?'

'What happened?' I ask. Stefan clicks on the table light, burning my eyes and filling the room with disorienting shadows.

'Your son was found in the basement of his block of flats. We've taken him to St Vincent's Hospital.'

'How did it happen?' I keep saying.

'We don't know. He wasn't able to speak. I regret to tell you that he may not last the night. Can you come immediately?'

'Yes, of course. Oh, my God. I'll be there as soon as I can. Please tell Scott I'm coming. Tell him to hang on.'

'Let me give you some phone numbers,' the Australian says uncomfortably, knowing there is precious little else he can do.

Stefan ruffles about the bedside table for a pencil. As I scribble the numbers of the hospital and police station on a scrap of paper, I glance at my boyfriend and catch the glint of sadness in his eyes, as if he senses our life together has changed for ever. My mind is already rushing halfway around the world; my body will soon follow.

I dial the hospital with shaky fingers and request the Intensive

Care Unit. A nurse answers and I explain who I am. 'How is Scott doing?' I ask, still unbelieving, still hoping to prove the policeman wrong.

'He's about to go into surgery,' the nurse answers in a kind but professional manner. 'We're trying to relieve pressure on his brain. I would suggest you come right over. Where are you calling from?'

'Germany.'

'I see.' The nurse quiets as she wrestles with the distance. 'Do try to hurry. The doctor will call when there is more news.'

Tears stream down my face as I pass the phone back to Stefan. I plead with God not to let my baby die. I want to hold him, to climb into bed with him and tell him all is okay, as I did when he was a small child afraid of thunder. He should not die without his family at his side. I take a deep breath and wipe my face. It's time to pull myself together. Time to be strong. I must get to Australia.

∾

Only a week before, my twenty-one-year-old son had called me from Sydney with glowing tales of life down under. The beach, the sun, the sense of freedom. The easiness of the people. His flat on Potts Hill was right on the ocean. He could watch the sunrises. He was in heaven. 'Mom, guess what: I'm going to play rugby for the Sydney Welsh Rugby Team.' He was over-the-moon excited, telling me that he would be training hard, sleeping more, running each day a little further, eating better. His enthusiasm was catching. I reminisced about how I'd go watch my boyfriend play rugby when I was a teenager, and how it was such a part of Welsh life: the singing, the playing, the roar of the crowd, and after the game, the camaraderie.

There and then I wanted to hold him but he was in another land finding out about himself. I could just imagine his big grin when he called to tell me about playing against the Kings Cross Bushwhackers: 'It was great, I scored twice and was given the Best and Fairest Players Award. We lost but that's okay; they're a big tough club.'

'That's wonderful, Scott.' I was so proud – such an impressive award.

'It's not a big deal Mom, the award,' he said with a disarming laugh. 'You see, my position was flyback. One of my mates pitched me the ball and I had a good shot at another score, but when I was tackled by this big fellow, one of their "piggies", he hit me pretty hard. When I was down he added an elbow.'

'That sounds awful,' I gasped.

My son was athletic, with broad shoulders and great strength for his size, but he was not the most imposing. Rugby is such a rough game.

'Are you sure you're all right?'

'I'm fine. My ribs are a little sore, but you know how it is when you're the new kid in town. He probably wanted to see if I'd get up. Anyway, a couple of mates said the ref should have called a penalty, but he didn't. So they were all steamed to lay out their flyback. I told them to forget it – it was probably an accident. Besides, Mom, you always said getting even doesn't solve anything. For some reason that tackle and scoring twice got me the award.'

Scott typically shrugged it off; in a couple of days he'd be right as rain. He could never accept that meanness was deliberate.

'You will love this, Mom. After the game in the clubhouse, the team sang the Welsh National Anthem, "Hen Wlad fy Nhadau" – Land of My Fathers. It's great; I'll sing it for you sometime. Well, I have to go now.' These were his final words. 'Love you. Have you heard of that song?'

'Yes, sweetie. I loved to sing it to you in Welsh when you were a child, and as a baby on those colicky nights.'

∾

Should I call Sammy, my eldest son? I can't even think what time it might be in Connecticut. What about Jonathan, my middle one? Knowing he faces exams and will run a marathon later this week, I decide to let him sleep. My concern is for naught: Jonathan calls a few minutes later, having already heard from Sammy. The Australians have called everyone they can locate. Jonathan wants to come with me but I tell him no, that he should let me go first and see the situation. I assure him Scott will be fine. Will he? I wish I was sure. Here I am trying to keep everyone else calm while I'm on the verge of coming apart.

After Jonathan hangs up, I sit with the quilt wrapped tightly round my body, drop my head onto my bent knees and close my eyes to gather strength.

Oh, Scotty, my Scotty, born in England, growing to exuberant manhood in America, near death in Australia. I will battle the world to be at your side.

∾

In emotional turmoil, I circle the flat wondering what to fit into the tattered suitcase lying open in the contour of the warm spot in our bed. What does one pack for someone in a coma? Memories perhaps, friendly and familiar? Scott's brown Paddington teddy bear is unearthed from my cupboard of keepsakes. And his music. Yes, I mustn't forget his music. The Spyro Gyro tapes Scott left at Christmas are assigned a corner niche. A few photos will be helpful when he comes out of the coma.

From the cupboard I retrieve a small antique cherrywood chest I had just bought the day before, a special place to keep my photos of the children, the few I could afford when they were still young, and select a handful. There's the one of us all walking on the beach in Westport, Connecticut, another of Scott fishing, and a more recent one of the three brothers laughing together over Sunday night dinner, their heads together as they compare peach-fuzz beards.

Yesterday was May Day and the first warm day of the year. Stefan's two brothers appeared out of the blue. Wolfgang had come from Munich, and Eckhert from outside Hamburg. Neither knew the other was coming. Wolfgang is an appraiser of castle antiques, and travels widely throughout Europe. Thanks to him our flat is adorned with elegant seventeenth- and eighteenth-century furniture. No sooner had Stefan's brothers arrived than we were off to the antique market in the small city of Tübingen. It was like a journey into the past, the open market crowded with eager shoppers, bright red and golden yellow flags snapping in the wind and string music from musicians in medieval garb. I bought the antique cherrywood chest in a fit of sentimentality.

After extracting the photos, I close my chest of memories, slowly run my hand over its polished top and return it to the cupboard.

After the Tübingen market, the three brothers rowed me about Lake Neckar in a flat-bottomed wood boat painted bright white with green stripes. Laughing and splashing, we were ecstatic about the return of warm weather, however temporary it would prove. Later, home for dinner, a headache suddenly overcame me. I rarely get headaches and found the throbbing pain in my temple odd. Slipping into the bathroom for aspirin, I glanced in the mirror and noticed my left eyelid had grown red and puffy. Stefan looked at my eye and suggested an insect had bitten me at the lake. Perhaps so, but I didn't remember it happening.

Despite the headache, an unusual sensation of warmth flowed through my body. Perhaps it was because I had raised three sons and here I was enjoying the company of three grown brothers. Later that night, as I drifted into a contented sleep, the warmth continued and I dreamt sweetly of my boys. We were so far apart, yet strangely I had never felt so close. That was when the phone rudely jarred me awake.

Hours later, at four a.m., as I haphazardly pack for Australia, my mind a jumble of emotions, the phone rings again.

'For you,' Stefan says.

I grab it from his hand and slide onto the bed next to my suitcase. 'Yes,' I whisper.

'This is Dr Croches calling.' The calm voice in my ear is distant and surreal, speaking from another planet. 'I'm a neurosurgeon at St Vincent's Hospital in Sydney. Your son has just come out of surgery. He's still in a coma, but we were able to relieve some of the pressure on his brain.'

'Do you know what happened?' I interrupt.

'Well, not exactly. It appears that he was hit in the left eye and fell about twenty feet. The evidence suggests his head struck the cement floor. I'm told he was not found for about ten hours.'

I touch my swollen left eye and recall my headache. 'Please, please save him,' I plead.

'We're doing our best,' Doctor Croches replies. 'We'll know more after we run some tests.' There is something in his voice that warns me he knows more than he is telling.

'I'll be on the next available flight,' I hasten to assure him.

∾

At the bathroom sink, I wash the tears from my eyes and study myself in the mirror. My sandy-blonde hair, usually a bit wild, has become a shoulder-length rat's nest. I must have gone to bed with my hair still damp from the lake. Thin bolts of red lightning accent the whites of my blue eyes; my left eye socket is now circled with a bluish bruise. Half-heartedly I run a brush through the tangles before giving up. Who cares how I look anyway?

Rooted by a sense of helplessness, I turn to gaze out the bathroom window into the first light of day. Although it is May the mornings are still dark, the trees still naked and the skies leaden with grey. It has started to snow. Tiny snowflakes drift gently earthward through stark-black boughs. Water drips down the windowpane like tears as I look out and think of Scott.

Where will I find the strength for this journey? I am frightened and dig deep inside me for courage. Just yesterday, the cold world outside this window had been so warm and friendly, filled with eternal hope. Today I am overcome with anxiety and a sense of urgency. A mother protects her children at all costs. I can do this. *I must do it.* I will make it to Scott and he will be waiting for me.

I stand before my open, half-packed suitcase wondering what else to include, but draw a blank. Snapping it shut, I stand it on the floor.

Stefan has been on the phone dialling one number after another, relieved to have something to do besides watch in helpless silence. He has me booked on a flight from Stuttgart to London Heathrow. The next 747 from London to Sydney leaves tonight, and to depart London I'll need an Australian visa. But it's Sunday morning and the Australian Consulate in Bonn is closed. Stefan tries the police. They are sympathetic but unable to help. Losing patience, I take the phone and dial the consulate's emergency number, finally rousing a clerk. With my situation stated and restated emphatically, I am eventually transferred to the duty officer.

'Sorry, but the consul is at a hotel for a private breakfast,' the duty officer explains in a drowsy voice. 'Call back tomorrow.'

I am in no mood for niceties. Polite but firm, I guilt him into revealing the phone number of the hotel. I dial again and insist on speaking with the consul. I am learning how to cajole and salt my pleadings with words like 'life' and 'death' and 'emergency'. Moments later an authoritative voice comes on.

'Yes, madam,' the consul responds crisply, his Australian patience strained, suiting a man dragged from his bratwurst and eggs.

Suppressing my frustration, I explain my predicament for the nth time.

'I understand your plight, Mrs Carl, but countries have strict rules,' he replies firmly. 'You will need a visa to enter Australia.'

His inability to understand confuses me. What is there about 'death' and 'emergency' this man fails to grasp? My voice raises one notch of urgency. Again, I explain the severity of my situation. Professionally polite, the consul invites me to visit his office the next morning.

'But it's a ten-hour drive to Bonn and then back,' I press. 'That's two days on the road; two days of lost precious time. Don't you

13

understand?' I press harder adding a steely edge to my voice. 'My son is dying *now*. I can't wait until Monday. *You're* the only one who can help me. How can you get me on the plane to Sydney tonight?' I refuse to let him off the phone and his breakfast is getting cold.

I hear an aggravated sigh. 'Truly, I'm very sorry,' the consul says again, this time with less conviction, 'but there is nothing I can do.'

I am near panic now. My mind is racing. There has to be an angle. Where's his soft spot? 'I must ask you one thing, sir. Do you have children?' I wait. The silence drags. I sense his discomfort.

The consul clears his throat. 'Perhaps I might fax the airlines an authorization, some form of waiver,' he says quietly.

'Yes. Yes, a waiver.' That would be perfect.

'I'll see if someone can meet you in Sydney, to stamp your passport at that end. We can try it. That's the best I can do.'

'Thank you, thank you.'

'I'll do what I can, Mrs Carl. Best of luck.'

༄

Stefan drives me the fifteen kilometres to Stuttgart's Echterdingen Airport. Absently, I watch the wintry German landscape slip by. Light snow still falls and traffic slows to a crawl. The windscreen wipers slap away the white froth. Sensing my mood of detachment Stefan drives in silence, a silence that seems only to magnify the growing gulf between us. I shift uncomfortably in the seat.

Stefan is a good man but not the same man I fell in love with a little over three years ago.

༄

I was with friends at Sunday brunch in the garden restaurant of an old inn in Westport, Connecticut when I first noticed him sitting behind me at another table. By chance we began to talk and I was instantly attracted to his quick laugh and the way it sparked his blue-grey eyes. Tall and athletic with a gentle face and a strong jawline, Stefan was thirty-nine at the time and a computer engineer doing work for Mercedes Benz. I was a few years older, raising three teenage boys. We dated for three years before he announced his company was transferring him back to Stuttgart.

'Come with me,' he had implored. 'You must experience Germany. I promise, if you don't like it I will stay only one year and we will return.' By that time my boys were sufficiently independent, and I agreed. One year would not be difficult, so I believed.

But I had not adjusted well. The winter was long, dark and wet. Stefan worked all day and quickly regressed into the way his mother and German society had raised him to be. On my own I worked hard to adapt, but there seemed to be an indecipherable code of strict rules and customs. I laboured to learn German, but feared to open my mouth because every word I mispronounced brought an instant and humourless Teutonic correction from neighbours and shopkeepers.

In our block of flats a large black placard appeared on our door when it was my turn to sweep the stairwell, shovel the pavement, or wash the windows, even when encrusted with ice. My easy-going lightheartedness silently died and I was left feeling joyless and empty. Stefan never again spoke of returning to Westport, as he had promised.

The full import of Stefan's German conditioning did not hit me until the first time we visited his childhood home to meet his parents. They lived in a comfortable, middle-class, three-storey house made of dark brick with a steeply pitched roof of grey slate. It was set behind a green hedge and flanked by a row of mature winter trees. Approaching their front door, Stefan overtly threw my hand away and moved two steps in front of me. Only later was I to learn he had been cautioned not to bring his previously married, mother of three children, Welsh girlfriend home with him.

The matron of the house, Madame Heller, short in hair, stature and temperament, greeted her son with nothing more than a firm handshake and a flurry of German instructions. She sternly whisked me away to a guestroom, well separated from Stefan's bedroom.

'You'll take this room,' Madame ordered in perfect English.

It was her house, and if she did not wish to acknowledge that her son and I slept together that was fair enough. Instead of recognizing my fatigue and offering me a rest while she and Stefan headed for the supermarket, Madame Heller ordered me to unpack the suitcases, iron her son's clothing and hang it in the fresh air. I kept waiting for Stefan to intercede and stick up for me but he accepted his mother's dominance without a hint of protest.

With Stefan's clothing dutifully waving in the breeze, I explored the rest of the house and joyfully discovered a piano in the living room. This alone would make my visit tolerable and I quickly reacquainted myself with the beauty of the instrument by wading into Beethoven's 'Moonlight Sonata', albeit raggedly and in my own key. I missed my piano. I had started playing on my grandmother's piano when I was four years old, just tapping out little tunes I would make up. During the war, under siege with the German bombing of my native city of Cardiff in Wales, my grandmother moved her piano down into the family air-raid shelter so they might enjoy music by candlelight during those long, dangerous nights. Stefan had promised to buy me one, but like his talk of returning to Westport, nothing had come of it.

My imaginative rendition of 'Moonlight Sonata' had drawn Stefan's father, Dr Heller, to the room. A kindly man in his sixties, grinning broadly, he withdrew sheet music from the piano bench and demonstrated his talents as a classical pianist with passion and grace. For the first time I felt welcome. At least we could communicate through our music. But our private concert came to an abrupt halt when Madame stormed into the room. Slamming the keyboard shut she ordered, 'Stop that noise! We have no time for such nonsense.'

Later, I asked Stefan why he never told me his father was such an accomplished musician. 'I didn't know,' he replied sadly.

After several days, when Stefan and I were about to depart, Madame appeared with a stack of freshly pressed underwear and pyjamas. The label 'Stefan Heller' had been carefully sewn into the waistband of each, as if she were sending her son off to summer camp. Stefan, who would have made great fun of this in America, remained silent, his eyes downcast.

∾

As Stefan manoeuvres his Mercedes onto the airport road, it strikes me that I am really leaving this place. Dressed in brown snow pants, a yellow silk blouse and laced-up fur-lined winter boots, I have nothing but a suitcase full of memories, several hundred American dollars and a heavy heart. Everything else I have left in Stefan's flat. My instinct tells me I will never see this man, or my belongings, again. I've always professed my roots are in myself, not in my possessions, and now my challenge is to live what I preach.

Stefan finally breaks the silence. 'When will you be back?' The thinness of his voice tells me he knows the answer.

'I don't know,' I say, avoiding his look.

But I do know. Germany will never be my home again. Still, my relationship with him feels uncomfortably unfinished. I think of my cherrywood chest filled with the rarest of all my treasures, the baby photos of my boys. Certainly I'll be back for that. Won't I?

Arriving at the airport departure kerb, I suddenly realize I have forgotten my jacket. The fresh snow has dropped the temperature back to winter digits and my teeth chatter uncontrollably. Clothing had seemed so unimportant when I was packing. Stefan assures me he will send it along to Australia, if I need it, then leaves me with a final silent hug. I hurry inside to join the ticket queue.

I've had only three hours' sleep in the last thirty-six, but still I cannot sleep on the London-bound plane. My body is a raging battleground between the forces of adrenaline and exhaustion. At least I'm moving forward, one step closer to Scott. After a few hours' stopover I'll catch a British Airways night flight to Sydney, via Dubai and Singapore. I pray to God that Scott will survive, that I will reach him in time and my love will piece him back together. Deep in my soul I know he's waiting for me. My guardian angels have never let me down. As long as the airline received the consul's fax, as long as I maintain momentum, who needs sleep?

But the stone faces of the agents at the British Airways counter at Heathrow tell me a different story. They have no idea what I'm talking about. 'Passports need to be stamped before you can fly,' states a round man with a balding head and thick sideburns. 'Those are the rules.'

'But the Australian Consul made special arrangements. Didn't you get his fax?'

'Oh that,' the round man says. 'Yes, we received that fax. But we don't accept faxed waivers. How do we know it's real? Maybe your Australian lover faxed you a visa waiver to spare you the trouble.'

My knees tremble in anger. I'm utterly exhausted, but furious at his insinuation. This time my rat-nest hair and blackened eye become assets. Looking a little crazy can't hurt. I lean into the counter and glower.

'It takes fifteen minutes to get a visa when the consulate is open,' I say icily. 'Do I look like the kind of person who would go to all this trouble to hunt down the consul on a Sunday morning just to save fifteen minutes? Look in my passport. Go ahead. I've never been to Australia before. How could I possibly have a boyfriend there? And even if I did, why would he break the law to spend a few days with me?' I lower my voice and say adamantly, *'My son is dying.* Don't you understand?'

The agent is unmoved. 'Then you'll need to get your passport stamped at the consulate in London tomorrow morning. That's how the system works.'

'My passport will be stamped in Australia,' I fairly shout, my face flushing red. 'The consul told you that.'

I try to calm myself. Pleading worked with the consul, and maybe that's the key here. But these stone faces have heard it all. Every bloody story mankind has invented has been tried on these people. I am in tears by now and if this doesn't work the wrath of a pious

Welsh mother who has been praying to God since early this morning will descend upon their heads. Reason abandons me and I persevere on willpower alone.

'You can call St Vincent's Hospital yourself,' I tell him coldly. 'If that doesn't work, call the Sydney police.' I tear a corner off a piece of official-looking paper and scribble. 'Here are their numbers. I will wait right here.'

The agent is taken aback. 'Most irregular,' he mumbles, reluctantly accepting the scrap of paper. 'Please, go and sit down. We will try to sort this out.' Turning his attention to the queue, he motions with a hand: 'Next in line, please!'

The 747 is loading while I sit in desperation on the concrete floor, my knees drawn tight to my chest, gently rocking. My yellow silk blouse is pasted to the perspiration on my back. My heart begins to race; my breathing builds fuller, louder. *I must get on this plane.* What's the key? What haven't I thought of yet?

Bolting to the counter, I demand, 'You must let me on that plane. Or else.'

Or else what? What could I do? What would make them feel threatened by me? But the breaking voice of this wild-haired woman teetering on the edge of destruction certainly has his attention. I look the little balding man directly in the eye, trying to connect with his soul. Surely he has a family. Surely there is someone he loves. 'What have you found out?' I demand. 'Did you speak to the hospital? Did you call the police?'

'We did.' The agent exhales exasperation and throws up his hands. 'Look, I don't doubt your story but that still doesn't solve our problem of no visa.'

The final call for the flight is announced. I have to act now.

Taking a deep breath, I launch my assault. 'How would you like it if I climbed up on this ticket counter and shouted to the entire airport what you're doing to me?'

His eyes widen. 'Most irregular,' he mutters. This is not proper British behaviour, his nervous hands tell me.

A few people have stopped to listen. I raise my voice. 'I'll call the newspapers; I'll call the television stations; I'll scream on the steps of parliament; I'll tell the whole bloody world that my son is dying and your stone-faced airline cares more about their stupid rules and stamped bits of paper than it does about a mother who is trying to reach her dying son!'

The agent swallows and silently surveys my determined stare. Sizing up my menacing five-foot-two Welsh frame and my seven stone of quaking fury, he wisely slips me a boarding pass across the counter.

Two

As the dead hours of flight drag on, I slip into a relaxed but frazzled space. No sleep can penetrate my shock and the determination that propels me onward. The flight attendant asks if she can get me something to eat, but I am not hungry. She suggests tea and I absently consent, but when the small china teapot appears on my tray, I take only a few sips. Noticing I am not dressed for travel, she kindly unfolds a blanket and drapes it about me. A few passengers, who had overheard my impassioned plea with the ticket agent, glance my way with sympathetic eyes, but I have no desire to speak to strangers. The flight attendant comes by again and whispers that there is a vacant seat in first class. She smuggles me up the stairs of the 747 into the top deck where I curl my small frame into a luxuriously wide leather seat with few neighbours. How I wish there were someone in the next seat, someone who loves me, someone to put their arms around me and share my burden. But it isn't to be. I am flying to a far-off continent where I am a total stranger, known to no one, knowing no one, without support or income, and no plan beyond getting to the hospital. It is not the first time I have found myself tackling seemingly impossible tasks, but I know this will be the hardest test yet.

∽

I was born Glenys Margaret in Cardiff on a wet and cold winter's morning. Within months of my birth, my father, Francis, was shipped to Burma by the British Army. He survived the war but did not return to his family. I would never know him and in later years, when I would ask my mother about him, she would snap, 'Don't ask such questions,' and so I never did.

My mother, Gladys, born the ninth of ten children into a boisterous Welsh family, was only eighteen when I arrived. My earliest memory of her is of a distant but beautiful woman, five-foot-five, of slender build with long legs and blonde, wavy, shoulder-length hair that framed deep-set blue eyes. She had an elegant smile that would light up her face, when she smiled, which wasn't often, perhaps due to the pain of being a teenage mother left with an unwanted child. Later, when deliverymen would stop by the back door, they would always ask me, 'Is your beautiful mother around?' To which I would invariably reply, 'No.'

No sooner did my father leave for Burma than my mother was conscripted into a bomb-making factory in Cardiff, along with hundreds of other healthy young women. I was handed to my mother's mother, who was too old for war work. She owned a house in Cardiff which she shared with my mother and I, but during the war she took me to be raised on one of the family's two farms, Marble Hall in Pembrokeshire, on the west coast of Wales. My grandmother's name was Margaret Elizabeth Best, but I knew her simply as Nanna. I remember her as a small woman dressed in navy blue, buttoned up, with a white collar. She had silver-white hair, brown eyes and a full mouth set in a rounded face. I loved sleeping with her in the softness of her big feather bed.

Nanna was a herbalist, and dabbled in astrology and numerology long before they were popular. People seeking her homegrown cures would come to the back door daily. She loved weaving. After the sheep were sheared, she would teach me how to spin and dye the wool, knit and weave. What I learned of colours and design at her elbow would serve me well in later years as I struggled to make a living. Nanna worked hard while singing all the time and she expected me to share the chores. At her side I felt safe.

Marble Hall was a seventeenth-century manor house of grey Welsh stone with a pitched slate roof, three storeys tall with drafty wood windows and damp stone walls. We were constantly cold from the harsh winds coming off the frigid North Atlantic, our only heat being sooty coal-burning fireplaces in every room. Nanna soon handed me a wire scrubber and my job, at the age of three, was to scrub the fire grates with black lead until they shone, whereupon Nanna would pile in the coal and light another fire. I was also charged with scrubbing the front stone steps. I remember thinking, 'Why am I scrubbing these grates when Nanna immediately lights another fire? Why am I cleaning the steps when, as soon as someone walks in, they are dirty again?' I soon forgot, though, as I made toast on a long fork over the fire, and ate it with the butter dripping all over my fingers and chin.

The house was surrounded by rolling green fields dotted with sheep and cattle. Relieved of my chores, I would make my way to the farmyard to mingle with the cows, sheep, horses, pheasants and chickens. They became my first playmates and introduced me to nature in its simplest form. My solitary walks across the moors instilled in me a strong streak of independence and rugged self-reliance. It was not uncommon for me, at four years old, to board a bus, even change buses, to roam the countryside in search of primroses and bluebells.

Those early days on my own toughened me up but also taught me the importance of reaching out to others. In wartime, people settle into the present moment and surrender to whatever life offers. They are joined in common suffering and, more often than not, try to relieve each other's burdens through small gifts and sharing what little they have. No opportunity to laugh, to enjoy and to feel human is ever missed.

After the war ended I was sent back to Cardiff to live with my mother and to attend school. Shortly after returning, at four and a half years old, I walked by myself, a mile and a half through open fields to Baden Powell elementary school and told the School Master, Mr Evans, that I was ready to start school.

'Where is your mother?' he asked in amazement.

'That doesn't matter,' I told him firmly. 'I am ready to start school, right now.'

Mr Evans sent me home to get my mother and eventually I was enrolled.

Walking to school each day, I would stop to collect broken china from bombed-out buildings. When I found a particularly beautiful piece, I'd fantasize about the house it came from, where it belonged, in the kitchen or the dining room, in the pantry or a bedroom, and who might have lived there. Instead of taking my treasures home, I'd keep them in my school desk. I suppose school was the safest place I knew back then.

As I walked around town, I would talk to everyone I met. Much to my mother's horror, I befriended Sam, the town tramp. He was a thick-set man with bright, dark eyes. He had a dingy handkerchief about his throat and wore an old woollen sweater with holes at the elbows and a dark, stained floppy felt hat. Sam survived part of the year by picking blackberries outside town to sell door to door. I often joined him in this endeavour after school. Although rejected by many of the townspeople, he turned out to be a wise man teaching me much about life through stories drawn from nature. I suppose I was too young to notice if Sam was really 'all there' or not, but he was my friend and I trusted him. I believe the trust of strangers I was to pass on to my boys was a gift from my days with Sam.

Upon my return from Marble Hall, I was also to meet my new stepfather, Edward Worth, whom Mum called Ted. Divorce was difficult to obtain under Welsh law, so Ted and my mum lived together for many years before they were legally married. But from the first moment I laid eyes on his compact, masculine frame with its broad shoulders, large sea-roughened hands and green-brown eyes accentuated by a shock of black hair, he became 'Dad' to me.

Mum had met Ted at a dance during the war. He commanded a minesweeper, which was part of the immense flotilla of ships and fishing trawlers that rescued the badly beaten British troops from the shores of Dunkirk in June of 1940. Mum was all of twenty, fourteen years his junior, and was no doubt swept away by this most distinguished man resplendent in his gold-trimmed naval uniform. Ted was a good man and to me, larger than life. He had an expansive sense of humour, a love of the sea, a passion for adventure and an unquenchable thirst for usquebaugh, his 'water of life', Scotch whisky.

After the war, Dad returned to his fishing trawler, the *Cardiff*

Lady, a beautiful boat about seventy-five feet long with a black hull, grey deck and topside. Dad would often take me down to his trawler before he put to sea. I can still smell the mix of salt and diesel and see the rigging strung with ropes and layers of sagging nets and hear the squawking of white seagulls that hovered in the stiff sea breeze over the stern. Dad led a hard life. With his crew of fourteen, he would roam as far as Greenland and Iceland for weeks at a time, battling freezing gales. Upon his return, the hold of the *Cardiff Lady* was filled with halibut, cod, hake, sole, and sometimes, shrimp. Afterwards, Dad would return to his favourite pub, the Moorland, and to his solace, Scotch whisky.

I loved Dad, when he was sober. And he loved me. Dad made me feel respected and understood, and with Mum affording me little attention, I would shadow Dad whenever I could. Because I would never speak around my mother, when I was with my Dad and had his attention I became a chatterbox. One time, when I wouldn't stop talking, Dad rolled me up in a fish net and hung me on a hook on the back door, then threw a blanket over me to quiet me down.

When I was five I had my tonsils removed and couldn't speak. Dad placed me on the sofa in the living room at night, while he slept on the floor next to me. 'If you need anything at all, Glennie,' he instructed, before snoozing off, 'you just pull on my hair.' I was very sick and had lost my appetite. To encourage me to eat, Dad would sometimes bring me bouquets of white tulips and make a great display of presenting them to me, as if I were a princess. To please him, I would take sips of warm soup.

Dad instilled in me a deep love of music. He took me to musicals and bought me Mario Lanza records. In the evenings, tucked into his lap, we would listen to Lanza sing 'Be My Love', and 'Ave Maria'. I first discovered my own singing voice with the Salvation Army choir. Churches were the best places to find live music. At six years old I started to venture out alone to Sunday church services, trying to locate the top performances. Mum and Dad had bought Nanna's house in Cardiff and long after the war her piano remained in the bomb shelter. I'd often tiptoe into the dark, through the cobwebs and filth, for my own private concerts. I had no formal music education, and mostly invented my own tunes as I went along. At Christmas, I would sing carols for my neighbours and they would reward me with a few pennies.

Dad would often read to me the works of Walter de la Mare, and the poems of William Wordsworth and Dylan Thomas. To this day I can recite a number of Wordsworth poems, including my favourite, 'I Wandered Lonely as a Cloud'.

Dylan Thomas grew up a few miles down the road from Marble Hall, in the Gower Peninsula. (Anthony Hopkins' family also lived 'just down the road', as did most families in tiny Wales.) As Dylan gained world fame, I remember as a child listening to adults talk about how they couldn't understand why Thomas deserved so much attention. 'Why's he so famous?' they would say. 'That daibach [boy] talks just the way we do.'

Dad enjoyed my gullible ways and was always pulling some prank on me. One time, I was anxious to camp out with my little girl-friend, Margaret. Neither of us knew what camping out meant, other than sleeping outside, or even what a tent looked like. Dad warned us we would get scared, but we were adamant. He also said we would have to stay out all night because the back door would be locked. It didn't dawn on me that the back door was never locked. I'm not even sure the door had a lock, but we agreed.

So Margaret and I hung a sheet across two kitchen chairs, put a rug on the ground and settled in for the night. In the fading light of dusk, we were just finishing a card game when from the yard came loud clanking sounds. Petrified, we peered out from our tent to see the lid of the steel dustbin bouncing up and down by itself. We dashed to the back door, begging to be let in. I heard a hearty laugh and looked up to see Dad hanging out of an upstairs window with a string in his hand.

Margaret and I went to see our first cowboys-and-Indians film together. We were amazed to see the Indians riding around, dressed up in paint and feathers, stealing the cowboys' horses. When we returned home, we sat in the kitchen boasting to each other about how we'd take care of those Indians if they dared come our way. Our fantasies grew more and more outlandish, with big sticks and rocks and ambushes and calling all our friends.

There was a knock on the front door. I went to open it with Margaret behind me, and in jumped an Indian! His face and teeth were black, his cheeks marked in red warpaint, and there was a band around his forehead with a feather sticking up. The Indians had heard us talking and now they'd really come to get us!

In terror, we ran through the house with the Indian in pursuit. We flew out the back door and tumbled headlong over a rock wall. We'd scraped our knees but there was no time to stop. We ran and ran all the way to Margaret's house, hearts pounding.

'My goodness, what's happened to you?' said Margaret's mother.

'The Indians are after us,' Margaret screamed. 'There's one with a feather and warpaint, and he's right behind us. Quick, lock the door!' Margaret's mother took our hands and led us into the kitchen. Both of us were starting to cry.

'Calm down, you two. There are certainly no Indians in Wales. You've seen one too many films, I'd say.'

'But he's coming! He was right behind us,' I insisted. 'We saw him at my house and then he chased us.'

'Well we won't let him in here, so you're safe. Just you stay here and we'll clean up these knees. There are no Indians here.'

We heard a knock on the door. 'That's him!' Margaret screamed. 'Don't open the door! Oh, please, don't open the door.'

'Don't be silly,' said Margaret's mother as she strode towards the door. We cowered in the kitchen.

We heard loud laughter and I realized it was my father. He walked in, still laughing. His face was coated with soot and marked with red lipstick, though he'd taken off the feather.

So here was our Indian, a Welsh sea captain having some fun. But for some time we were still quite nervous about the Indians coming to get us, and whenever we talked about them, we whispered and made sure we were alone.

But let Dad near his usquebaugh, and he was a different and sometimes violent man. One day, when I was about seven, he took me out to a destroyer in the harbour to visit the captain, an old friend from the war. While they retreated to the captain's cabin to share stories and a drink or two, I was left to wander and watch the seagulls swoop down on the deck. Evidently, after a couple of hours, Dad left and it was not until the destroyer had put to sea that I was discovered. I remember the captain saying, 'Christ, Ted forgot to take his daughter.' In open waters, pitching on the swells, I was handed off to the coastguard for safe passage. They turned me over to the police, who asked if I knew my way home. I replied, 'No, but I know my address,' and they took me home in a police car. Dad was not surprised to see me. I don't think he even knew what he had done.

For some reason, even as a child, I don't remember being scared. I was never afraid of boarding strange buses or being left on a ship. I have always felt God was with me. I always believed there was a higher being, but maybe this being would not be found in church. I also believed in fairies and angels. Why not? Someone was looking out for me.

When I was ten, my mother decided I should be enrolled in a Catholic convent school, Heathfield House. I'm not sure what got into her. Perhaps it was because Dad claimed he was an agnostic, or perhaps Mum wanted to get even with him for showing me so much attention. I found his agnostic claim difficult to believe: at nights, he would read me the Bible, and he knew it inside out. Maybe that made him an expert agnostic. But mother insisted, and so I was enrolled and stayed there until I was sixteen.

The rigidity of the convent school nearly killed me. First, there was my dreary uniform: a pleated brown gymslip over a cream-coloured blouse with a brown belt loose about my waist, and a brown and blue striped tie. On the left breast pocket of my brown blazer edged in blue piping, was the school's coat of arms with its motto, 'Serve Others Before Yourself,' embroidered in Latin at the bottom.

I also objected to what the Sisters were teaching. I just knew they couldn't be right. God could never want people to be so inflexible. If God was everywhere, how could He be limited to a certain ideology or organization? How could He just love some people and ignore the rest? Repeating the rosary like parrots before every lesson seemed ridiculous. Not that I thought all religion wrong, I just felt it had more to do with each person's experience than a group decision. The Sisters incessantly talked of love but were not kind to us, so wrapped up were they in their own beliefs and rules. They must have seen how I dropped from the top of my academic class to the bottom but they never asked why it was happening or how I felt. They taught us constantly to guard against the seven deadly sins, but seemed to take special exception to the eighth, noise, and the ninth, colour.

My favourite class was art, but under the guidance of the Sisters we were required to copy precisely the art of others. When I tried to use my imagination, my hands were slapped. If there was a tenth deadly sin, it had to be creativity. Later, during my first pregnancy, I would return to art. The overflowing happiness of becoming a mother unleashed my artistic impulses and fertile imagination, and I gradually developed my own style.

In my second year at Heathfield, the Sisters allowed us to have a Christmas party. Instead of our uniforms, we were allowed to wear long dresses. There were no boys to dance with, of course, but the girls could dance together under the watchful eyes of the Sisters. This was a big event and Dad took me to a store where he bought me a beautiful ankle-length dress of pale blue adorned with netting and delicate sleeves. One of the girls, Ann Pledge, arrived at the dance still in her uniform. I asked her if she had a dress and she answered no. The next day I asked one of the Sisters why my friend, Ann, couldn't have been given a dress for the party. I remember I was told, 'She lives in the orphanage. She'll have to get used to that.'

I was outraged. How could someone who talks about love be so mean to a young orphan girl? My bitterness over their hypocrisy, their obsession with their own spiritual purity to the exclusion of the needs of others, settled in me as a challenge to always try to be truly kind to others, a conviction I tried to carry forward in my boys.

Remembering my convent experience, I was loath to subject my children to formal religious instruction. Rote recitation of an ideology had not made the Sisters any kinder or more compassionate. So I taught my boys one simple rule: be kind to others. Most of all, I wanted to provide my boys with a moral shield to protect them in the world. Kindness became the basis for this shield. 'Brothers don't fight,' I would stress repeatedly. 'Brothers are kind to each other and to strangers. Right and wrong is easily determined by the effect our actions have on others.' This simple belief gave me a certain fearless trust of others, a trust that would carry me into the unknown, to Australia, and to America again.

Life at home was getting more difficult as Dad was drinking more and getting wilder. Sometimes he would show up at Heathfield in the middle of the day, plastered. He would walk the halls yelling, 'Glennie, Glennie! Which classroom are you in? I've come to take you home. It's time for an adventure.'

The Sisters, unwilling to confront him, would send me out to quiet Dad down. But if Dad were bent on an adventure, an adventure would be had. We would go for a walk in the country, or wander through a bookshop, or listen to music. Sometimes, we would arrive home late after dark, fresh from a musical, and Mum would be waiting anxiously by the door. Not willing to face Dad herself, she would scold me and say, 'Glennie, why didn't you bring your dad home earlier?' As if I had any say in it.

At one point, when I was about eleven, I decided to run away to London. I recall thinking there must be more to life than Dad's intermittent drunken binges, Mum's cold aloofness and the forced rules of the Sisters at the convent. So I scraped together what change I had and boarded the morning train. It took me most of the day to get to London, but when I arrived and was standing in Paddington station, I suddenly realized I had nowhere to stay. After walking up and down Paddington Street I reboarded the train and returned home late that night. My mother, not even asking where I had been, sent me immediately to my room and said I could not go out that weekend – end of story. I felt helpless and couldn't fight back.

One day in early June, when I was twelve, my greatest prayer was finally answered. Every year in December, Dad would ask me, 'Glennie, what would you like for Christmas?' And every year I would answer the same: 'I want a piano and a baby brother.' The piano remained a dream, but on this particular June day my mother returned from the hospital with my belated Christmas gift, a baby brother, John. At seven pounds, John was a healthy baby, but he had colic and would not stop crying. I remember peering into the baby bed in wonder, not quite sure how to react to this little pink, fuzzy-headed creature that always seemed to be crying. Even though I loved the idea of being an older sister, I was crestfallen at the discovery that it took a long time for him to talk. That's why I wanted a brother – to have someone to talk to, to have someone to cure my loneliness – but all he did was clamp his eyes shut and cry.

Bewildered, I would pester Dad, 'When's John going to talk? How long do I have to wait?'

Even Mum had little patience with his crying. When I walked into the house from school, the second floor reverberated with Johnnie's colicky cries. As the front door closed, Mum would often lean over the railing and shout, 'Glennie, take him out of the house.' So I would bundle my baby brother into his black and white Silver Cross pram and take him up and down the hall, or back and forth across the porch or up and down the street. Later, when Johnnie learned to walk, perhaps sensing sibling rivalry, he became a little devil, pulling my hair and kicking my legs to get his way. For all the mischief, I did love my little brother. He was my dream come true. I just wished he had come equipped to talk.

Our family's economic condition in the fifties, if truly stated, was no economic condition at all. The coal mines were closing and fishing had turned meagre. After finishing at Heathfield, I was awarded a scholarship to Cardiff University, but Mum insisted that more education would only ruin me and encouraged me to marry instead. Then I proclaimed I wanted to be a midwife, but Mum said no again. 'It's too messy,' she said. Denied midwifery and not having found an acceptable suitor, I finally enrolled at the university in an eighteen-month vocational course in Early Childhood Training. But my dreams lay elsewhere. America had always fascinated me since I was a small girl and I had always imagined that someday I would go there.

I was eighteen when I met Samuel Carl. An American, he said, visiting his distant Welsh roots, Samuel was twenty when we met in a coffee bookshop on High Street and fell into a discussion of art and jazz. I was immediately attracted to this vibrantly handsome man. With broad shoulders, adventurous brown eyes over high cheekbones and a full head of blond hair, he swept me away with stories of America and exotic travel. We dated for two months before he was drafted into the American military and had to return home for training. Months later, when Samuel was stationed in France, he would cross the channel to visit me whenever he could.

On one of his visits, we went for a long walk through the open green fields overlooking the sea outside Cardiff. Returning home exhausted, I fell asleep on the couch. When I awoke, Samuel was cleaning the mud off my shoes. A great warmth settled over me and I remember looking up at him thinking how much he must love me, and I suddenly knew that I loved him. I knew I had found my husband and that I would have a peaceful home of my own.

When he returned to France a few days later, I followed and we were married at an American military base near Poitiers in France. Soon I was pregnant with my son Sammy. My husband told me that if I wanted our child to be President of the United States, he must be born in America. So, near the ninth month, without a great deal of thought, alone and very pregnant, I boarded a flight to America. Sammy was born in a military hospital in Georgia, after which I returned to Britain. When my husband's army enlistment expired he rejoined me and within the next three years we had two more sons, Jonathan and Scott.

Of all the boys, Scotty's birth was the most fraught. Two months premature, at five pounds nine ounces, he was the most delicate thing I had ever beheld. I still see that tiny face looking up from my belly minutes after entering this world. Scott's face seemed that of an angel, perfectly formed without a newborn's wrinkles and creases.

He was also born with gossamer-white hair, an arresting feature that would later become his trademark.

From the very first, perhaps a foreshadowing of what was to come, little Scotty was forced to fight for survival. With a poorly developed digestive system, he couldn't get enough to eat, and when I finished feeding him, he would throw it all up. In and out of an incubator, Scott continued to lose weight, slipping well under five pounds. The doctors were at a loss, as nothing seemed to help. Then, miraculously, at three-and-a-half months, he stabilized then blossomed into a healthy baby.

I was twenty-five by this time and Samuel was twenty-six. After Scotty was born, Samuel became increasingly frustrated at his loss of freedom and extinguished dreams, and withdrew into himself. He had always wanted to be a writer and travel to exotic places, but in our short marriage our only exotic travel had been limited to trips to the delivery room. I knew he was suffering, and in sympathy I suggested he take the little money we had and travel through Europe to work off some of his unhappiness and rekindle his dreams. So Samuel left and, after a period spent apart, we agreed to divorce and go our separate ways.

Like so many young and naive couples, we had never thought of asking ourselves the tough questions of life before committing to marriage. We were simply in love with being in love. What else was there? In spite of the growing distance between Mum and me and my determination for a life better than hers, I had unwittingly shadowed her path.

Alone again, I searched for a way to support my family but it was exceedingly difficult. In those days, no one would hire a young mother with three children under school age. Then I thought of the vocational class I had taken in Early Childhood Training from a visiting American professor. He had offered to help if I should ever come to America. With that slim reed of hope, I set out for that far-away land with a three-year-old, a two-year-old and Scotty in my arms. There we would do better than our meagre life in Wales; we would do better than merely survive. Finally, I had a family of my own and all the struggles of raising them would never feel like a burden in any way. On the contrary, my children always inspired me and raised my spirits.

∿

I am jarred into the present by the skidding bounce of the 747 as we land in Dubai, United Arab Emirates. I was warned when I boarded in London not to show my unvisaed passport to anyone, and not to leave the plane until I arrived in Sydney. I watch with some dread as uniformed police with machine guns walk slowly down the aisle. These are strange, cold and unsmiling faces and a chill comes over me as I realize just how great a leap I am taking. I pull the blanket about me and pretend to sleep as they pass by.

After the police leave, my guardian flight attendant kneels at the seat to tell me the captain has received a radio message from Dr Croches: Scott is alive but still in a deep coma. I am amazed and grateful they care so much. 'Keep fighting, Scott,' I whisper to myself. 'Mom's on the way.' We are airborne again, heading for Singapore. I turn my back to the aisle, curl more tightly into the big leather seat and slip into my past.

Three

Our first American home was in a suburb of Detroit. We arrived shortly after Detroit was rocked by race riots. The Black Panthers were at war with the Nixon administration and even the local police rarely ventured from their squad cars. Perhaps I was overly naive and trusting, but every day I would walk, with Sammy and Jonathan clinging to my skirt and Scotty in my arms, through neighbourhoods where we were the only white faces, passing burned-out cars and stores with smashed windows.

The American professor found me a job in a pilot Head Start programme for underprivileged children. To qualify for the job I had to live in the black ghetto where I worked. One Christmas, Santa Claus visited our programme. I still have a photo of that occasion showing little white-haired Scotty sitting in the red lap of a huge black Santa surrounded by a sea of tiny, bright-eyed black faces. Much as I appreciated my boys having the chance to mix with children of other races, they did have to endure prejudice for being different. One day, Jonathan returned from school and related his typical day as, 'Mom, you always tell me not to fight, so I gave them my money again. But then they hit me anyway.'

Money continued to be a problem. I never asked for help from the boys' father or my own parents. My pay barely covered the living expenses of a single person, let alone three growing children. But aid always came right when we needed it. I might sell something that I had made – a painting, a weaving or a dress – or I might pick up an extra job for a few days.

Two years later we moved to Berkeley in California. I had been offered a job at Far West Labs to instruct others how to teach early childhood education. My American professor friend had visited my Head Start class in Detroit one day and was intrigued by the programme I had developed to teach my pre-schoolers mathematics, colours and shapes.

When I began working at Head Start, I soon realized my children were not learning by the traditional method of holding up a 2 or a 4 or the colour green and having the class just watch and repeat what I said. So I designed a little game where I cut out squares, circles and triangles from coloured paper and scattered them about the class. I would ask a child to bring me three blue squares, or five white triangles, and so on. As the children scurried about the room they would have to apply a conceptual understanding of colours, shapes and numbers to fulfil their assignment. By today's learning standards, this system is nothing extraordinary; it's everyday fare on *Sesame Street*. But my professor friend was intrigued. My approach was revolutionary, he told me, and recommended me to Far West Labs.

I had hoped Berkeley would offer the boys a more normal life, but we encountered riots of a different kind. The Vietnam War had split the nation into two camps and Berkeley was one of the battlefields. One day, as I rested at lunch in a coffee shop, I met a sensitive and angry young man named Ron Kovic, who was a disabled Vietnam veteran. We began a lengthy discussion about the injuries he had received in Vietnam and the humiliation and indifference he had suffered at the hands of veterans' hospitals.

'I was nineteen and idealistic when I was sent to Vietnam,' Ron told me. 'I believed in Audie Murphy and apple pie and the American dream, but Vietnam destroyed all that. And the VA hospitals nearly destroyed me. I survived Vietnam only to nearly die from infections in the hospital.'

It was only as I was preparing to leave that Ron told me he was writing a book about his experiences, *Born on the Fourth of July*. Inspired by my first-hand experience of the terrible consequences of this insane war, I joined anti-war protests and even took my small children to a few passive sit-ins.

But a year in 'Berscrkley' was enough. Going from the battlefield of the Detroit ghettos to another was too radical for my boys. I longed for a quiet place in the country where I could provide a healthy environment and the boys could have more freedom. When a friend mentioned he knew of an inexpensive country cottage outside Los Gatos in the Santa Cruz Mountains, I left my job, packed us up and moved. In those days no one wanted to live in the hill country, so rents were low but jobs were scarce. I kept food on the table by waitressing at a local diner called The Summit, and helped develop a pilot learning disabilities programme at Redmond Elementary school.

Our little two-bedroom house, with its weathered cedar-shake shingles, grey redwood siding, and large old wood windows that rattled from years of wear, was nestled into three acres of towering redwoods. I forsook curtains in favour of light, and our windows soon became small greenhouses, crammed with red, pink and white geraniums, purple chrysanthemums, marigolds, and pots of California golden poppies. Guarding our family were two old English sheepdogs, a white bunny, a family of grey field mice, a copper-coloured guinea pig, a calico cat and a funny little rat named Rootbeer, who would climb on the bunny's back and just sit there as if he were the king of the mountain. The boys couldn't wait to get home from school and play with them. Rats, dogs, cats, boys and all, we were an extended family with each receiving equal love and attention.

The two mop-like sheepdogs had been a gift from the previous tenants, and while the boys were overjoyed, my enthusiasm was short-lived. Within two weeks our tight little home was filled with fourteen crawling puppies. I moved them to a pen outside with straw on the ground and soon they were bounding about like spring lambs. Before long they were demanding more than mother's milk and so I began to feed the puppies cooked hamburger laced with cottage cheese. As their appetites grew, so did our food bill until, like the little old lady who lived in a shoe, I began to wonder what to do. Finally, after three months, I laid down the law. The puppies had to go.

It was little Scott, of course, who objected the most strenuously. 'I'll get a job, Mom,' he pleaded. 'I'll take care of them and feed them and you won't have to do a thing.' But knowing better, I insisted.

On a Saturday morning we put red, white and blue ribbons and bows about each of the puppy's necks, brushed their short black and brown hair, and loaded them into three cardboard boxes for the trip to Old Town in Los Gatos, where I instructed the boys to find new homes for the puppies. 'I'll be back in three hours,' I told them as they unloaded the boxes on to the sidewalk in front of a small market.

When I returned, I found a group of people gathered around the boxes, purring over all fourteen puppies, who, by this time, had chewed each other's ribbons to shreds. Not one puppy had been awarded to a lucky recipient. I pulled Scotty aside.

'Why haven't you given these puppies away?' I asked, not in the least bit happy.

'Look, Mom,' he said, holding up a paper. 'I have a list of people who want a puppy, and I have their phone numbers. But I have to interview them first. I can't give my puppies away to just anybody.'

That evening I heard Scotty and Jonathan on the phone. They were calling those who had signed the list and peppering them with detailed questions scrawled on a sheet: If I give you a puppy, what will you feed it? Will you walk the puppy every day? Do you work during the day, and if you do, who will take care of the puppy when you are gone? Will you give the puppy a pillow to sleep on? He will miss his brothers and sisters so he will need a pillow to sleep on. Will the puppy have a friend, or will he be all alone? Do you promise to take the puppy to the doctor for his shots and if he gets sick? Do you have any children who can play with the puppy? Will you keep the puppy inside or do you have a yard for him to play in? And so on.

Scotty's questions were detailed and in-depth, more than I ever anticipated from a five-year-old. Whoever was on the other end, no doubt greatly amused by his grilling, good-naturedly played along. Eventually Scotty would say, 'Well, I guess you can come and pick up a puppy, but if you don't want him you have to promise to call me back and I will come and get him.' Just what a single mother with three young boys and fourteen puppies wanted to hear.

Within a week thirteen of the puppies had found a home (Scotty kept his favourite), with two of the duly vetted foster parents driving eighty miles from San Francisco to pick up their 'children'.

A short time later I met Tony Perez, a disc jockey at a San Jose radio station and a professional jazz musician who played the trumpet and piano. We'd get together in the evenings and play music. Tony wrote a song, which he later recorded, called 'Scotty's Bounce'. It nicely captured the vibrant energy of my youngest. Tony introduced me to Pat Metheny, Russ Farrante (who was to gain success with the Yellowjackets), Nate Pruitt, who later worked with Quincy Jones, and other jazz greats. Tony arranged for Russ to be my children's music teacher. Scott played the trumpet, Jonathan took up the trumpet and piano, and Sammy the clarinet. Tony had been a running back on the Santa Clara University football team and helped the boys excel in football, baseball and softball. He was the passion of my life for the next five to six years and my sons and I are still great friends with him. We had warm times together.

A great advantage to living in the country was that it limited the boys' access to the temptations of junk food. I had forbidden them to drink soda pop and eat deep-fried snacks. I also regulated their reading of comic books. Then came Mother's Day. Unknown to me, the boys pooled all their money together to buy me gifts. With the three gathered around the kitchen table giggling and barely containing their glee, I unwrapped a six-pack of Coke, a large bag of potato chips and a Marvel comic book. They also announced they were baking me a cake. When I checked the oven, set at a mellow 100 degrees, I found it baking away in a large pan filled with dry chocolate cake mix, mashed bananas, strawberries and two raw eggs stuffed in the middle. They didn't know to add water or that it had to be mixed up.

'Where did you get these ingredients?' I asked Sammy, trying to be pleased, but concerned the boys had broken a family rule against hitching rides with strangers. 'How did you get to town? Did you hitchhike?'

Little Scotty placed his hands on my arm and with a great show of concern, said, 'Mom, we stopped every car going to town, but I promise, we didn't ride with anyone we didn't know.'

The two older boys had always looked out for Scott, but he also stood up for them. One time the school bully had cornered Jonathan in a local park. Just as the bully was about to take a swing, little Scotty rushed him and knocked him over a bike rack. Jonathan grabbed his brother's arm and they raced into the hills, the bully in hot pursuit. The boys hid under a wooden bridge on a hiking trail for some time before Jonathan ventured out to see if it was safe. Finding the bully gone, he gave a whistle to let Scott know the coast was clear. During the seven years we lived in the Santa Cruz hills, that whistle became their secret signal, indicating that it was safe to come out.

As Scott grew older, he took to fishing before school. I often caught him running out the door at five a.m., jumping on his bike and heading for his favourite fishing hole at Lexington reservoir. He'd gut his catch of the day, crappie, sunfish, or small-mouth bass, and distribute the gifts on the front porches of our elderly neighbours, mostly retirees. Unlike many boys his age, Scott loved to visit the elderly and would sit for hours listening to their stories.

Like boys everywhere, my sons weren't always angels. Once, when I came up short of money to pay my water bill and was faced with disconnection, the boys slipped out of the house at night and hiked to the water company office. Somehow they broke in and dug through the files until they found my bill and ripped it up. They deposited the shredded paper in the waste basket next to the filing cabinet, tossed a couple of eggs against the walls to make it look like vandalism, and hiked back home.

The next morning, while the two older boys were in school, a policeman came to the door. 'It looks like a child did it,' he told me, and produced the reconstructed water bill, all taped together. I was devastated. My boys, guilty of breaking and entering? When I explained that Sammy and Jonathan were in school (Scotty had mysteriously disappeared), the policeman went off to interview them. Later he called, and with a barely concealed chuckle, told me: 'They're not bad kids. They were trying to help you. I let them off with a strict lecture.' That night, I unleashed my anger. The two older ones were already taller than me, so all I could do was yell. It was one of the few times I resented having to raise the boys alone. Where was their father? After a bit of shouting all was forgiven. They were, after all, my best friends.

After seven years in the hills, with the boys older and in need of greater stimulation, and with my need for greater income, I began to consider moving from our comfortable cottage. But where? Back to the bay area? Even then it was very expensive, so I turned my eyes southward believing Los Angeles, with its creative energy and opportunities in music and fashion, might be the answer. It was summer and a few weeks remained before the boys would have to be registered for school, so I rented a small cottage at Carmel, telling the boys we would take a holiday on the beach before moving on to Los Angeles.

As the boys beachcombed, I began to paint in earnest. One day, having set up my easel with a stunning view of the swelling green bay against a dark peninsula of Monterey pines, I was furiously painting away when a stranger stopped to watch over my shoulder. Comparing the bay scene with my canvas, and finding little similarity, he finally asked, in a tone of puzzlement: 'What is it out there that you are painting?'

'Oh, I'm not painting that scene,' I told him. 'I'm painting what I see; I'm painting from my imagination.' He watched for a while longer, then asked if the paintings were for sale. He owned a gallery in Carmel, he explained, and would like to exhibit my paintings. Eventually, I sold a series of six through his gallery. I thought back to the art training I had received at the hands of the convent Sisters and smiled. Surely this was my redemption.

One quiet morning, with the sun's slanting orange rays illuminating a wall of grey fog hanging a mile or so out to sea, I was on a solitary walk along the beach when I ran across the boys, dressed in shorts and T-shirts, furiously at work on an old, wooden rowing boat mired in the sand. Sammy and Jonathan were bailing sand and seaweed from the interior while Scotty was pounding away with a hammer. After a while I asked the boys what they were doing.

Scotty stopped hammering. 'We found this old boat, Mom,' he said. 'We're fixing it so we can go sailing.' I circled the boat for a closer look. It seemed cheaply made, about ten feet long with salt-weathered, sun-baked plywood sides stripped of all colour, a flat bottom layered with sand, and a square stern with a jagged hole near the floor about the size of a cantaloupe, now half-patched with scraps of wood Scotty had already nailed in place.

'Do you really think this boat will float?' I asked. All three shot me looks of incredulity, as if I had suggested that the earth was flat, or a beach ball square. 'Good luck,' I said brightly, not wanting to spoil their fun. 'I'm off on my walk. When I return, we can all go for a sail.'

Upon my return, I found the three boys heaving the old boat across the white sand towards the water. Finally, with the gentle waves lapping the bow, the two older boys insisted that Scotty, being the lightest (or perhaps the most gullible), should hop in for the maiden cruise. With Scotty on his knees in the bottom clutching a broken paddle, Sammy and Jonathan shoved him into the surf. Surprisingly, the boat floated.

'Start paddling,' Jonathan instructed.

Scotty leaned over the right side and flailed away with the broken paddle, drenching himself with fifty-five degree spray and sending the boat into a gentle left-hand circle.

'The other side,' Sammy yelled. 'Paddle on the other side.'

Scotty switched sides, furiously paddling to correct his earlier mistake, sending the boat into a right-hand circle.

'Paddle one side, then the other,' Jonathan shouted.

Scotty energetically paddled two strokes on the right, then shifted to two strokes on the left, then back to the right, jumping back and forth until the boat began to rock dangerously.

By this time the boat was about ten feet from the shore. I noticed it had taken on a serious list to the rear. In fact, it was sinking rather quickly. The older boys also noticed, and careful to avoid getting wet themselves, jumped about on the sand waving their arms and calling out new instructions: 'Scotty, paddle back to shore! Turn it around and come back! Not that way, Scotty! The other way!' But by now the boat was heavy with water, uncontrollable and half-gone.

'Abandon ship! Abandon ship!' Jonathan yelled.

'Jump, Scotty, jump,' Sammy called.

Scotty was standing upright, frozen in the middle of the boat looking down into the water as it rose to his knees, and then to his waist, as the boat grounded bottom. Stepping over the side, with broken paddle held high and a look of crushing embarrassment on his face, Scotty waded ashore while his brothers rolled with laughter.

I gave his chattering body a hug and after suggesting he might want to go home and change to dry clothes, told him with the straightest face I could muster, 'I'm very proud of you, darling. After saving all hands, you went down with the ship.'

Head downcast, unsure if he'd been tricked or not, Scotty looked at me sideways, his blue lips twisting in uncertainty, as if to say, 'Gee Mom, you wouldn't kid a kid would you?' Turning around, dejected, he trudged off in the direction of home.

At the end of summer the boys and I moved to Venice, Los Angeles, but we were not destined to stay long. I had no idea what LA would be like, and was soon struggling to make a living. Again I resorted to waitressing. Russ Farrante, who had also moved to Los Angeles, asked me to act as his agent and I booked a few gigs for him at local nightclubs. But LA was immense, overpowering, and too fast-paced for us. My dream of living on the beach in Santa Monica remained a dream. I limped around town in an old broken-down Toyota searching for jobs. Then in the spring of 1979 I got a small break.

Through a contact, I found an entry position with Warner

Communications writing music and lyrics. But I had to live in New York City. So the boys and I once again packed up and headed east, finally settling in Westport, Connecticut, in a small house with a back garden, as I wanted my boys in a more natural setting within commuting distance of the city. But the position at Warners didn't last long. I had hoped to write music for films but my bosses wanted pop music, which I found uninspiring. The ultimate problem was that I lacked formal music training. I learned and played by ear, believing creativity and imagination would trump professional training.

So again I turned to waitressing and catering in Westport for regular income, supplemented by occasional trips into the city to sell a painting or a dress design. I had not met with much success until the Chavari stores bought a few of my original dress designs. Then Barneys bought a couple, primarily black evening wear cut along classic lines. Perry Ellis bought several heather-coloured tweed coats, and several wool scarves I had designed and woven, along with a design for baggy pants of English tweed. But the fashion world was erratic and often cruel, and I was growing tired of the commute. With three teenage boys at home, I became increasingly reluctant to venture outside Westport. A few months later, I meet Stefan Heller on a Sunday morning at a garden restaurant and we began to date.

Erica Jong frequented the Mushroom, a health-food cafe in Westport where I worked, and one day asked if I might take care of her daughter, Molly, on occasion. Erica was in her early forties then. I was struck by the intensity in her eyes and her quick intelligence. I didn't know until later that she was the author of *Fear of Flying* and was working on *Fanny* when we met, but sensing she was under considerable pressure, I agreed to her offer.

Molly was a red-haired toddler who quickly won the hearts of my sons. For Christmas, Scotty made her a wooden rocking horse. When he was showing it to me, I noticed the head was not well attached. It could be turned around 180 degrees without much effort. When I pointed out this defect to Scott, he replied: 'But Mom, that's so the horse can turn to face Molly so she can talk to it.' Jonathan and Sammy dressed up in Santa costumes and with Scott in tow, we delivered the horse to Molly on Christmas Eve. Erica and her husband John responded with books for the boys and gracious invitations to their home and our friendship continued to grow.

∾

Sensing a change in air pressure, I sit upright as the 747 descends into Singapore. In spite of being warned not to leave the plane I feel trapped, with an insatiable craving for exercise and fresh air. Parked at the gate, the cabin door opens. Not having slept in nearly two days, my mind has degenerated into silly abandon. I bolt down the causeway and into a bathroom to regain my composure.

The picture I confront in the mirror is disturbing: sleepless, dark eyes in sunken pockets; a pallid face drained of life. I flail at my rat's-nest hair with a brush hoping to rearrange it over the bluish bruise, but it's hopeless. And my clothes, the nylon ski pants and fur boots, are unsuitable for the sub-tropics; my body swelters. Splashing water on my face, I take slow, deep breaths to gain control. Sydney remains eight hours away. Still, I'm almost there.

Scotty is waiting for me. I know. I trust. Again, I am lucky my papers are not checked and my journey continues.

∾

The last time I'd seen my youngest son had been five months ago at Christmas with the Hellers in Stuttgart. I was expected to accompany Stefan to his parents' house, as was tradition. Scott had arrived the day before and would go with us. I warned him that Stefan's mother was not very friendly, but all I expected was that he be true to himself. Scott handled the situation in his usual disarming style, happily greeting Madame Heller as if she were a revered relative. He helped with dishes and other chores without being asked. Spying the taboo piano, he sat right down and played up a storm of jazz right in front of her. I actually witnessed Madame Heller crack a smile. With his natural quality of lightness, Scotty could melt even the toughest heart.

When Jonathan arrived shortly after Christmas, we all went skiing in the Austrian Alps. Although I had provided skiing lessons for the boys, I had never skied myself. But always the optimist, I was up for an adventure. Noticing I had no hat, the boys bought me a stocking cap only to discover it was twice my size, flopping down to the bridge of my nose. After thanking them for the gift, I headed for the ladies' room to salvage my dignity. Failing to fill the hat with my rolled hair, I stuffed the extra space with a wadded stream of toilet paper, tucking the end under an elastic hair band. The hat fit snugly and I thought myself pretty clever until I reached the ski lift. Riding high above the snow, a gust of wind sent the hat airborne and the stream of toilet paper unravelled behind me in a wavy twenty-foot tail. The prim German couple sharing our lift were beside themselves with embarrassment. My boys, equally embarrassed, pretended not to notice as I spent the balance of the ride reeling in my paper hairpiece.

Paper tails paled next to the larger challenge of descending the mountain in one piece. I had been a pretty fair waterskier so I understood balance. But I didn't know how to make snow skis behave. With Scott behind, sharing my skis, his hands around my waist, we pushed off. It was a thrill, flying down that slick mountain through lightly falling snow. Faster and faster we went, laughing like children, until it came time to stop. Heading directly into a milling group of skiers at the bottom, we had no choice but to fall over and tumble into the base of a tree. Hardy pillars of German decorum we were not.

❧

It is daylight outside the porthole of the 747. The plane sweeps across Sydney in a looping approach to the airport. Miniature white sails criss-cross the flat blue waters of Sydney harbour below. The white clamshells of the Sydney Opera House slip under the wing. And then we are taxiing to the gate.

Two Sydney policemen escort me from the plane and through immigration where my passport becomes legal. I'm in too much pain to ask if Scott is still alive. I fear the answer. The policemen's grim efficiency tells the story. Why else the hurry; why the deference? I am hustled outside to a police car parked at the kerb. Squinting in the bright autumn sun, I ask about my bag, though I hardly care as I am guided into the rear seat. 'It will be delivered later,' one of the policemen says, sliding behind the wheel. We edge from the kerb and aggressively meld into Sydney-bound traffic.

'St Vincent's is in Darlinghurst, about ten kilometres north,' the driver says over his shoulder.

'Do you know what happened?' I ask, wide awake now, a second wind of adrenaline kicking in. After nearly twenty-four hours in the air and God only knows how many time zones, I am only minutes from rescuing my son.

'We don't know the whole story,' the other policeman says. 'We do know your son had played rugby earlier in the day and had come home after dark. He may have startled a burglar. He was pushed, or maybe he fell, two storeys into a basement.'

'Why did it take so long to find him?' I demand.

'A neighbour reported hearing something to the building manager, but he thought it was a drunk, or maybe a couple of dogs. Unfortunately he wasn't found until morning.'

We head up Victoria Street towards St Vincent's. Everything is so green and lush, just as Scott had said. I've seen these tropical plants before, the red-flowered bottlebrush, purple jacaranda, the yellow and red bird of paradise, in California, but only planted in straight rows. Here they are scattered everywhere, almost at random, growing wild. The grey snows of Germany are a faded lifetime away.

❧

Scott was so excited about moving to Australia. It had been his wish since he was a little boy in California. He had tried living in Denmark to be near Jonathan, but had little interest in learning Danish. 'I speak English,' he had said. 'I'm going to Australia. I want to study architecture. And they play rugby in Australia,' he had added with a twinkle in his eye. After visiting me in Stuttgart over Christmas, he had gone to England, met up with his friend Niall for a day or two, said goodbye to his Nanna and his many friends, then set out for Australia.

The day he left Germany, Scott gave me a hand-painted wooden duck. Tucked inside its hollow body was this touching note: 'This magical duck is a token of my love to a great mother that I will always have love for in my heart. And when you look at this magical duck I will feel your eyes of love upon me wishing only the best for me wherever I am. Love, Scott.'

After a meandering voyage through several countries, upon reaching Thailand he called to check in: 'You'd love it here, Mom. There are pineapples galore! And mangos!'

After settling into Sydney, he called again: 'It's so great here, Mom. It's sunny and bright. The people are fantastic. I'm running every day – I'm getting so healthy. Best of all, I'm playing rugby.' He had also picked up a part-time job, tiling for a building contractor, as he had done in Westport. I was proud of him. He was happy. Life was delicious. What could possibly go wrong?

∾

The police car winds through the suburbs of Darlinghurst before pulling up to a long grey-stone structure with a small tower on top set in a lovely field of green grass. St Vincent's resembles a school more than a hospital.

Now I'm frantic. I crash through the doors and demand of the nurse: 'Where is the Intensive Care Unit? Which room is Scott's? How is he doing? Has he improved?'

At last, I ease gently through the door into Scott's pale-green silence. My baby is alone, covered with a white sheet on a single bed, eyes closed, as if dreamily asleep. I don't see the wires and tubes that connect him to cold, clicking machines. I don't see the black eye or the white bandage that wraps his head. I see only the little boy in his blue flannel pyjamas sprinkled with yellow and black circus animals that I would check on each night, to kiss and allay his fears, to assure him he's safe and that I would be there for him in the night.

With tears flowing, I wrap my arms around him. 'It's okay, Scotty,' I tell him firmly. 'Mom is here. You can wake up now.'

Four

But Scott does not wake up. I sit at the foot of his narrow steel bed in a trance-like state, unblinking and disorientated. My son lies inert, his chest rising and falling in shallow moves that barely ruffle the white sheet tucked at his neck. Beside his bed, the respirator hisses and throbs as it artificially inflates, then deflates his lungs. Suddenly, I am overcome with an aching fatigue that pushes me towards despair. What if my baby never wakes up? What if it's hopeless? What if he sleeps for years in that twilight zone suspended between life and death, in my arms yet beyond my reach, perpetually on the edge of slipping away? What if it's years? Years . . .?

I sit up straight and forcibly shake clear the cobwebs of defeat. I will not allow fear to crush my hope. Your mom has arrived, Scotty, and now it's time to take charge. Where are the nurses? Where are the doctors? Let's get to work! When you open your eyes I will be right here, holding your hand. I can't wait to see your cheerful smile and hear you say: 'Hey, Mom. What are you doing here?'

I hear a low cough and turn about. A white-coated man stands in the doorway. He is thinly built, of average height, in his late thirties with small blue eyes in a patrician face and fine black hair. With a gentle nod he enters the room. My eyes search his for answers.

'Mrs Carl?' I nod slowly, not knowing what to expect. 'I'm Dr Croches,' he says in a soft Australian voice, with a steady gaze that brims with compassion. 'I'm the head of the Intensive Care Unit. And I'm very glad you're here.'

Immediately I am put at ease. 'How is my son?' I ask. He does not attempt to evade my pleading eyes. I trust him already.

'Your son is in a deep coma. Unfortunately, traumatic brain injuries are exceptionally complicated. Because of the delay in getting medical attention, Scott is suffering from sustained cerebral oedema. Brain swelling. He has what we call a subdural haematoma. That's a blood clot beneath the dura, the membrane that covers the brain and spinal cord. Our first operation, the one I called you about in Germany, was to release the pressure on his brain. We are about to take him in for another operation, for a tracheotomy to help him breathe.'

'How long will he be like this?' I ask.

Dr Croches presses my hand in his own, a hand not much larger than mine with thin, surgeon's fingers. 'I don't know,' he says quietly. 'We'll have to wait and see. But the longer he's in a coma, the less likely he will fully recover.'

'Can't you give him something to help him wake up?'

'Quite the opposite, I'm afraid. The medication we've given him is to deepen his unconscious state. He needs to be kept deeply immobile. By controlling his breathing, blood pressure and other functions, we hope to reduce the damage from swelling. You see, the swelling that occurs in the first few days after a head injury can cause death if not treated immediately. So far, we've managed to control the swelling. But he's in a very critical condition. If we do manage to save him, and the prognosis is not positive, Mrs Carl, he may well suffer permanent brain damage.'

I hug the wall as a pair of white-coated orderlies wheel Scott from his room.

'We will do the best we can,' Dr Croches adds. Squeezing my hand in reassurance, he follows the trolley down the hall.

I sit in the waiting room in a dreamlike state, having travelled thousands of miles, halfway around the world, where night is day and day is night. I have lost all sense of time and place. Are these people speaking English, or is it German? Is it snowing outside, or is it sunny? How will I eat? Where will I sleep? And on so little money? I must find my strength. My thoughts drift back twenty-one years to another time of white coats and pumping machines where I fought for the life of baby Scotty. I had felt so helpless as, undernourished and losing weight, he seemed to slip towards death. And now here I am again.

The couple sitting next to me introduce themselves. He is Richard Neville. Tall and slender with a hint of reserve, Richard is a writer and producer for Australian television. His wife, Julie Clarke, younger, gregarious, lighthearted and engaging, is also a writer and producer. Julie's mother has just been admitted to the ICU and the three of us bond immediately. I tell them my story. When I mention my own black eye and headache on the day of Scott's accident, Richard turns my way. His dark eyes flicker with interest. He is working on a TV miniseries on psychic phenomena, he tells me, and asks probing questions. Julie later introduces me to her brother Rollie and his wife Robin, both local artists. These four become my first and fastest friends, my anchors during my stormy months in Australia. Even after Julie's mother is released from St Vincent's they visit often to stand by Scott's bedside, to hold my hand and share my burden. Richard's mini-series on psychic phenomena would eventually be syndicated.

Dr Croches enters the waiting room and I spring to my feet for the news.

'He's breathing easier now with the respirator through the trachea,' he tells me in that soft voice that wraps me like a down quilt. 'One thing Scott has in his favour is youth. If he wasn't an athlete, his heart might have stopped long ago. You know, it rained the night he fell. He might have died of hypothermia, but in the long run it may have been a blessing. The cold probably kept the swelling of his brain to a minimum. If it had been warmer, he might not have made it to the hospital at all.'

I stand in solitary guard by Scott's bed. With the tracheotomy added, the scene is surreal. I've never seen so many tubes and wires attached to a body; so many machines flash and click, hiss and pump, to their own impersonal rhythm. Where is the life in this intertwining of technology and flesh? In the eye-catching flash of lights or in the drugged deep sleep of my son? What can *I* do to help? While I fear dislodging a tube or disconnecting a wire, I sit on the edge of his bed, take his cool, limp hand in mine and feel for his weak pulse. Surely Scotty must sense my presence. I feel his energy. He must feel mine. Machines are no match for our human bond.

My mind flies back to when he was so little, to when he would entwine his small fingers in mine looking for reassurance. 'Mommy, Mommy, hold my hand,' he would say in such a tiny voice, his clear brown eyes looking up into mine. 'Hold both my hands.' I would grasp them both and swing him around until his feet left the ground, then lift him to the sky just to hear his cheeky outcry of delight. Scotty loved that, to be thrust into the sky where the birds live and to look down upon the land and believe he was a giant. But that was yesterday. Now I hold his hand for my own reassurance, knowing we cannot go back.

A woman enters on cat's feet to stand in silence at the foot of the bed. She is dressed in the white uniform and blue cape of a nurse. 'How is Scotty doing?' she asks after a long pause, in a quiet but solid voice. I just look at her, unable to respond. I have no idea.

'My name's Jenny,' she says with a reassuring smile. 'I have the day shift for this room. Scott is my patient.' I notice first the glow in Jenny's face. She is in her mid-thirties, mid-height and smartly trim in her uniform, with blue-grey eyes and long blonde hair swept back in a bun. But it's the lovely inner glow of her face to which I'm drawn. I know for certain, now, that my baby is in good hands.

Jenny removes her cape and sets about checking the machines and tubes, talking to me as she moves efficiently about the room. 'Some medications cannot be delivered through the drip system so we've inserted a central line, this one, into his chest. This is the gastronasal tube used to feed and rehydrate his body. These are the wires that monitor his heart.'

Jenny moves on to wipe Scott's mouth, ears and nose. 'Fluids build up when you're in a coma,' she adds. 'Have to keep everything clean.'

When Jenny finishes, she returns to the foot of the bed to look down on Scott. 'You know, Mrs Carl, there is something special about your son,' she says wistfully. 'I don't know what it is, but it's there. During his last operation, when the tracheotomy tube was inserted, I just couldn't stay away. I wasn't needed but I felt I had to be there. Something made me stay.'

Picking up her cape, she pauses for a brief moment to lay a thoughtful hand on my shoulder. 'I'll be back to check on him soon.' And she slips out the door.

The ICU staff employ every diagnostic tool at their disposal. Scott's severe brain damage clearly shows on the CAT scan. His pupils are tested for reaction to light and there is no response. Scott's low reading on the Glasgow Coma Scale predicts a slim chance of recovery.

I later discover that Scott had also broken his clavicle in the fall. Dr Croches had known this, but his priority was to relieve the pressure on Scott's brain. And because everyone believed Scott was going to die anyway, the clavicle was never set. Now it's too late. They can't administer anaesthesia to a coma patient. The pain from the broken clavicle will only become a problem if Scott wakes up, which is thought highly improbable.

I gather together some coins and call Stefan from a pay phone. To my surprise, Madame Heller answers. As soon as I identify myself, she slams the phone down. Giving her the benefit of the doubt, I try again. Again, she hangs up. Have I caught her by pure coincidence during a brief visit to her son's house, or has she moved in to comfort him? I conclude it's probably better to write.

With nowhere to go, I sleep in Scott's room curled on the foot of his bed, or in a chair in the waiting room, depending on what procedures are scheduled. The hospital staff do not interfere, giving me free rein. Usually I require darkness and quiet to sleep, but I soon learn to cope with constant light, the round-the-clock racket of rapid footsteps, urgent voices and the trundle of trolley wheels in the hallway. As long as I can stay next to Scott, I will manage. One night, though, I wake up needing to go to the bathroom only to find I am twisted up in Scott's spaghetti of tubes and wires. The side rail is up and I cannot slide out. Caught between the fear of having an accident in his bed and tearing out a tube, I struggle on the verge of panic. Gradually, methodically, I work myself free just in time.

I stay with Scott most of the time, holding him, often singing the old Welsh lullabies he loved as a child: 'Callwynllan'(David of the White Rock), and 'Gaellaen yr Nowstyr' (Golden Slumbers). 'Where are you, Scott?' I whisper. 'Are you among the stars? Are you running through the clouds between two worlds?' And I know he's answering. Is it his fault I cannot hear? Deep inside this shell of a body Scotty's spirit lives, an inextinguishable spark that rages against the dark. 'What are you thinking, Scotty? Do you remember how much I love you? I know you do. When you return I will love you stronger than ever. I will love you for ever.'

I am told coma patients often react to familiar voices. So I purchase his favourite childhood book, *The Wind in the Willows*, and read it aloud. I hold his hands and pray. Certainly God has kept him alive for a reason. Certainly he will awaken soon. But what if he awakes and is still lost? What if he is paralysed or deaf? Or blind? Will he understand language? Or will he have to start over again like a newborn baby? Will he recognize me? Will he recognize his brothers? Will he still laugh, sing, whistle? Will he smile? I clench his hand tightly. What was that? Didn't his eye just flicker? Didn't he squeeze me back? I lean forward to study his face for a sign, any sign. He looks so peaceful. Am I going crazy?

But Scotty was squeezing my hand even without his knowledge.

He was having allergic reactions. At first Dr Croches had prescribed Dilantin and other medications for relaxation and to prevent seizures, but the swelling in Scotty's face indicated an allergic reaction. I don't know how I knew, but intuitively I did. I knew what the doctors weren't picking up. I also sensed his liver was being damaged. When the tests came back and I was right, the medication was suspended and his liver soon repaired itself. Often, when I held his hand, I would detect something, often nothing more than a twitch or a flicker in his face. I would pray this was the beginning of his awakening, but again and again I was disappointed.

Early one morning, on the verge of complete exhaustion, I attempt to swallow breakfast in a nearby cafe. A fellow at the next table notices my tears. 'What's the matter?' he asks. I glance his way. There is something familiar about the man, his piercing eyes and deep masculine voice. Briefly, I explain my situation. Pulling a napkin from the holder, he asks the name of my son, writes a quick note and hands it to me. 'Dear Scotty,' the note begins. 'When you wake up, hope you get well fast. Love, David Bowie.'

The days drag on, days of holding Scott's hand, of reading stories, of prayer and silence; days of fitful catnaps curled on the foot of his bed and hours of pacing the hallways in search of hope. Throughout the day, I move him gently. I rock his heavy weight trying to alleviate bedsores and I adjust his arms. I rest his feet on pillows and wonder if they are cold. Perhaps I should knit him socks? I could buy knitting needles and wool. I could knit him a sweater and a hat. My imagination spins out of control. Slow down, I tell myself. Slow down.

Members of Scotty's rugby team drop in to visit a fallen comrade. Big, brawny boys, they stand at the foot of his bed in shock and uncertainty before the mute, tubed and wired body stretched out before them. After a few minutes of agitated silence, they engulf me in their thick arms, offer a few words of comfort, then quietly slip away.

About two weeks after I arrive, the 'system' catches up with me. The hospital asks to see Scott's passport to ascertain when he entered Australia. Hospital care is free for Australians and for visitors with emergencies, up to a point. Surely they won't discharge a patient in a coma. Or will they? My experience obtaining an Australian visa in Germany has taught me the hardness of state rules and I sense a looming battle.

With dread I catch a taxi to Scott's apartment on Potts Point to sort through his belongings. I will force myself to confront the scene of Scott's dreadful fall. The taxi drops me at the kerb on Potts Point Road, in an upmarket section of beach property with chic shops, cafes and a few seedy-looking nightclubs stripped of their dark glamour by a bright sun. I walk 150 feet to a four-storey, vanilla block of flats with small, decorator balconies scattered across its face.

On the concrete pad before the glass front doors, I stop to calm my nerves. There, to my right, is the black steel-pipe railing that barricades the yawning open pit where I was told Scott was found. About forty feet long, ten feet wide, twenty feet deep and lined with greyish concrete, the pit runs the length of the building on either side of the front doors. What is its purpose, other than a death trap? Ventilation? Light for basement apartments? Storage?

With clenched teeth, I force myself to lean forward over the railing and stare into the shadowy bottom littered with sweet wrappers and mulched leaves, soggy from evening rain. What happened that night? An accident or an assault? Painfully, I try to imagine the scene. It is dark with dim light flowing from the inside hallway. If Scott had stumbled surely the railing would have saved him. So it had to be a mugging, the black eye. But why? For revenge? For money? The police reports were vague with no mention of a missing wallet. Still, someone could have hit him, taken his wallet, then pitched him over the railing, tossing his wallet after. Or perhaps he had been shoved under, or dragged around the railing and . . .

I begin to cry and wipe my eyes. What does it matter? It's done. I can't reverse life.

I climb concrete stairs to the second floor, turn left down a long hallway, find Scott's flat and let myself in. The living room is untidy and typically male. Rugby posters are taped to the walls. A small stereo is tucked into a mostly empty bookcase. Next to the bookcase is a small wooden desk with a green plastic chair. In a corner of his bedroom is a pile of dirty clothes. The double bed is unmade; blue sheets and a thin green blanket. Above the headboard is a colourful poster of the Great Barrier Reef. I search his bureau, then the drawers of his desk and find his British passport tucked into a bundle of old letters, most from me with German stamps and some from his brother. Flipping through the passport, I come to his Australian visa and search for the expiration date. It's a three-month-from-date-of-entry visa, and I mentally calculate: twelve weeks, minus five weeks in the country, minus two weeks since my arrival, and breathe a sigh of relief. Five weeks left, enough to quell my panic, if only for a moment.

Clutching his passport and letters, I stand before the picture window in his living room with a view eastward out over the South Pacific where Scott told me he would watch the sunrise. In the distance, ant-like and impersonal, a few people walk the beach. The breaking waves are moving white streaks on a broader plane of greenish-blue. I stare at the horizon, a razor line that imperceptibly separates the purple-blue of water from the whitish-blue of sky and my mind drifts again to the grey cabin of a destroyer forty years earlier: I am a little girl surrounded by sailors. Towering over me is the captain. I hear him boom out in a salty voice, 'Christ almighty! Ted's bloody gone off and left his little girl.'

Will Scott leave me, too? I shudder and return to the waiting taxi.

The taxi driver takes me to the post office where I clean out Scott's mailbox. The letter I sent him before leaving Stuttgart has arrived. I rip it open and tuck the much-needed money into my purse. There is another letter from Germany addressed to Scott. Puzzled, I open the envelope thinking it might be a get-well card only to discover it is from a Stuttgart woman who worked for the United Nations. She had hired me to improve her English and I had taught her by playing scrabble. But the letter is written to Scott. I skim the brief note until my eye stops: 'How is your mother doing after her accident? Is she still in a coma?' How could this woman be so confused? Unless . . . Of course! Only Madame Heller could be behind such mischief.

Back at St Vincent's, I gather another mountain of change to call Sammy and Jonathan. I need to keep them informed. Or maybe I am desperate to hear their familiar, stabilizing voices. 'Your brother is going to be fine,' I lie. 'Scott's situation has improved.' Jonathan insists he will come immediately. But I tell him, 'No. There is nothing you can do, my dear. Finish your university exams first, then come.' But that will be six weeks. Can I last that long? I want him here so desperately. But I also know Jonathan must lead his own life. When I return to Scott, I whisper in his ear, 'Your brothers are coming. Hang on, Scotty.'

But Scott continues his slow decline. He suffers raging bouts of fever. His kidneys become infected and the antibiotics they administer cause allergic reactions. His temperature fluctuates between a bone-chilling 88° and an oven-like 106°. I am sure there is a problem with Scott's internal thermostat. Sometimes he is so close to death all I can do is lie with him and share his suffering. In those moments, when I can no longer bear his pain, I whisper in his ear, 'Scotty, do you hear me? You have my permission to die. Don't suffer for me. It's okay to let go.' But my heart is bursting and I also tell him, 'If you choose to live, baby, I will do everything in my power to heal you.' As if he has heard me, he struggles back, time and time again, but at an ever-greater cost to his strength.

Unannounced, Sammy arrives from America. Dressed in a brown business suit and carrying an impressive leather briefcase, he storms into the hospital loudly offering to pay for everything. 'I'll sign any papers,' he announces to anyone willing to listen. 'Spare no expense. If it takes the rest of my life, I'll pay you whatever it takes.'

I am deeply touched by his display of charity, but in his youthful exuberance he has forgotten his chequebook and I know he has no money. 'Money is not what your brother needs,' Dr Croches explains. 'What your brother needs is a miracle.'

When Sammy enters Scott's room, his face turns pale. Removing his St Christopher's medal, Sammy lovingly hangs it on the bed above Scott's head. I am so grateful he is here, but with no work permit and a limited visa, Sammy can only stay a week. When he finally leaves, I pitch even further into the black depths of despair and loneliness.

Scott is moved from his private room into a larger 'holding' ward with twenty beds in two rows of ten. Now, at night I sleep on his bed surrounded by the suffering of the dying. People enter and are rolled away at all hours. Family members ebb and flow like waves on the sand. Their grief becomes mine, and mine, theirs. At the bedside to Scott's right sits a businessman whose wife fell and broke her legs while he was away on a business trip. When he returned after thirty-six hours both her legs had to be amputated, as she was a diabetic, and infection had set in. Now she is dying, and he is constantly by her side. When she passes away he is overcome with guilt and despair. I put my arms around him and tell him there are things in life more powerful than our best intentions; that life is painted in broader strokes than we can imagine and all we can do is our best. I want to think part of him hears me and that my words have helped.

On Scotty's left, a young man also lies in a coma. His girlfriend left him and in his despair he hung himself. I look at his contorted body, and see how it relaxes imperceptibly as his life passes. I'm shocked to the core.

Across the aisle, a youthful girl with brown stringy hair, who has had nothing in life but pain, lies in an overdose coma. I am touched by the many homeless people who surround her bed to stand vigil, and I am so very thankful this hospital is open to everyone. One of her friends places a weeks-old baby, kicking and crying, at the young woman's feet, but that baby girl will never know her mother. This time drugs provide the ultimate escape. I am in tears as a woman from Social Services removes the crying baby to her first foster home.

I am deeply grateful my boys never developed a drug or alcohol problem. They knew how much I detested alcohol from my childhood of suffering Dad's binges. I've always suspected that they experimented with pot, as most young people seem to do, in spite of parental denial, and I've always known they drink beer, but that's a far cry from a thirst for usquebaugh.

In the depths of night when I cannot sleep, I slip from Scott's bed to walk the empty and shadowy corridors in the worn linen pants and yellow silk blouse I brought with me. I pass quietly through darkened wards and peer into empty rooms. I float past a nurse bent over an open file, her face half-lit by the glow of a work light and I pass empty trolleys covered with fresh white sheets abandoned in a line along a wall. I hear muted voices and shallow breathing. I hear quiet crying and moans of pain. This is a house of lost souls and I feel at home. I see their shadows and hear them cry out: mothers lost to their children; fathers to their daughters; sons to their mothers. And I see myself, another lost soul. Where is my justice? they plead. Where is my God? Why my daughter, why my son? But I can do nothing. I have no power to change their fate, or mine. I tell them I am as helpless as they are, trapped in an ever-changing bubble of emotions, grabbing at every sliver of hope. We have no choice but to trust in our angels and let it be.

At four weeks, Scott contracts golden staph, an infection that lives in hospitals. He is removed from the ICU ward and put into a single room to isolate him from other patients. Other infections set in, wreaking havoc on his defenceless and undernourished body. With Scott allergic to antibiotics, Dr Croches can do nothing. The incision where the central tube enters Scott's body festers with pus. All the tubes that breathe for him, feed him and pump his blood have become contaminated with life-threatening micro-organisms,

70

and he develops septicaemia, blood poisoning. Against my will, the doctors try new antibiotics. Instantly, I detect swelling from another allergic reaction. Dr Croches informs me he intends to remove the respirator to see if Scott might breathe on his own. I prepare myself for the worst, saying a silent prayer of goodbye, but when the machine is disconnected, Scott continues to breathe. In fact, his condition seems to improve slightly. Miraculously, we have made another step forward. The doctors cluster about the bed in quiet wonder. Later, Dr Croches tells me they were all sure Scott would die but no one had the courage to tell me. I understood. No one wanted to destroy my faith.

After weeks of emotional turbulence watching Scott gradually gain strength only to weaken and slide to new lows, I begin to sense a subtle pattern to his cycle of health. When the doctors increase his medications, his body begins to fail. When medications are decreased or terminated, miraculously, Scotty begins to rally. Could it be that the very drugs intended to save him might actually be poisoning him, deepening his coma and pushing him towards death? I have always known Scotty and I have high-frequency energy fields and low blood pressure. We are also allergic to most drugs. Does this mixture of high energy and low blood pressure and allergic reactions have anything to do with healing? I begin to suspect it might.

I've read of an oncologist in a London hospital, Dr Darius, who has researched why certain people diagnosed with high-frequency body energy seem to heal better with little or no medication while other patients who are under heavy medication languish even though they both share similar signs. Dr Darius is able to identify the presence of high energy through his own intuition and the detection of abnormal amounts of heat by lightly holding his hand over a patient's head. These same patients also have low blood pressure. While many would dismiss his technique as paranormal medicine (some would even say mumbo jumbo), he has been successful in helping patients heal by linking their level of medication to their levels of high-frequency energy.

As a child, Scotty was always allergic to medicine. I learned early the best way to treat his childhood diseases was not to treat them at all but to let nature work her magic. Scotty's body had a way of healing itself as long as it was left alone. This had always been true for me, as well. I believe medicine interferes with my body's self-healing process but have found this phenomenon curiously unexplainable until both of us were diagnosed with high-frequency energy and low blood pressure.

Mother's Day passes with me at Scott's bedside. A thoughtful Indian doctor, Vijay, brings me a bouquet of colourful flowers and a small box of chocolates. I receive motherly notes from the boys. Increasingly, members of the hospital staff, doctors and nurses, make Scott's room a regular stop on their rounds, even those not assigned to his case. They ask about his condition and about his life before the injury. I tell them of his loving nature and dynamic energy. Their concern warms my heart and makes the unbearable less so. I understand why Scott loved Australia and its people. This is a country founded in the hardship of a penal colony, but its people are warm, spiritual, grounded and open.

Nurse Jenny, increasingly concerned with my emotional and mental state, escorts me to the staff psychologist for an evaluation. The psychologist asks me to evaluate myself. How am I coping? he wants to know. Am I getting enough rest? Am I drowning under the burden? I secretly believe he is evaluating my emotional capacity to handle Scott's death, which seems, to all but me, a foregone conclusion.

'I have made my peace with what may happen,' I tell him. 'I have given Scotty permission to die. But it hasn't happened yet, has it? And I am willing to be patient.'

This is what he wants to hear and I return to Scott's room. I sit on the floor at the foot of his bed with a large sketchpad before me. I draw a figure sitting up in bed, a rendition of both Scott and me, with attributes of both of us, with the face shown turning in three directions. I draw the psychiatrist sitting behind us asking questions. When I finish, I stare at the drawing and wonder what the psychologist might think if he saw this.

To escape the pain of reality, I rise early and walk ten minutes to the bluff over the bay to witness the sunrise. Each new beginning is announced in brilliant reds and purples until the fireball, perfectly round and blazing glory, rises majestically from its perch on the horizon to light the world and offer fresh inspiration. Nature renews me and offers a reprieve from the sterile atmosphere of the hospital. On my walks, white cockatoos scream and swoop down from eucalyptus trees. A pair of ibis birds strut across my path. I gather nature's art for Scott's room. A gnarly branch becomes his window altar, with bits of flowers, feathers and leaves strung from the twigs. I find wall posters of red sunrises and cool fields of golden flowers for Scotty's walls. Gradually, I transform his antiseptic cocoon into a work of nature. The hospital staff never interfere with my nesting ways.

After my morning walks I usually eat in the canteen, mostly oatmeal and coffee. With few people about at that hour, I find quiet corners and use the time to reflect. Sometimes I cry out, but when

I find myself spiralling into despair I turn off the tape in my head. Why suffer unnecessarily? I think of happier times. How I handle this challenge is my choice and it works, most of the time.

I begin to receive phone calls from Stefan telling me how much he misses me and his intention to visit me in Australia some time, not in the near future, but some time. I begin to feel finally at peace about our relationship even though somewhere in my psyche I realize it's all over.

Dr Croches often enters the room on his rounds and simply leans against the wall. 'How are you doing, Glenys?' he asks in that soothing voice.

'Up and down,' I reply, always with a smile but never really looking at him, to mask my exhaustion and fear. 'Up and down Paddington Street.'

That was my private joke, which Dr Croches would never understand. The last time I felt so small, so insignificant and so terribly alone was when I ran away from home at eleven and took the train to London, walking up and down Paddington Street, a little girl in a big, noisy and impersonal city.

'And how is Scott today?' he asks. I tell him the first thing that comes to me: 'He's not any worse,' or, 'There may be a kidney problem,' or, 'You need to check his liver.' In every case, the tests they run show a problem in the area I suggest. Dr Croches seems to enjoy this daily exchange and pays close attention to my suggestions.

Richard and Julie often invite me to their home. I relish the brief respite that their caring friendship affords. Rollie and Robin often stand beside me at Scott's bed in silence, with fingers intertwined. They bring me warm clothes for the Australian winter, and Scott a tape player with tapes of gentle music. They add hand-painted woodcarvings and other personal treasures to Scott's window art. They have a vacant flat near the hospital and give me a key for those few times when, driven by exhaustion, I dare spend a night away from Scott's bed. How can I repay such loving concern?

It has now been six weeks since I arrived, six weeks of coma, trauma, exhaustion, and endless disappointment. Jonathan is taking his year-end university exams now, and when he finishes he promises to join us for a long stay. My joy swells as I anticipate his arrival. Every day I whisper in Scott's ear, 'Your brother is coming, Scotty. He's coming soon. Be strong.' But as Jonathan is finishing his exams, Scott takes a turn for the worse. The usual team of doctors converges again. They remove the feeding tubes, a major source of contamination, but there is no improvement. The tube that pumps and filters his blood continues to infect him. If they remove that tube, Scotty will surely die. But it is a losing battle. Blood poisoning is on its death march. His blood pressure drops to a critical 36 over 22. His fever rages at 106°. His entire body, including his face, bloats with infection. His vital signs are fading.

Dr Croches takes me into the hall. 'The infection is killing Scott,' he tells me. I see moisture in his eyes. 'We need your permission to remove all the tubes and stop the medication. It's his only chance. But, honestly, I don't think it will help. I think you should prepare yourself.'

I feel suffocated. How can I make such a decision to deliberately end his life? I can't. I turn and run down the hall and outside to the green lawn, to inhale deeply the fresh sea air and absorb the warm winter sun. On a wooden bench under a huge eucalyptus tree I fall into uncontrollable sobbing. Oh, God, I pray, why can't I trade places with Scott? Why can't he lead his life and follow his dreams? I feel a hand on my shoulder. Dr Croches has followed me.

'I'm so sorry to have run out on you,' I sob, trying to blot my flow of tears.

'He's your son and you've fought hard to be with him this long,' he says, quietly. 'I understand your grief. I have two sons of my own.' His hand gently squeezes my shoulder in support. 'But I'm afraid it's time to let go.'

'His brother Jonathan is on his way,' I plead. 'Scott can't die without seeing his brother. Please keep Scotty alive just a bit longer?'

Dr Croches is quiet for a long time, an eternity it seems. 'Tell your son to hurry.'

I collect another pile of coins for the pay phone. 'You must hurry,' I tell Jonathan. 'Scotty needs you. Can you leave tonight?'

'I've sent my passport to the Australian Embassy in Copenhagen,' Jonathan tells me. 'They still have it and it's Saturday. I can't do anything until Monday.'

That's too late, my mind screams. Tears run down my cheeks in thin rivers. I'm coming apart, but I can't let Jonathan know. 'Come as soon as you can,' is all I can say, and hang up quickly before I break down completely.

When I return to Scott's room, two nurses are rigging a sheet tent over his bed. They set up a pan of ice with a fan to blow cool air into the tent to break Scott's fever. His signs stabilize until suddenly his body temperature plummets to an icy 88°. We turn off the fan and cover him with thermal blankets: within hours, his raging fever is back and we remove the blankets. 'Please stay with me,' I plead over and over. 'Jonathan is coming. You want to see your brother, don't you?'

Time seems to fly by, as if making it impossible for Jonathan to arrive in time. But at the same time, each moment seems endless, eternal. Scott is still with me. I am still with him. I lie by his side, singing softly, hoping it gives him comfort. Hours pass, or has it been days? Maybe no more than minutes.

Dr Croches comes to my side and tells me Scott's vital signs are fading. The end is here. Dr Croches hands me the papers granting permission to donate Scott's organs, and I sign. Then I hug my son a last time. I tell him how proud I am to be his mother. I tell him what a wonderful son he has been to me. My tears fall across his face. Doctors and nurses have quietly slipped into the room to gather around his bed. Many are openly weeping. I hear myself saying, over and over, 'No, no, no, no . . .'

'Mom?'

I swing around. Jonathan is standing in the doorway. Blurry-eyed and dishevelled, he throws his arms around me in a tight hug. 'I came as fast as I could, Mom. I hope I'm not too late.'

I frame his face in my hands. 'Oh, Jonathan, Jonathan. Scott is dying, honey,' I tell him between sobs. 'Go tell him your goodbyes. Tell him that you love him.'

Jonathan approaches the bed with a quiet reverence. The tubes have been removed and Scott lies under the white sheet, angelic, in a deep slumber. Jonathan leans over and whispers in his brother's ear. I can't hear what is said and I won't ever ask him to tell me. It is his private moment. He continues to whisper, then gives a long, low whistle, the same whistle he and Scott had shared as children, the whistle that meant, 'It's okay to come out now. The coast is clear.'

Inexplicably, within minutes, Scott's vital signs begin to improve. His blood pressure strengthens, his pulse quickens and slowly colour returns to his face. The doctors who have gathered round are dumb with wonder. How could this be? their expressions ask. The word 'miracle' is whispered. As his condition improves, the tubes that have been removed from his body are reattached. His tracheotomy tube is changed, his IV line and feeding tube are reinserted. The respirator is not needed, as he is able to breathe on his own.

Stunned by the rapid turnabout, I find myself lost in a fog of mixed emotions. My baby may live after all. But then, is this for real? I have been down this rocky path before. So many times my heart soared at the faintest sign of life. So many times I witnessed Scott fighting back only to lose ground in the end. Could it be different this time? I want so much to believe, but my optimism and faith are captive to sheer exhaustion.

Months of hospital life have taken their toll on me. There has been persistent pressure from well-intentioned doctors who wished to abandon Scott to the nursing home. The endless hours of holding his hands, working his fingers and gently bending his arms to stimulate blood flow and exercise flaccid muscles. The reading aloud of his favourite books. And the one-sided conversations: How are you feeling today, Scott? . . . Can you hear me? . . . Did I tell you I talked to Sammy? . . . Oh, Jonathan called to say . . . Nurse Jenny stopped by . . . Followed by the inevitable disheartening crash of Scott's silence.

On and on, over and over, looking out beyond Scott's window with its altar of branches and bird feathers and flowers, I watch the days evaporate into weeks, the weeks into months. In spite of it all, I continue to gather the courage to keep going. Secretly I wonder how long I can tap my reservoir of strength before it runs dry. How deep is that pool? How shallow? I am in uncharted waters.

With money a persistent and nagging worry, I write to Stefan asking him to sell my BMW. Soon the envelope arrives with much-needed cash, but it will last only so long, and I have nothing else left to sell.

Even as the grey storm clouds gather, I am gripped by a stronger determination to seek the sun. Scott is depending on me. I promised I would be here. I will make his life whole again. I will carry his weight and fight the system.

Still, so many times in the night, as I lie curled at the foot of his bed, the ugly monster of self-doubt appears to attack my resolve. I am frightened, terrified I will not have the strength. I do not want to fail. After all, it's not my failure.

But now I am helped by Jonathan's presence. I am overwhelmed by his love and gentleness with Scott. He spends many hours with Scott, reading, talking to him, helping the nurses and making suggestions in his quiet manner.

Suddenly Scott shows signs of waking up. Another battle begins.

Five

If Scott's story were a Hollywood film, he would awaken with a yawn and a lazy smile, casually reach out for my hand, and ask for a huge dish of chocolate ice-cream. But films are fiction, and not how someone wakes after three months in the deep freeze of a head-injury coma. Muscles atrophy and lose mass. Tendons and ligaments contract, causing knees to bend and arms to crook. In a prone position, the body's blood is evenly dispersed. The heart relaxes and nearly forgets how to pump, so that even the smallest movement can lead to over-exertion and rapid exhaustion. Lacking stimulation, the brain shuts down to the point where even simple thoughts require great effort. Sometimes a part of memory is erased, as if a videotape has been passed over a magnet. Waking from a deep coma takes weeks, sometimes months, of tedious therapy with uncertain consequences. As well as suffering from the after-effects of the coma, Scott has damaged nerve and brain tissue from the fall.

The first sign of Scott's awakening is the imperceptible flicker of an eye. I am sitting on his bed, his hand loosely cupped in mine, when I catch the flicker. Shifting forward to focus intently on his face, I watch and wait for what feels like an eternity.

There again, another flicker, but this time it is more a shallow blink. He blinks once, then again, and one of his lids is partially open. It is only a crack, but I see his eye. Is he looking my way? My heart races, my breath quickens and turns shallow. My hands perspire. For months Scott has lain with tightly closed eyes, till I began to doubt even their colour. Now suddenly, finally, he is opening from that world. Could my butterfly be emerging from his chrysalis?

Firmly I grasp his hand. 'Scotty,' I whisper, 'can you hear me? If you can, squeeze my hand.'

I await his response while fighting to calm my chills and control the roar of my own rapid breathing, for fear of missing another sign. After several minutes, I slowly repeat my command and wait again in the vacuum of expectation. Then I feel it. A squeezing pressure on my hand, so slight it might have been a feather landing on my skin. But the pressure is unmistakable and deliberate. My heart leaps.

'How are you doing this morning, Glenys?' a quiet voice says from behind. I didn't hear Dr Croches enter. But I dare not turn around. Scott and I are communicating. It is more than that: I am sending him my energy, refuelling my son's spirit with mine, and giving him the strength and desire to break the bonds of his sleep. To turn away now might set him back.

'Scotty's waking up,' I hear myself say. 'He opened an eye. I've been talking to him, and he responded, he squeezed my hand.'

Dr Croches moves to Scott's side, leaning across the bed to pass his hand in front of Scott's face, checking for eye response. Noticing nothing, he gently lifts Scott's eyelid. His eye seems fixed in an unfocused stare, but his brown iris constricts in reaction to light. Dr Croches steps away from the bed and crosses his arms, deep in thought.

'I guess there are miracles,' he says quietly, more an inner thought than an outer comment. I feel the warm touch of his hand on my shoulder, a silent affirmation that I have been right all along, that my faith has been true, and we have surmounted unbelievable odds.

But my thoughts are elsewhere, sorting through unknowns. My son has begun to wake up, but to what? Where is the joy in this small victory when such a heavy burden remains? Has he returned a vegetable? Will he ever walk again, or even talk? How long before the hospital evicts us? Scott's visa has long expired, so I know it's just a matter of time. Where could we go? Live in the moment, my inner self commands. Do what you can today, trust you'll be able to handle the morrow.

The next day brings even more stress. Unannounced, the immigration doctor appears, a burly no-nonsense man. He walks briskly into Scott's room and stands at the end of his bed looking through a sheaf of papers, which I imagine to be Scotty's medical records. Clearing his throat with a loud harumph, and without turning my way or looking me in the eyes, he begins to speak. In the silent confines of the room, his voice roars.

'So what are we going to do with this young man? Obviously he is in no condition to go anywhere, but his visa has expired, and that means he's here illegally. You are also here illegally. So pray tell me, what are we going to do?' Moving to the side of the bed, his eyes run the length of Scott's immobile frame while he nervously tugs at the tip of his chin. 'His visa has expired and our records show that you do not have acceptable insurance for rehabilitation. That's a problem. Yes, that's certainly a problem. He is certainly not well enough to travel.' He glances at his sheaf of papers, then leaves the room, saying, 'I'll be back. I'll call you.'

When the doctor departs, I sit for a long time staring at the wall over Scott's head. What can I do? Immigration has already informed me they will not renew Scott's or my visa. If we did have renewed visas, we could claim additional benefits, but the Australian government will hear nothing of it. Where could we go? I have no idea. But, it hasn't happened yet, has it? I resolve to make the most of the time I have.

Gradually Scott gathers strength. Within days both his eyes open. He remains too weak to move his head, but as his brain re-engages, his eyes shift and blink as they slowly roam the room to gather and process intelligence before exhaustion sets in and he drifts back into sleep. Other times he opens his eyes only to stare into the ceiling, disengaged, unblinking and unfocused, as if his mind is unable to escape the gravitational pull of his alternate world.

I tell him, 'Do not be afraid. You cannot speak yet because you have a tracheotomy tube in place. When the doctors remove it, you will be able to talk. You were hurt, Scott, but you are now beginning to get better. I want you to feel safe, and concentrate on getting better.'

In the ensuing days I redouble my efforts to further his rehabilitation. I read to him longer, and with a firmer voice, believing that even while he sleeps my words are stimulating his brain. With renewed vitality I massage his hands and fingers, slowly and gently move his good right arm, and manipulate his feet to stretch the Achilles tendon. But I sense I am walking a thin line. Too much stimulation might be more dangerous than too little. Overloaded, Scott's brain might shut down to seek refuge in the protective tranquillity of his coma. How much is too much? Where is the trigger? How will I know? Don't ask questions, my inner voice instructs; trust your feelings, trust what Scotty tells you. As if responding to my determination, his body responds. Each day he stays awake a little longer. He flexes his fingers a little more, and with my gentle help, he moves his good arm and his head slightly.

At the end of that week, a steel tilt table is wheeled through the door. After months on his back, Scott's heart, organs and muscles need introduction to the stress of vertical living. Reborn into his new life, like a baby, he will need to relearn the most elemental of skills. From across the room, I watch the orderlies carefully lift Scott from his bed to the brown cushion of the tilt table where his body and each limb are carefully strapped into place. A physically fit patient would assist in his own transfer by stiffening his muscles, but Scott's muscles are shrunken, making the short lift from one bed to another a delicate manoeuvre.

At first the tilt table is raised only a few degrees for one to two minutes, while a technician checks his pulse and carefully monitors the colour of his face. If Scott's face turned ashen, a sign the heart was overworked and blood was pouring to his feet, the table would be lowered immediately. But his pulse remains strong and his face looks healthy. The table arrives daily, and gradually over the next five weeks the incline is increased: five degrees, ten, fifteen, then forty-five, while the length of time is also increased from one minute to five, then to ten, fifteen and up to thirty.

But as the table slope increases, gravity weighs in with its own consequences. The tracheotomy tube still inserted in Scott's throat takes on a new weight as its angle changes slightly, and sometimes causes pain at the incision. Arm and leg muscles, long accustomed to the horizontal support of the bed, find themselves hanging vertically with an unaccustomed weight that strains their attachments to the bones. Internal organs that had found a new nest within Scott's horizontal body are now being stretched from their comfort and forced to reposition themselves normally. Yet through all the pain, barely a moan escapes his lips.

Suddenly I feel weak and insignificant. Could I be unworthy as a mother? My own self-indulgence, suffering, my weeks of self-pity, loneliness and guilt pale next to Scott's struggle. Who is being healed here, and who is the healer? Rather than my nurturing him, Scott inspires me. He gives me the spiritual and emotional strength to carry on, to be a better person.

In the second week of the tilt table therapy, a speech therapist appears, pushing a small white cart on wheels. 'I'm here for Scott's swallow test,' she announces with a cheery smile. 'We've been feeding him by tube, and now we have to see if he can feed himself,' she adds, as she jockeys the cart closer to the bed. 'People in a coma forget how to eat; their swallow muscles get lazy. So what we're going to do now is see if these muscles still work.'

From a bottle she pours a few drops of dark liquid into a spoon, and supporting Scott's head with her left hand, slips the tip of the spoon into his mouth to see what might happen. The muscles in his throat constrict as he swallows the drops. 'That's very good, a good first step,' she says, as if Scott were an average patient with an average broken neck. 'It seems you haven't forgotten everything. Now how about we try some jelly, something nice and soft.' With a spoon she places a small amount of jelly into his mouth. Again Scott's throat muscles ripple as he swallows. 'Swallowing is more difficult than you think,' she says, while closely observing Scott's responses.

I am deeply amused by her unusual chattiness. Perhaps like so many others who daily enter our room, she has been inspired by Scott's struggle and miraculous recovery.

'We take swallowing for granted, don't we?' she bubbles on, 'but when you have forgotten how to swallow, you have also forgotten so many other things, like coordinating your tongue and breathing with swallowing. Of course this is unconscious. It's really a brain problem, you see. If Scott tried to swallow this jelly at the same time as inhaling, he might suck food into his lungs. So his brain has to sort it out, to relearn its old habits.'

She spoons another small helping of jelly into Scott's mouth, which he handles fine. 'He's doing so well, Glenys. We'll do this for a few more days. If he passes with good marks, we can probably remove the tube.' Gathering her equipment, she wheels the cart from the room.

I feel an immense sense of relief and accomplishment. Another small step. No, not a small step, a big, big step, a more-than-monumental step towards life. Slowly my fears are being tamed. I know now he can eat, but can he speak? I won't know the answer until the tracheotomy tube is removed. In the meantime I will work on Scott's language comprehension.

Next morning, I find a large piece of cardboard, about two by three feet, and with a black marker write words in large letters across it:

red black hot cold sleepy music yes no.

I prop up Scott's body with pillows and sit on the side of his bed holding the sign about two feet in front of his eyes. 'Now then, Scott, I will say a word and I want you to point to it. Just point with your eyes. I'll know what you mean. Do you understand?' I search his brown eyes for an answer. They are looking at the board, but reveal little understanding.

'Good.' I continue the game. 'Now find the word "hot".' Scott continues staring at the board, then slowly his eyes begin a crawling search until several moments later they focus on the word 'hot'. I breathe a deep sigh before continuing. We work through my list of words. My confidence grows that his brain is capable of processing abstractions. I also notice that as his eyes search, he is trying to move his arm, as if driven by a compulsion to point.

'Scott, can you point to the word? Is that what you want, to point? If it's yes, squeeze my hand. Do you understand? Squeeze my hand.' Clasping his good hand in mine, I wait. His response is not immediate, but I am learning patience. Somewhere in his brain a neurological battle rages. Electrical impulses fire and misfire in chaotic order while his confused brain feverishly works to sort it out. But there it is, a squeeze. Awkwardly, Scott bends his thumb into my flesh.

I begin the routine again, asking him to identify various words, while this time I support the weight of his arm, letting him guide his finger to the correct response. In the days to come, lifting and stretching his arm to model the act of pointing will consume many hours.

A few days later, Dr Croches strides through the door. 'It's about time to remove the tracheotomy tube. He seems to be handling things on his own. With your help and determination,' he adds with a knowing smile, 'I don't think he'll starve.'

'I've been meaning to ask you something,' I say. 'I've been reading in the library about brain damage. I read that a brain can learn new pathways, and that it can rewire itself to compensate for damage. Is that true?'

'There is research to that effect,' Dr Croches says a bit guardedly, 'but it's not definitive. It is possible. I mean it hasn't been disproved. With the proper stimulation, Scott's brain might well learn new pathways.' Dr Croches silently appraises Scotty with thoughtful, narrowed eyes. 'Knowing your son, Glenys, I would think anything is possible.'

'Well then,' I reply, 'as soon as the trachea is removed I would like to put Scotty in a wheelchair and tour him about his new grand house, the hospital!' I was giddy with anticipation. 'He needs to travel a bit and see the sights.'

Dr Croches' face clouds over. 'I'm not sure he's ready for that. How long has it been? Three weeks. I don't think he's strong enough to sit up.'

'We can make it, I know we can. I'll prop him up with pillows and strap him in. We both need this.' With a sigh and a raised brow, Dr Croches nods assent.

True to his word, a few days after the incision in Scott's throat is sewn up, a wheelchair appears. After propping up Scott's body with pillows and strapping him in, we set off down the same long corridors I so often walked alone in the solitude of night. Now I'm exhilarated and walk with a wide smile and the full stride of a conquering heroine. Never have I felt so free and full of life, even though Scott cannot hold himself up. Repeatedly, his body slides toward the floor and I am forced to stop and pull him upright, rearranging the pillows before continuing. This is my first experience of dealing with Scott's full weight. Sobered, I wonder how I will ever manage without the assistance of hospital staff.

Turning a corner, we enter the lift and down we go to the basement cafeteria for his favourite treat. With a plastic cup of chocolate ice-cream set before him, I push a silver spoon into Scott's good hand, and wrap his fingers around the handle. But he has trouble grasping the spoon, and even more trouble manoeuvring it into his dish. So I help him scoop, and when he cannot get it into his mouth, I help again. With the first taste of ice-cream, Scott's eyes glow with excitement and the right side of his mouth breaks into a crinkled, wooden half-smile.

Several more times we practise eating, but it is a slow process and he grows frustrated. Dropping the spoon, Scott reaches out awkwardly and jabs his fingers into the bowl, scoops the ice-cream, and erratically pushes it into his mouth, leaving a broad brown smear across his face. I wipe his fingers clean with a white napkin, and as I lean forward to clean his face, Scott clumsily hooks his right arm round my neck and pulls me forward, planting a sloppy, chocolatey, flat-lipped kiss on my cheek. Stunned, I pull back to look into his sparkling eyes, and for just a second detect the faintest flash of his old devilish sense of humour. Tearing up, I blot my eyes with the back of my hand, wipe at the streaks on my face, and in the process smear chocolate everywhere.

I am desperate to run off to the bathroom for a mirror, but I dare not leave him alone. Propping him in his chair, I quickly turn for the lift. Upstairs I move as quickly down the hallway as I dare while keeping my head lowered. Surely I won't be noticed with chocolate all over me. But I am. Nurses see me coming and grin as I pass. Orderlies notice as they push loaded trolleys fresh from surgery. Even ambulatory patients, normally preoccupied with their own travails, stop hobbling on their crutches to give me a quizzical look.

By this time I've decided I don't care. I hold my head high for the world to see. My son has just given me a kiss. In his room I check the mirror and I'm surprised to see a clean face. What are these people looking at, I wonder, or were they looking at all? What's happening to my mind?

I make flash cards from pieces of cardboard, each with a word written in large black letters, and hold them up to train his voice. First I pronounce the word, then encourage Scott to do the same. It is difficult and exhausting work, but it must be done. Like any newborn, he must learn to speak. He must learn to purse his lips, to shape sounds, to use his tongue, and to control his breathing. Somewhere locked in his mind, the circuitry of speech lies dormant. Through repetition and modelling I am determined to find and energize that circuit. At first Scott's responses are muted or exaggerated, sometimes only gurgles, sometimes loud grunts. Eventually he modulates his responses, and as breathing, muscle and sounds converge, his speech patterns improve to the point where we can carry on halting but often difficult conversations.

Thankfully, Scott's burden is no longer solely mine. Jonathan with his solid and caring nature has his visa extended and settles in for a longer stay. His wife Ulla has also come to help and to see for herself how Scott is improving. We don't tell Scott Ulla is coming so he is surprised when she walks into his room, and immediately picks up her hand and starts kissing it. I'm sure he's gratified that his extended family are rallying around. And Ulla is touched by his exuberant greeting, knowing how much pain he is in. Having Jonathan and Ulla there ends my isolation and provides a needed sense of family. We make Scott's room our home and at night we alternate sleeping on the waiting room couches or on Scott's bed.

Hold My Hand

Scott's old apartment on Potts Point is still available as the rent has been prepaid, and I persuade Jonathan to move in. We devise a schedule of twelve-hour shifts. Night or day, one of us will always be at Scott's side. When the apartment rent expires, my friends Rollie and Robin offer Jonathan their spare bedroom. Every day he rides a borrowed bicycle twenty-five miles from their home in the suburb of Sutherland to the hospital for his shift, then rides back at night or the next morning after I take over. Jonathan's a very strong bicyclist.

Jonathan passes the hours reading to Scott. Over the next several weeks they manage to consume the entire *Lord of the Rings* trilogy. Sometimes he straps Scott into the wheelchair and takes him to the hospital roof for a small amount of sunshine. When we leave Scott at night, we always make sure a tape is playing so he has at least a half hour of music.

For the first time in months, I am able to enjoy a few luxurious days of freedom. On my days off, Julie Clarke's mother, Johnnie, invites me to her home near the beach in Gymea. Rising early in the mornings, I walk the sand, inviting the sun and breeze to restore my depleted spirit. After a long nap I return to the beach to swim and swim until I can barely crawl from the surf. I didn't know how exhausted I was, how close I was to an emotional breakdown, until I experienced the freedom of the sea. How does one express gratitude to another for the simplicity of their friendship, a private room, a soft clean bed and a hot cup of tea? Whom do you thank for a swim in the ocean, for the luxury of solitude on a deserted beach, for your health and serenity? I am beginning to love life again.

After five weeks Scott graduates from the tilt table and a staff psychologist comes round to assess my son's mental competence. Mid-height, in his late thirties, unsmiling in a sterile white coat, he enters the room under a halo of gloom. One can tell so much from a person's eyes – warmth, humour, sincerity, fear – but his are flat and empty. I wonder if he isn't depressed himself. Certainly he lacks the most essential ingredient of happiness, a sense of humour. Sitting on the side of Scott's bed, the psychologist methodically runs through a battery of questions in a monotone voice while I sit tight-lipped in a chair against the side wall.

'What time of day is it, Scott?'

A long pause. Finally Scott answers. 'It seems I've lost my watch.' The psychologist frowns and makes a mark in his file. I know Scott has no clue – there are no clocks in the room, and even a glance out the window reveals little more than filtered daylight. I say to myself, I must get Scott a watch.

'How did you get here?'

Scott's face creases as he vainly searches his mind. With the short-term memory loss that comes with head injury, I already know there will be no answer that satisfies.

'UFO, and they're not coming back,' Scott finally says with that crooked, half-frozen smile that signifies a joke, a smile the psychologist misses as he frowns and makes another mark. But I am amused. Scott knows he doesn't know, so why not throw out something wild? He chooses humour over despondency.

The third question: 'Do you know where you are?'

'The Ritz Hotel.' I've forgotten to tell him the name of the hospital he's in.

The psychologist grows agitated. His patient is not cooperating.

The questions continue for another twenty minutes. Scott's answers are short and off the point, perhaps slyly so, and to me humorous. When the man leaves, I am sure Scott has flunked his mental test. But then I realize that might be a good thing. Wouldn't the hospital be less inclined to release someone detached from reality? Unknowingly, Scott may have bought us some more time.

I have just pulled my chair to the bed and am about to read to Scott when Jonathan unexpectedly appears, pushing a wheelchair seating a young man with a badly disfigured face. They are on their way to the roof for some sun, Jonathan tells me, but he wanted to swing by to say hello and introduce his friend Tim. I have seen the young man before. Often I look up from one of my daily tutorials with Scott to see Tim at the door peering in, but before I can say anything he is gone, leaving me with that uneasy feeling of having encountered another lost soul.

Tim was one of the nineteen other patients in Scott's old ward, Jonathan later tells me, the one whose face was swaddled in white bandages after he put a gun in his mouth and pulled the trigger. The bandages are gone now, and even after several reconstructive surgeries, his face remains shattered. His upper jaw is mostly gone, as is his nose, cleanly shot off leaving two gaping holes for nostrils. Tim is deeply depressed, and bitterly angry with the surgeons who saved him, for they rescued him from one hell only to thrust him into another. Knowing his disfigurement and his visceral impact upon others, Tim hides in his dark room, refusing to be wheeled outside or to meet others. For some reason, however, he has found a friend in Jonathan and allows himself to be taken to the roof.

After Tim is introduced to Scotty and me, he appears more often at our door, sometimes even wheeling himself in to quietly observe.

I talk to him obliquely, but not directly facing him, as I soon learn this drives him away. Years later I will find myself thinking back to the bitterness of Tim, a victim of his own hand, and to the bitterness of Ron Kovic, victim of a war that left him a quadriplegic. And I think of other victims I've met, who cope not with bitterness but with smiles and soaring spirits. Why is it some people emerge from adversity with a will to conquer, and others with a will to die? The great tragedy is not our death or disfigurement, but what dies inside us while we are living. Sometimes we forget our responsibility to ourselves and drift through life into nothingness.

If it hadn't been for a phone call from Stefan in Germany, Christmas might have passed with scant notice. 'I'm flying into Sydney to see you and Scott,' he tells me. It is strange hearing that distant voice after so long, and I'm unsure how to respond. But I can't say no. Not to someone I have known so well. A firm anchor to my past might be just what I need. When Johnnie hears Stefan is coming, she kindly invites us to spend Christmas with her. Stefan arrives, and with some foreboding, Jonathan, Ulla and I check Scott out of the hospital and move to Johnnie's for three days.

It is a wonderful time, and a bright spot into what my future may be like with Scott at home, finally.

We all exchange Christmas gifts. Scott's trumpet has been sent from America by friends who are storing some of his possessions. We hold it up for him so he can use his good hand to play the notes, and see if he can blow it. We all laugh at the funny sounds coming out. Even Scott laughs at himself.

Even though I relish the sanctity of her home with its gay Christmas tree and carols and a strong feeling of family, Scott is a little out of his element, and I realize, more difficult to manage. We sleep little, and I'm emotionally spent. With Stefan pressing to rekindle our relationship, given my burdens, the holidays lose their edge. Soon after, I return Scott to the hospital and Stefan departs for Germany, leaving me emotionally disorientated with unanswered questions. He's a good man, and thinks so much of me; perhaps I should have been more receptive. Will I ever enjoy another relationship? But I can't live in Germany, and I can't sacrifice Scott's future to my own confusion and uncertain desires.

That night I overhear Scott and Jonathan reminiscing about the times in Denmark when they both lived in Copenhagen and how little time they actually spent together compared to how close they were growing up. Scott says, 'Hey, you had your reasons. A new lady [Ulla]. That part of your life was just as important as us being together as brothers and friends.' This means a lot to Jonathan, because he is battling missing his little brother and a lifetime of memories and trying to accept Scott in his new injured form. Scott was Jonathan's shadow for their entire childhood and they never got tired of each other. They never understood friends who didn't want their little brother or sister around. But it seems to dawn on Jonathan that all he had with his little brother is still there, right in front of him. It's nice that we can all be together this special Christmas, feeling the warmth of everybody's caring.

∾

I will never forget that sunny morning when Dr Croches walked into Scott's room with a smile on his face. 'I have good news for you, Glenys,' he says quietly, so as not to wake Scott. 'We believe your son is well enough to be discharged. But better yet, arrangements have been made for him at the Coorabel Rehabilitation

Hospital. It will take a day or two to sort out, but you might want to pull your things together.'

I am so stunned that I can only stare at Dr Croches in disbelief. I'm not even aware that he has walked out, or that I am fumbling about for a chair, fearing my lightheadedness and shortness of breath presage a collapse. Four months in this small box of a room, six months of nights curled on Scott's bed, four months of struggle to push back the pall of defeat, finally to be told Scott is well enough to leave. And not simply to leave, but to be transferred to a rehab hospital, even after the immigration doctor has emphatically stated, 'Impossible! Your visa won't allow it.'

I leap from my chair and with nervous excitement pace the room, my mind racing. The word 'rehabilitation' echoes like a church bell. Now we will make real progress. Now with professional help, Scott will learn to walk. He will learn to talk. Now his brain will mend and he will be made whole again. It will be hard work, I know that, but now it will happen. All my prayers, all my dreams, all my hopes are being answered. I dream that night of the Coorabel Hospital, but what I don't dream of is what I actually find.

Coorabel, formally known as the Royal Ryde Rehabilitation Hospital, is twenty miles from St Vincent's, on Charles Street in the suburb of Ryde. I might just as well be in another country. It's a single-storey building with a red tile roof set in a verdant garden with a wall. Coorabel houses about sixty patients in wards of four to ten patients each. Scott is placed in a small ward with three others, all bedridden. One has suffered a debilitating stroke. Another has an inoperable brain tumour, and the third has a head injury. No longer allowed to spend the night, I seek refuge with Johnnie who arranges for me to borrow a small car for the forty-five-minute daily drive.

Jonathan also rearranges his commute, which is now longer than the twenty-five miles he used to pedal.

Unlike St Vincent's, where I was allowed to decorate Scott's room and where the doctors were open and supportive, at Coorabel I am treated as an inconvenience. The doctors seem secretive, with no one person in charge of Scotty's treatment. It is nearly a week before I meet the senior doctor. I am massaging Scott's right hand, working as always on both hands to build strength and circulation, when a heavy-set man briskly enters our small ward. 'I am Dr Rosen, head of the hospital. And this is Scott Carl?' I nod yes, but he isn't looking; he is flipping the pages of a brown file. What strikes me is the cool distance of his voice and the fact he speaks to me in the abstract, as if I am little more than a translucent shadow, even though I am now at his side.

'You've been here how long? Yes, it says here a week. Our facility is different from others. Our patients have severe problems. They are here for therapy and cannot tolerate noise or disruption of any sort. So you will be asked to conform to our rules precisely. Limit your time to visiting hours. No visiting at night. And you are not allowed in the therapy rooms. It is for the good of the patients.'

Finally Dr Rosen turns my way. 'Scott is here for therapy,' I say, gathering courage. 'But he has a problem. When he fell he broke his left clavicle, and because he was in a coma it was never fixed. I know it's giving him a lot of pain. What can we do about his left arm?'

Dr Rosen appraises Scotty's upper body, then glances at me. 'I suggest you forget he has a left arm.'

My amazement leaves me speechless. How can he say that in front of my son?

97

'Doctor, there's nothing wrong with Scott's hearing,' I say coolly, my temper rising. Scotty is in fact quietly absorbing every word.

'You have to stop being in denial,' Dr Rosen responds. It hits me then that this doctor, who knows nothing of Scott except notes in a chart, has already written my son off as hopeless. Later I come to understand how a lack of money forces Dr Rosen to make hard choices regarding the kind of treatment he can offer but now I am really angry.

'How would you like it if I chopped off your left hand?' I spit out. Immediately, I regret my outburst, but I'm only human and this man is destroying my hope. Dr Rosen looks at me with wide eyes.

From across the room, Scott's voice growls, 'You don't know it, but you're dealing with my mom. I feel sorry for you.'

Dr Rosen's jaw tightens. Abruptly he turns on his heel and walks out the door. I go to Scott's side. 'Don't worry, we'll get it moving.'

'I know we will,' he says, giving me a one-armed hug and an awkward kiss.

How could I say otherwise? He believes in me and I believe in him. Together we will move mountains. But I have a nagging premonition that Scott and I may have unknowingly joined Alice on her plunge into a mad-hatter wonderland of frustration and illusion.

Each morning after arriving from Johnnie's, I wheel Scott to the therapy room where I leave him for two hours until I collect him for lunch in the small cafeteria, surrounded by many other patients. There I notice a young man, a policeman who was shot on duty, who always sits at the table next to us, unmoving, with his head slumped over his food. After a while, an orderly appears to remove his untouched food. I find this strange, and one day I ask the orderly why the policeman never touches his food. 'I don't know,' the orderly says. 'I'm not sure he knows how to eat. Doesn't matter really.' He shrugs. 'The nurses will feed him later by tube.'

The policeman's mother, nicely dressed and very tidy, often joins him for lunch. She sits at the table, nervous and ill at ease. Her eyes show her pain. Sometimes she encourages him to eat, but never lifts a spoon to help him. After a few minutes, flustered and unable to cope, she gets up and hurries from the room. I taught Scott to use a spoon, and it occurs to me I might teach this young man as well. After his mother leaves, I sit beside him, hold his hand, and gently wrap his fingers round the spoon handle, then model the motion of eating. Within three weeks he is eating on his own. I know the hospital staff are overstretched and I have the time to spend with him. Helping this young man seems the right thing to do.

I have never been afraid of sick people. They aren't so different. As a six-year-old in Wales I would board a city bus for the ten-mile trip to take sweets to my granddad in Whitchurch Hospital, a sanatorium for shell-shocked veterans of the First World War. A large man with a kindly face and white hair, he had one eye covered by a patch and another which was very, very blue. He had lost his eye in a German POW camp. Dressed in a stiff brown uniform with medals on his chest, he would greet me with a formal salute. Then he would sit down and play cards with me, or let me read his coloured comic books, or we would go for walks around the grounds. I would curl my hand in his, and he would hold it tight. I felt very safe with him. Sitting down among the trees and flowers my shyness about singing in front of him disappeared and I sang most of the new tunes I had recently learned. I knew they meant something to him because his face lit up and he would gently touch my cheek with his hand. I would watch the other crippled and shell-shocked soldiers in their stiff uniforms march proudly by in twos and threes, saluting each other when they passed. I'm sure it was strange behaviour, but I thought nothing of it. I loved my visits to Granddad.

But I am concerned with what I am seeing at Coorabel. Another strange thing is happening in the cafeteria. Sitting with Scott, I notice many of the patients are obsessed with the wall clock. They look at their food, then up at the clock, shake their heads, and look down at their food. Soon, unconsciously, I am doing the same thing. What is there about that clock, I wonder, that so fascinates everyone? Then it strikes me. It is six hours fast. The patients are eating breakfast at noon, lunch at six and dinner at midnight. The scene is so bizarre I want to burst out laughing. How can patients rehabilitate themselves, how can they tell the psychologist the time of day, with a clock like this? I fully expect a white rabbit to run through the cafeteria crying out, 'I'm late, I'm late for a very important date.'

Every afternoon in Scott's ward, an orderly brings a plate of French fries, sets it on a side table and leaves. I watch this go on for several days, before finally saying to her, 'You never have time to sit down and eat your French fries.'

'Oh, these aren't mine, these are for the patients.'

'But none of them can walk,' I tell her. 'How are they supposed to get them?'

She shrugs: 'I am only allowed to bring them in, not serve them.' So unless one of the busy nurses are free they remain uneaten.

After more than two weeks of wheeling Scott to therapy, I begin to wonder when I pick him up why he is always in the same place where I left him. I begin to doubt he is receiving therapy at all.

When I ask one of the nurses, she tells me Scott isn't responding, so therapy is pointless. How could this be? I wonder. But I too notice he is not as responsive as he was in St Vincent's. It isn't for another two weeks that I learn the reason. Usually Scott's medical records are kept at the nurses' station, but for some odd reason when we return from therapy one afternoon, his records are on his bed. Is it a mistake, or a secret message? As I review the contents, I know instantly what is wrong. The doctors have been medicating him without my knowledge. No wonder he's not responding. He's been drugged. This is a disaster and I start to cry. After five weeks I know our days at Coorabel are numbered.

I insist on meeting Dr Rosen. When we finally meet, I relay my experiences and concerns about Scott's lack of progress and how he is being medicated without my permission. I tell him how terribly upset and discouraged I am, not only for my son but also for the others in Coorabel with similar conditions. I tell him emphatically that the situation is unacceptable, that even though I'm not a citizen of Australia and am appreciative of all their help, I feel sabotaged.

Dr Rosen pushes back from his desk and tells me with an air of finality, 'We've done the best we can. You are still in denial, Mrs Carl. I would recommend you place him in a home and return to your friends in America. When he improves, you can come back to get him.'

I am speechless. All I can do is stare. 'I would also suggest,' he continues, 'that you give serious thought to having his tendons cut. It would make it easier to care for him.'

My mouth drops and my wits return. I stand and lean over his desk. 'Then Scott would be like a rag doll. Certainly he would no longer need therapy. Wouldn't that be convenient? You would only have to water him like a vegetable. Scott and I are leaving this place as soon as I can find a flat.'

'There's no way you will be able to manage him. I will be seeing you again.'

'Dr Rosen, you will never see me again. On that you have my promise.'

It turned out that Dr Rosen was right; he would see me again later, but in vastly different and far happier circumstances.

Six

Flushed with excitement, I gaze from my kitchen windows into the small and wildly overgrown garden behind our new flat. I'm not seeing the yellow and orange flowers choked with brownish mid-summer weeds, or the purple flowers of the jacaranda tree that flag the garden boundary. I am thinking of our new-found freedom and of Scott lying on the couch in our small living room. I'm thinking of the immense effort it took to get him this far. And I'm thinking, now what? What's next? I have no idea. My mind is blank.

When I stormed out of Dr Rosen's office, I wasn't thinking of the next step. Only that I must take control of my son's future, that I could no longer place my faith in the warehouse mentality of state institutions. If Scott were to have a chance, I would need to create my own therapy programme. What would it be other than love, massage and lavender oil? I didn't know, but I would be open to anything – acupuncture, herbs, Feldenkrais, hypnosis, t'ai chi, physio-therapy, moxa, magnets, craniosacral, even crystals, and most of all, people. I would be open to anyone and everyone willing to help, for I knew I would need lots and lots of help.

The very night I announce my intention to leave Coorabel, as if guided by divine hands, I receive a phone call from nurse Jenny at St Vincent's. She has a friend who is moving from a small one-bedroom apartment in the bohemian Five Corners area of Paddington. It will be vacant within days, she tells me, and it has basic furnishings – a double bed, a chest of drawers, a couch and a wood kitchen table with two chairs.

The next morning, with great anticipation, I take a bus and walk to Glenmore Street and stand in front of a narrow, four-storey red brick building holding eight flats, on the crest of a slight hill. Mine is on the bottom floor, with an outside stairway that leads directly from the pavement to a partially submerged front door.

My heart races with excitement. Finally we have a home, our first in Australia, and it is perfect. No hallways to navigate. No lifts to fight. Within blocks there is a large park to wheel Scott for fresh air. There's Paddington Market for shopping. And at the rear of the flat a small garden for sunning and tasting nature. It's all so perfect, I'm bursting with joy.

A few days later, in a daring daylight operation, I bring Scott home from Coorabel. As I struggle to manoeuvre him from his wheelchair into the back seat of a cab, an orderly comes running from the building. 'I'm sorry, but you can't take the wheelchair,' he says, huffing and with beads of perspiration on his brow. 'Your visa doesn't allow it.' My fear kicks in, and I am horrified not to have anticipated this. Pulling myself together so as not to sound hysterical, I ask, 'How will I manage without it? Depriving him of a wheelchair is like cutting off his legs.' The orderly shrugs, and rolls the chair away.

In the back seat, I struggle to support Scott's weight and keep him upright. His stiff body slides about on the slick seat as the cab weaves through traffic. I tell myself, 'Be brave, be calm, take deep breaths.' Several times Scott slithers onto the floor, and I exert great effort to pull him upright again. Once, as the cab turns sharp right, he tumbles on to me, burying me under his frame. As I struggle to extract myself from his crushing weight, our eyes lock. 'Mom, we've got to stop meeting like this,' he quips. We both burst into laughter at the absurdity of our situation. In his mirror, our cabby, a young man with a blond pony tail in a Hawaiian shirt, eyes our layered bodies with curious disbelief. Pulling up in front of our new flat, the cabby turns and, laying a tanned arm along the seatback, says, 'How will you get him into your flat?'

'I haven't thought of that yet,' I reply. My eyes sweep the busy street, but I am dumbfounded.

'Should I call the police?' he asks.

'No, no,' I say, 'I'll work something out. Wait here.'

I step from the cab to clear my brain. The front door seems so far. How will I do this? Coming down the pavement is a man in black racing tights on a red, thin-tyred bicycle. I step out, blocking his way.

'Do you have a strong back?' I ask.

He brakes to a stop within inches of me. 'Sure. Why?'

I explain about my invalid son and how I need help getting him into our flat. With a shrug he lays his bike in the grass. I snare two other men, both strong and burly, with the same question. Now I have three, and need one more. Catching the cabby's eyes, I motion for him to join us, and we negotiate Scott's inflexible body out of the cab, down the stairs and through the front door onto the couch. I thank them profusely, and they leave me to manage my new reality. Now we are really alone.

Moving into the kitchen, I look out the window at the yellow and white flowers and the purple jacaranda tree, numb with the seeming hopelessness of my task. It took all that exhausting work to move Scott a few feet with no wheelchair, and now there is just me, weighing in at seven stone. How can I possibly cope? How can I get him from the couch into the bedroom, or to the table, or to the bathroom, or anywhere without a wheelchair?

I do have Jonathan, but Ulla is with him and he must divide his attention. Plus, they are staying twenty miles away. Besides, they have their future to decide. In any event his visa will soon expire and once again I must cope alone. I will need lots and lots of help.

I call Jonathan the next morning realizing that I cannot get Scott in the shower by myself; I don't seem to have the strength to lift him. He says he'll be right over, and pedals his bicycle to where we live.

He tries to stay somewhat dry as Scott sits on a chair with the water running down him. Scott suddenly coughs water that has flowed into his mouth all over Jon and puts his arm up as if to say 'Ooops!' and at the same time does his characteristic slow look up: his eyes look first, and then his head slowly rolls, saying, 'Sorry about that, Jon.' Jon says, 'Hey buddy, don't think twice about it,' and then breaks down. He can only think of Scott, who despite hardly being able to move, only recently out of a coma after such a long time, still has it in him to worry about whether Jonathan gets a little wet. It is so hard to cope with Jonathan's sadness.

Another time Jonathan has helped him shower and Scott is naked apart from a towel, his arm around Jonathan's neck, unable to stand by himself. The body that a few months earlier was playing rugby is now bent over and lopsided, his left foot not reaching the ground. About to move down the hall, he catches sight of himself in the mirror outside the bathroom. I see the surprise and shock on his face, which seem to say, 'Shit, I don't look too good!' Then the sad silence.

In general, his injury has created a condition that keeps him unaware of how bad he really is. We are lucky in this respect because, during this period, he really isn't depressed.

Dismayed at how much help I will need, I search my mind and think of the volunteers I have to press into service. It dawns on me that every minute, dozens of potential volunteers pass my door. Each hour, hundreds are shopping in Paddington Market. I need only a few. Not many, just a few at a time. Tearing pages from a large pad, I make flyers. With a pen I write, 'I need help with an invalid son. Please if you can spend even one hour per month, come by,' and give my address. I ask Scott if he will be okay for a few minutes, then walk down Glenmore Street pushing them into the hands of pedestrians.

Returning home I can only wait, but in the meantime I set my mind to procuring a wheelchair. Towards evening there is a knock on my door. I open it to two women and a man. One of the women, in her fifties with grey hair, holds my flyer. 'I brought my husband,' she says, nodding towards the man who is dressed in work clothes and carries a brown paper sack. 'And we've brought a little food. What can we do to help?' I motion them in while turning away for fear they will see my streaming tears. My prayers are being answered. Scott and I are strangers, yet these people care.

Together we move Scott into the bedroom and make him comfortable. I put on music and light a few candles. Sandwiches are passed out and we sit and talk. They tell me with warm smiles they will be back. After my guests leave, I lie next to Scott and read aloud until he falls asleep, placing his entire trust into my unqualified hands. But I do not sleep well. Every two hours I need to lift and turn him to a more comfortable position. And I will have to get him into the bathroom or bring it to him. Still, I'm wonderfully excited, and my blood pounds with exhilaration. We are winning. Scott and I, I tell myself, are winning.

The next day my three volunteers return. I create more flyers and they fan out, pinning them on bulletin boards in the supermarket, the library, St Vincent's Hospital, a bookshop and other public places.

Moments after they leave I open the door to the pony-tailed cabby in the same Hawaiian shirt. His name's Tim. 'I've been thinking, mate,' he says with a clever grin, 'that maybe we should go find ourselves a wheelchair.'

When the volunteers return, they stay with Scott. I get in Tim's cab and we are off, pulling to a stop at the entrance of Coorabel. 'The hospital?' I ask.

'Why not?' he says with a twinkle. 'If you need money you go to a bank.'

We walk into the emergency entrance. The hall is deserted except for a row of empty chrome and black wheelchairs against a wall. He shushes me, then motions for me to sit down. The cabby spins the chair around, wheels me rapidly out the swinging doors, helps me into the back seat of the cab as if I were a patient, then quickly tucks the folded chair into the boot. 'We're just borrowing it, mind you,' he says, flashing a bright smile as we speed off.

That afternoon two other volunteers knock on my door. The leaflets are working. The next day three more show up and we move Scott to a bed on the living room floor where he can be more easily handled. As the days pass, and as the word spreads, the numbers increase. Most are neighbours. Some spend an hour massaging Scott's muscles and stretching his ligaments. Others volunteer to do our mountains of laundry or run errands.

I try to take Scott out for a walk every day. It is not easy for me, standing five foot two, to manoeuvre a wheelchair carrying a man much taller and heavier than myself who has trouble keeping upright. The first challenge, especially when I am by myself, is to get the wheelchair out of the flat, up the steps and onto the street. Sometimes I wheel Scott to the steps and lift him out of the chair, which I am able to do by myself, lay him on a blanket, lift the wheelchair up the steps to the pavement, then find somebody who will help. We each take hold of one end of the blanket and carry Scott up the steps to the wheelchair. Then I'll try and get Scott on his knees and into the wheelchair. We often overbalance, Scott pinning me to the blanket. It causes much amusement among the passers-by. Some ask if they can help, and others hurry on and pretend they haven't seen anything.

Once Scott is secure in the chair, we head off down the street. He takes some bumps as we negotiate the kerbs and other obstacles along the way, and rates me on my skills, grumbling, 'Gee, Mom, that was a minus six!' Or, laughing, 'Great, Mom! Plus two!' The rating game is a regular feature of our walks over the coming months and years. It is a way for Scott to express himself, and he always keeps a generous sense of humour. And of course it keeps me on my toes.

In the evening I light candles and play tranquil music – sometimes opera, sometimes Mozart, sometimes New Age inspirational.

After a day of therapy Scott is usually exhausted with pain, but in the evening he and I have our special time of quiet. Sometimes I lie beside him and hold his hand, neither of us needing to speak.

Sometimes Scott asks me to dance for him, which I gladly do, pretending I'm a ballerina, moving around his wheelchair, laughing at how good it feels even as I realize how much more flexible I was in my younger days. When we do talk, it is of neither the past nor the future, for they have ceased to exist. We live only in the moment, for that is all we can count on, and we live each golden drop of these moments as if we'll never live another. Or we simply talk to hear each other's reassuring voice. He never says to me, 'Mom, why do you think this happened to me?' Sometimes I wonder about this. I'm not sure the question ever occurs to him.

I'm rubbing his head and hair as I used to when he was a little boy. Without thinking I look into his eyes and say, 'Scott, are you afraid to die?' as he has been to the edge so many times.

In a loud voice he replies, 'I LOVE LIVING.'

After he is tucked in bed, I watch the candles glowing, making shadows on the wall. In my solitary daydreaming, I get lost in the shadows. It is my way of meditating, to revitalize my mind and soul.

As the numbers of volunteers increase, they present unique challenges. Most know nothing of head injuries or physiotherapy, and must be trained. So I contact a Dr Freeman whom I have read about as an advocate of home therapy. He agrees to come for a visit and advise me how I can help best. In the meantime, I become a teacher and demonstrate exercises and techniques. I show how to pick up a leg, how to push an arm, how to find and stretch tendons and ligaments, and how to support Scott's broken clavicle. I encourage and praise, but most of all I express my deep gratitude, always reminding them the main thing is that they have to feel comfortable with Scott and Scott must feel comfortable with them.

When Dr Freeman visits, he agrees with me that there is more to Scott than the doctors have taken the time to see. He says the essence of any treatment must be to keep Scott moving at all costs, constantly stimulating his brain through repetitive exercising, in the hope the brain will make new neural pathways. 'It is very hard and tedious work,' he said, 'but if you have the patience, the reward may be a big increase in Scott's ability to move by himself.' He promises to come back in six weeks, and agrees that I should continue training people.

Another challenge is to coordinate the increased numbers of volunteers. I calculate I will need ten a day, seven days a week – seventy volunteers a week, nearly three hundred in a month, although hopefully many will repeat. Overwhelmed at the sheer numbers, I continue to pass out leaflets. After my phone is installed, they call to reserve times. In addition to teaching, I now manage schedules. I tack a large sheet of paper to a wall and create a monthly calendar for bookings. Dutifully I write names in squares, but find I must adjust to changing circumstances, and my calendar fills with cancellations, scratch-outs and transferred names.

I am taping a leaflet on a post near the bus stop when I sense the gaze of someone over my shoulder. Turning about I look into the composed blue eyes of a woman in her sixties, tall with silver hair swept back in a bun and only a hint of make-up. She is dressed in an understated grey skirt and vanilla blouse with a delicate ivory brooch at her neck. Her features and countenance are lovely, hinting at great beauty in her younger days. 'Is this your son?' she asks in a firm and soothing voice. I nod yes. 'My name is Shirley. I have a few minutes and would love to meet him.'

That's how Shirley and I met. She lives in the neighbourhood and comes by often to sit and talk with Scott. She asks about his life and his dreams in the way grandmothers do best, without judgement or condescension, and works on his vocabulary and articulation. I know how Scott missed having a grandmotherly figure in his life, as my mother lived in Wales and he rarely saw her. Now I hear a lot of laughing and whispering going on between them.

When other volunteers are available, Shirley joins me in the kitchen for a pot of hot jasmine tea and we discuss Scott's progress, as well as art, music, and broader family issues. Gradually she becomes part of the Carl family. I am delighted Scott has a grandmother, and I an intimate friend.

Scott once presented Shirley with a card written in his handwriting, promising that someday, when he could, he would take Shirley to Bondi Beach and dance with her after eating crackers and cheese. A sweet dream.

Months later, Shirley confides she doesn't know why she was drawn to Scott and me. 'I've never volunteered to do this sort of thing before,' she tells me. 'I just felt I had to do something.'

In the coming months, many of my volunteers would say the same sort of thing: I don't know why I was drawn to you and Scott but I couldn't say no ... I'm usually not a do-gooder but I had to help ... There was no posturing to impress others, no egos on sleeves, just a selflessness that was heartwarming.

One morning I open the front door to a young man in black leather with chains on his shoulder, long, spiked, blue hair, and silver earrings. He extends a hand and in a soft, respectful voice, introduces himself as Robert. 'I've heard about what you are doing,' he says. 'Would you mind if I watch?'

My first instinct is to tell him, 'Thank you, we're fully booked.' But I hesitate. I had vowed never to turn anyone away. So I step aside and welcome him into our apartment, with its calm atmosphere of incense, candles and classical music. To the discomfort of two volunteers who are massaging Scott's arms and legs, Robert leans against a wall and quietly observes for two hours before slipping out of the door.

That night, a three-course dinner is delivered along with a glorious bouquet of summer flowers and a tape of the Bruch violin concertos, with a note on light blue stationery saying, 'Thank you for inviting me into your home. Love, Robert.' I feel sheepish that I almost turned him away. To this day, Robert is a reminder of the danger of judging people by their looks and not their hearts. I wish to write back to him, but I have no address, and can only hope I will see him again.

Many volunteers walk in the door seemingly as their muse dictates. Strangers show up unannounced and pitch in. I quickly abandon my schedule, to rely instead on whomever providence deposits at my open door. By the end of the first month my volunteers exceed a hundred, and I notice increasingly they are coming from beyond the neighbourhood.

That night I check my finances, only to confirm my worst fear. The expense of living a normal life has quickly drained the money Stefan sent from my BMW. When the volunteers catch wind of my situation, they rent a stall at the Paddington Flea Market to sell whatever the neighbourhood might donate. Word circulates on the grapevine, and soon cardboard boxes and brown bags of used clothes, books, tapes, art, furniture, tennis rackets, shoes, pots and pans appear at my door as neighbours empty their closets and garages. Twice a month, volunteers man the 'All proceeds go to Scott Carl' booth, and for the remainder of my stay in Australia, the money they raise pays our expenses.

I pray for good weather, because when it rains we have to cancel the stall and I'm inundated with all kinds of objects until the next market day, and I simply have no room for them.

Quite unexpectedly, two months later, Robert appears again. His hair is washed and trimmed. The earrings have been removed, and he is dressed in crisp, dark blue trousers and a light blue sport shirt. It is even ironed. He works with Scott almost every evening and reads to him from books on spirituality. They become good friends.

Months later Robert sadly announces he will return to school and may not have time to continue with Scott. I remember him saying he was a dropout, and I am pleased he will continue with his education, although Scott and I will surely miss him. 'Where are you enrolling?' I ask casually, to show my support. 'I'm returning to medical school,' he says with a soft smile. 'I left because I saw no point. But after working with Scott I found my purpose.'

About the time Robert enters our lives I also receive a phone call from a man with a deep husky voice. His name is Billy, and he is calling from the Blue Mountains, a couple of hours west of the city. 'I've heard about your son,' Billy rumbles over the phone. 'I'm a masseur and I have a special technique that I learned from my papa. He worked with Sister Kinney in the old days, in her polio clinic. She taught him some secret techniques, and I think they might help your son. I'd like to come and volunteer.' I give Billy my address, but he doesn't appear right away and I forget about him.

A week later I open the door to a bull of a man who fills the doorframe and blocks the light. He is huge, at least six foot three, and weighs at least seventeen stone with a shaggy mane of red hair, a full red beard with a tuft of white at the skin, hairy, muscular arms, green, deep-set eyes and a barrel of a chest. 'My name's Billy,' he says. 'I called you about volunteering, and I'm here.'

I step back as Billy, toting an old leather suitcase, advances into the room and looks around. 'Where do I sleep?'

'You're not just here for the day?' I ask, rather intimidated.

'My special treatment takes three weeks. I always move in. Can't do it any other way.' What can I do? How can I refuse such dedication? So I lead him into my bedroom and say, 'This is where you'll sleep.' He throws his suitcase on the bed, and I gather my things and move into the living room to sleep with Scott.

Standing over Scott, Billy looks around the room and asks, 'Where's your massage table?'

'I'm sorry, this is what we have,' I say.

Billy shakes his head. 'Not good enough. I have one in my truck.' He leaves and soon returns with a massage table in pieces, which he assembles next to Scott. It's homemade and very sturdy. Getting on one knee, Billy lifts Scott from his floor bed, deposits him on the table, and after pondering the situation, proceeds with his special technique. He has a particular way of kneading the muscles very actively, while at the same time rocking the body. Billy's moves are so nimble, his hands melodically smooth as his stubby fingers probe and stroke, that before my eyes he has transformed himself into an artist, a maestro of massage. I am speechless. Two other volunteers watch in quiet awe as Billy's hands work their magic.

After a week, Billy is not only working intensely with Scott, but has hung a sheet to divide the living room and started a side business taking in clients from the neighbourhood. Some knock on the door while others call and say, 'My back is hurting,' or 'I woke up with this terrible kink in my neck. Is the magic mountain man working today?' Suddenly I am the madam of a massage parlour. But I couldn't be happier. Billy is kind and compassionate and Scott shows considerable improvement in arm and leg flexibility.

After his promised three weeks, Magic Man packs up, breaks down his table, and departs as mysteriously as he arrived. For weeks after, people call to enquire about him. I have no idea when he'll be back, I say, maybe never. But Billy does return. Several months later he surprises us all with a knock on our door and continues his work with Scotty. Soon he has set up a successful local practice with his own place.

All day, every day, we are visited by a cross-section of Australian society. People drift in and out. I lose track of who is volunteering and who is there to socialize, bring food or flowers, or pick up laundry. Neighbours check in and musicians arrive unannounced. A beautiful high-school girl with long brown hair stands over Scott and plays a violin concerto. Two university students with African djembe drums pound out rhythms. A leathery fellow from the outback with a didgeridoo entertains us with three friends on flute, tambourine and guitar. When the music isn't live it's recorded – classical, meditation, folk, jazz. Day and night our little apartment overflows with music and laughter.

From a nearby Feldenkrais school an instructor volunteers his students. Another day we are visited by Sai Baba devotees, and some Hare Krishnas who normally spend their time asking for donations, but who end up volunteering and bringing wonderful food. We enlist a decathlon runner, taxi drivers, schoolteachers, plumbers, lawyers, architects, policemen, actors, nurses, medical interns, students, foreign students, teenagers who run errands, retired couples who take away our laundry and bring in meals. A woman named Rose who owns a used clothing store (called Second Hand Rose) brings me vintage clothing. I am amazed by their generosity and humbled by their gifts and blessings.

Janet, a young gymnast from England, visits Scott. She is tall and athletic, with shoulder-length blonde hair bound in a pony tail and a pink, glowing face. They become a little enamoured of each other. Janet always has a big smile and doesn't seem to have any sense of boundaries as to what Scott can or can't do. She treats him as if he's not disabled at all. She often takes Scott for long trips around Paddington (I wonder what kind of scores *she* gets on pushing the wheelchair). I can relax, knowing that with her muscular frame she can handle Scott and he will be safe. One of Janet's favourite amusements is to park Scott on the pavement, walk a half block in front of him, and do back-flips the length of the block until she lands on her feet right in front of his chair.

I look up one day to see Janet at Scott's side laughing about something, and think about how many attractive young women, and not-so-young women, I see Scott hugging and sharing a laugh with. Even as an invalid, he has a certain charismatic quality that women find attractive.

Once, when Scott has to go back to St Vincent's and stay in the neuro ward for three days for tests after he's suffered a seizure at home, she comes to cheer him up, turning cartwheels up and down the ward, to everyone's delight. Her energy is boundless. During that short stay, Scott is very scared watching people come in and go for tests. Some return with red marks from radiation and hair missing. Some are coming back from surgery and some do not come back at all. So for Scott, Janet's visits are quite uplifting. He is so scared that he makes me put taxi money in his drawer, in case he has to get out of there quickly when I'm not around. But that never happens.

Two world-class boxers volunteer. Frank, a lightweight from Dublin, is seventy now, but full of care and compassion, and is battling poverty himself as nobody will employ him because of his age. At the slightest hint of sadness he breaks into an old pub song with a full tenor voice. His friend, a quiet and very large man from Nigeria, is introduced simply as The Champ. Much younger than Frank, he is a one-time Commonwealth heavyweight champion. The two work on Scott's left arm to get more flexibility. It is tedious and torturous for Scott. His face grimaces, but he never complains or loses his sense of humour. 'You want to arm wrestle?' Scott chides the Irishman. 'I'm not sure you're up to it, so I'll use my bad arm to make it easy on you.' The Irishman laughs joyously and eggs Scott on. 'Come on now, mate, you can't go through life without a good left jab.'

Two little boys, five and seven, arrive with their mother. While she talks with Scott and stretches his right arm, I ask if they would like to rub lotion on his feet. They reply, 'Can we really?' I say, 'Of course,' and give them the bottle of lotion, and leave them to their own devices. Too often, we shield children from life's ills and infirmities, and in the process we deprive them of the skills and com-

118

passion needed to cope. It is a shame how we lock children out when tragedy appears. They should be allowed to share in these situations, so they learn not to be afraid of sickness or death. It is mainly the unknown that is scary for them. With Scott, I saw children learning to exercise their natural compassion and healing energy.

Many volunteers bring their young children who laugh and giggle as they romp through our small apartment and play outside. Fathers bring their babies and balance them on Scott's stomach. He loves having the babies the most. He strokes their heads and it takes his mind off his pain while their parents pull at his legs. After all, babies are pure love.

A young Israeli woman named Haiki appears at our door. She is short and stout with dark, thick, curly hair around a cherubic face. Haiki is a medic in the Israeli army and informs me she possesses an intuitive sense of how to work with disabilities. She is drawn to Scott and when the other volunteers leave and I am in the kitchen cleaning up she lies on her back next to Scott and they talk of sex. I shut the kitchen door to leave them alone. I am sure their relationship is just talk, but sometimes mothers learn things they should forget.

Keith walks in unannounced and introduces himself as an osteopath with spare time who wants to help. He is slightly built and about thirty-five years old with over-the-collar blond hair and blue eyes that brim with enthusiasm. I introduce him to Scott and he immediately begins a neck massage treatment. As he works, Keith asks my son about his injuries. 'I don't remember how I was injured,' Scott explains briefly. 'But I'm getting much better.'

'That's wonderful,' Keith replies. 'Miracles do happen, don't they?'

Scott laughs. 'Maybe so, but I don't live on 34th Street.'

Jonathan comes when he can to take Scott for afternoons at the beach. One day, rolling Scott's wheelchair along the boardwalk, they pass two young women. Reaching out his good hand, Scott pinches one on the bottom. Whipping round in surprised anger, and confused by the sight of an invalid in a wheelchair, she turns her wrath on Jonathan, who wheels briskly on in embarrassment as Scott convulses with laughter.

Scott wants to put his feet in the ocean, but wheelchairs do not go through sand, so we have to devise another way. With Jonathan and Rollie's ingenuity, we cut off the legs of a chair and nail poles in their place, put Scott on the seat, tie him in with Ace bandages, and bear him like a maharaja across the sand to the water. After we lay it down in the ocean, a big wave comes and wipes him out with sea spray. Scott can't move and he doesn't care; he just laughs. I think he feels safe strapped to the chair. We also carry him to the rocks and put a fishing pole in his good arm. To everyone's surprise, he catches a little fish. Luck is on his side. By summer's end, Scott's face fills out and shines with a healthy copper glow. Unfortunately, those outings become few and far between as Jonathan's visa expires and he and Ulla depart for Denmark, leaving me to continue my crusade.

I receive a call from the Probation Department, asking if I could use the help of an osteopath, as they have one who could come every day. He is on probation for financial impropriety. I don't care and eagerly say yes. I laugh to myself each day when I have to mark his card to say that he has been there all day. He is a gentle soul. I can see where he would have money problems. He lives in the moment and only his work matters. Even after he is off probation he still comes, almost every day. He works wonders.

Three housewives become regulars. One is mired in an unhappy marriage, but can't break out as she's been diagnosed with cancer and can't work. The second has a schizophrenic son and a husband who's just left her. The third is raising four children alone. They quickly bond with Scott and with each other. Like Scott they are not bitter, they are just trying to get on with their lives. They initially arrive individually but soon carpool together and become fast friends. It takes an hour each way for them to reach our apartment. I found that level of commitment very moving. The women work as a team to exercise Scott's arms and legs, rolling him on the bolster.

One day I watch them turn him over on his stomach and bend his legs back to stretch muscles. When they finish, in the process of repositioning his body, they lift his upper body. Instinctively Scott thrusts his thighs forward, and quite suddenly he is upright on his knees. Stabilized and encouraged by two of the women, he awkwardly puts one knee forward, shifts his body, and slides the other knee forward while they hold him up, one on each side.

I catch my breath. Slowly and haltingly, Scott is walking, if only on his knees. He cannot balance, he cannot take more than a few steps, but he possesses some control of his thigh muscles and his hips. Might Scott someday stand on his feet? One leg is longer than the other, and one bends at the knee, so it is a little shorter. Haven't I just a few minutes ago seen him walk on his knees with help? If he can go from a coma to balancing on his knees, surely he can make another leap forward. All of a sudden the possibilities seem limitless.

He has a rag doll someone made from wool and rags so he could stretch his fingers around it as part of his therapy for his left hand. At the end of the day he mimics us, becoming the physio trainer telling the doll everything we say to him repeatedly: 'Stretch that leg, hold it, you know you can do better, you know you can do it.' I wonder what is going through his mind. Sometimes he calls me Hitler's Wife, laughing, making me get down and do push-ups. 'One more,' he says, 'you know it's good for you.' Sometimes he jokes, 'I'm going to get out of this place and go to the army; I'd be treated better there. Maybe it would be better in basic training.'

I also listen to him taking his aggressions and frustrations out on the doll. One time he throws it on top of a cupboard and says, 'You're staying there for a week and not coming down.'

Whatever anger he feels, he never carries it into the actual therapy. If it is an older person working on him, and a lot of pain is being inflicted, he will sometimes pick up their hand and kiss it as a way of saying it's okay. He never gives up. Each step of the way his courage never falters.

'Isn't it Saturday tomorrow? Will I get the day off?'

'What do you think?' I reply.

'Okay, okay, I get the message,' he says.

Sometimes when we talk during the middle of the night and he can't sleep, he'll say, 'I have a pain here; will you massage it with lavender oil, make the pain go away?' as if I have that power. Later, he'll fall asleep with a peaceful look on his face. I wonder where he goes in his dreams.

Another time when he sent me a birthday card he wrote, 'I love you, you are the best mom in the world. I love how you take care of me, but I hope you never get sore like I am.' When I asked him about his pain, he replied, 'It won't be for ever.' When I asked him what he missed most, he replied, 'I miss running. I miss my buddies and friends in America that I played ball with. I miss my roommate Niall from Copenhagen, the sports we did together, flirting with the ladies and working at Burger King while planning the next step of our future.'

One of my regular volunteers is Brendan, a young physiotherapist from St Vincent's who used to stop by Scott's room. He appears at our door in his white coat, asking if he can be of help. He is of modest build with short brown hair, narrowly set brown eyes and a wide smile in a slim, pale face. He is also very British, but to his credit he is willing to bend the rules. Inspired by Scott's walk on his knees he says, 'I believe it's critical to try and splint his legs and to keep his spine straight.' So Brendan and I build what he terms a sentry box, a three-sided wooden box that Scott can sit in with his legs forward. Once he is seated, I pad him up so he can't slump, and put a padded wedge between his thighs to drive them apart and to stretch and build his inner thigh muscles – a necessity if he is ever to stand. I also paint a chessboard on top of the table that keeps his legs open, so he can amuse himself by playing chess while he stays in the box for an hour.

Scott's leg is still bent at the knee and one day as Brendan and I sit at the kitchen table discussing therapy strategies, he looks at me with a devilish glint in his eye. 'I know what to do,' he says. 'We sneak him into the hospital, get his legs as straight as possible, and put them in casts to stretch his tendons.'

'Is that possible?' I ask. 'Won't we be caught?'

Brendan smiles. 'Trust me, I know these people. They won't suspect a thing.'

In preparation for the splinting, we intensify our efforts to loosen up Scott's leg muscles and tendons. I set a schedule of a solid week of six-hour days of pulling, stretching and holding Scott's legs for fifteen minutes at a time, with volunteers working in one-hour shifts to get his muscles stretched and pliable before they are cast in plaster.

We will have to transport Scott to the hospital, and once his legs are locked straight in casts, we'll need an even larger car to get him home. Fortunately, one of the volunteers offers his station wagon. On D-Day it appears. We move Scott up the stairs and into the back seat and are off to St Vincent's. Brendan borrows a wheelchair and soon we are in that part of the orthopaedic ward where the casts are set.

True to Brendan's word, the staff pay no special mind, believing Scott has been transferred in from somewhere. On the casting table the technicians lean into his knee, causing Scott to grimace in pain, until each leg straightens as far as possible, and they apply full leg casts.

The next trick is to get him home with the plaster still wet. Scott is back in the wheelchair, but he has picked up front-end weight, and his thick white legs stick straight out at a right angle, making it difficult to manoeuvre in the hall. 'Normally,' Brendan says with a wide grin as we prop and shore Scott's legs, 'people with both legs in a cast are kept in the hospital. But that would be pushing our luck.'

At the flat, volunteers help Scott down the stairs and onto his bed where he lies in considerable pain as his straightened legs pull against the frozen tendons behind his knees. All I can offer is Tylenol. After three days his flesh swells and turns red around the cast, and I'm fearful of an infection. What have we done? I am haunted by doubt and worry. I call Brendan.

'Does he have a rise in temperature?'

'No,' I answer, 'but he's in a lot of pain.'

'I told you he would be,' Brendan says. 'Give him more Tylenol. They have to stay on for seven days or it won't work.'

During those agonizing days, Michael, a Maori from New Zealand, spends hours at Scott's bedside to take his mind off the pain. Dressed in psychedelic colours, Michael has a handsome South Seas look with an engaging smile and great warmth. He hangs a small animal-skin pouch around Scott's neck and tells him it contains a sacred coin. 'You are on a special journey,' he solemnly tells Scott. 'When you travel you should always have money.' Michael eventually tells me he has been inspired to enrol in physiotherapy school because of Scott, so he can be better at helping others.

At the end of a long and painful week, especially the endless nights, Brendan and I return Scott to St Vincent's where the casts are sawn off. The stretching has worked and Scott has more flexibility in his knees, but at the price of considerable loss of skin. So I face a new problem: healing the skin on Scott's legs. Back home, I call Keith and ask for treatment. Keith arrives and rubs drops of aloe vera squeezed from one of my house plants into Scott's raw skin. Then he brings out his needles and gives Scott a full acupuncture treatment. The treatments seem to help, and within days Scott's skin is repairing itself.

About six months have passed since I took the apartment, and nearly one hundred and twenty volunteers pass each week through my door. Scott shows great improvement from his six-hour days of therapy. I'm content with my life, enriched by our friends and much laughter. But suddenly I am rudely reminded of reality. Once again the system, like a wolf lurking in the woods, comes knocking. A letter arrives from Immigration informing me that I am in Australia illegally and I must check in, answer questions on Scott's health, and fill out new forms.

It turns into a lengthy process. Trusting Scott to my volunteers, I wait at Immigration for hours before a case officer tells me to return in two weeks with the new information. After visiting Immigration several times only to be interviewed by the same man who asks the same questions, I blow a fuse and complain bitterly to the poor man, who can say little more than, 'I'm sorry, love, but we have to have some sort of procedures.' When I return home, I tell my volunteers of my frustration. I am sure I will have to leave the country.

That night, after Scott slips into sleep, I step out the back door to breathe the dark air. It is a clear and lovely night. The moon has not yet risen, and the stars dance above me, twinkling specks of diamonds in a charcoal-black sky. My mind is drawn back to that little girl in Marble Hall who trusted her stars. And I can hear Ted, my wayward sea-captain Dad, say as he did so often, 'Trust in your stars, Glennie. Those stars have saved many a drifting man.' Whenever I have faltered from life's course and my future seems uncertain, I think back to Dad's advice and turn skyward for guidance. What do my stars tell me tonight? What course shall I follow?

What I do not know is at this very moment my dear friend Shirley is launching a campaign of rescue. Across Sydney, hundreds of phones are beginning to ring.

Seven

Letters pour in from volunteers, neighbours, friends, even strangers. Not form letters, but individually written and signed letters addressed to Immigration. Please let Scott and Glenys stay, the letters say. She won't be a burden on the state ... We'll provide dinner for them every Wednesday ... We'll provide food for one week ... We'll make sure they're fed ... I will help Glenys with the rent ... I will do her washing ... I will help care for Scott ... Some are written by children who draw happy faces in the margins with crayons, and plead, 'Please let Scott and Glenys stay.'

Their calls to local newspapers set off a storm of media attention. My phone rings for a week, reporters wanting a statement and friends and volunteers offering their support. We're fighting for you Glenys, they say. Others are indignant. How could the government treat you like this? Over the next few weeks, articles appear in Australian newspapers.

My greatest concern now is being deported. It hasn't happened yet, but I realize it's inevitable. With all this publicity it's impossible to hide. How much time can I buy? A few weeks, a few months, I don't know. Perhaps the negative publicity will induce amnesia, a thin hope at best. Immigration may be a muddled bureaucracy, but they are obsessive in their muddling. One day they threaten, the next they purr and smile with understanding. This can't go on, and I know it and am worried.

From outside comes the loud slam of car doors. I peer out my front window to find a TV van parked in front of my flat. As I watch, three casually dressed men load up with camera equipment and walk towards my steps. Behind them on the pavement, a few neighbours have gathered to watch. When I open my front door, an attractive young man introduces himself. 'Mrs Carl, I'm from *The Ray Martin Show*, and I'd like to interview you about the fine work you're doing with your son.'

In a trance of disbelief, I step aside and allow the film crew entry. Roaming our small flat, they film everything: Scott on his bed, the volunteers, me with tangled hair, the living room, the bedroom, even the kitchen. The interviewer thrusts a microphone in my face and barrages me with questions: Where are you from? How long has Scott been in Australia? How did it happen? Tell me about the coma. How's his progress? Rate your medical care. How? Why? What? Where? When? The questions fly, fast and furious. I throw out answers helter-skelter without thinking. They ask my volunteers about themselves and how they feel. Then the crew is outside shooting our apartment, and cutaways of the knot of neighbours. Finally, after loading their van, in a swirl of wind they are gone, off to stage another ambush.

The next afternoon, I watch myself on the programme, a fifteen-minute afternoon segment about Scott, his head injury, our volunteers and the progress he's made. I am amazed at the programme's polish and control, how chaos has been turned into coherence, and I'm fascinated with that look-alike on the small screen. Is that how I look? No, that's not me. Oh, that could have been a better angle on Scott. I don't remember that question . . . But I'm impressed. The answers are eloquent and interesting, more so than the ones I remember giving. Scott is great at hiding his pain. He cooperates fully, even though he is lying down all the time. He even burps and slowly says, 'I'm only human.'

While I was caught unawares by the Ray Martin interview, I am totally unprepared for the whirlwind that follows. Overnight we become minor celebrities, and the phone rings for several days. Many call about volunteering, and I happily explain my needs and give out my address. Several calls are from men with offers of marriage, so Scott and I can stay in the country and receive treatment. Amused, I politely decline, while my volunteers have a great laugh.

A few days later, two men walk through my open door. Both are tanned with firm bodies and dressed in wild colours. One has streaked blond hair and a pink shirt and green slacks. The other, shorter with dark hair and a single earring, is in a bright red striped silk shirt with a purple boa about his neck. The taller one opens his arms wide and with a theatrical flourish, announces, 'Glenys darling, I am Rick and this is David, and we are here to marry you!' And they engulf me in a grand hug. The volunteers cheer, laughing. 'And where is Scott?' David announces, his eyes sweeping the room with irrepressible panache. It is obvious of course, but David makes a great display of discovery, as if Scott were normal. The two men sit beside my son in deep discussion, before coming my way. 'Sign us up, darling,' Rick declares, 'any time, any place.' And so I do. Rick and David, part-time actors, full-time showmen and gay lovers, join the team and become fast friends.

The duo appear often at our door, mostly without warning,

wildly dressed and outrageously charming. 'Time for coffee! Go, go, go,' they order, swishing me out the door. When I return an hour later from coffee or the supermarket, Rick, Dave and Scott stage hilarious scenes from Shakespeare or comedian Robin Williams. The duo does most of the acting of course, but they throw nonsensical lines to Scott. He replies with his usual wit, fully engaged. They are a riotous pair, with unabashed charisma and deep feelings for Scott, and they are insistent about marrying me. 'Darling, you can marry one of us or both of us, whatever makes you happy,' Rick tells me more than once. 'What a party!' But I never take them seriously.

After several weeks of this, the volunteers decide to have some fun. Late one afternoon, a man delivers a wedding cake of creamy frosting on double layers of chocolate cake. Stuck on the top are a single white-laced bride, and five tuxedoed grooms. The two dozen volunteers who have gathered for my wedding reception play wedding music, light candles, toast my fortune with champagne, and have a grand time, all pretend.

As if Rick and Dave weren't enough, another David walks through our door, in blue jeans and black tennis shoes, with a guitar slung across his back. He is about thirty with a fringe of wiry brown hair around a bald spot, a stubbly beard, and impish green-blue eyes in an angular face. Concerned over the beads of sweat that line his brow, I ask if he's ill.

'No, I'm not sick,' he replies.

'You're sure you don't have a temperature?' I ask, laying my palm against his face. He shakes his head. 'Then why are you perspiring so?'

'I'm on meds.'

'What are you taking medication for?' I ask, growing cautious.

'I'm schizophrenic.'

'I see. And when you're not on meds, what happens then?'

'I'm a different person. I think I'm the fifth Beatle. That's what the doctors tell me, and I think they're right.'

'That's charming, David. How do you know you're the fifth Beatle?'

He shrugs. 'Isn't it obvious? Ask my friends, they'll tell you. And I have all the music.'

My guess is David's on lithium, which produces the side effect of sweating. But he seems gentle and harmless, and working with Scott might be good therapy. So David too joins my ever-expanding team of volunteers. He comes three times a week in the evenings, after the others have left, and helps Scott wash and dress for bed. When David arrives, I take notice if his brow is perspiring, if he is on his meds, to ease my mind. Sometimes I can't tell, and I move through the quiet flat, keeping an ear open to what he's saying. But David is cheerful, gentle and full of stories, and I begin to question if being the fifth Beatle is such a bad thing. He and Scott talk for hours, and when Scott tires, David softly strums his guitar and sings songs.

Some days later as I'm absorbed with training a new volunteer to stretch Scott's leg ligaments, I glance up to find a nicely dressed man in my doorway. Behind him is a younger fellow with a camera on his shoulder. 'Mrs Carl, I'm Walter Pearson, and I'm the news anchor for Channel Five,' he says with an easy smile, in the measured voice of a professional announcer. Dark and attractive, in his early fifties, with light brown hair and humorous brown eyes, his every move comes with confidence and a comfortable grace. 'You're making a name for yourself, and I'd like to interview you for tonight's programme.'

Many of the male volunteers who work with Scott are attractive, but this man is different, and I find myself staring at him. Quickly I regain my composure and shift my eyes to his cameraman, who seems excessively impatient next to Walter's calm demeanour.

With a sense of weariness, I ask them in. *The Ray Martin Show* was a warning of the pitfalls of being a celebrity. Still, publicity attracts volunteers, and if my privacy has to be a casualty, so be it. Again, I tell Scott's story and answer questions about his health, the medical system and his treatment. The cameraman shoots his film, and the highly edited story is broadcast that evening, although I'm much too busy to watch.

A few nights later I am surprised to receive a call from Walter. 'Did you see the programme?' he asks. I tell him no, I was much too busy with my son. 'Well, I just wanted to check on you,' he says. 'Is there anything you need?' I assure him we are well taken care of. 'That segment on you and Scott drew quite a response,' he adds. 'What you're doing for your son is an inspiration.' I thank him politely. 'If I'm in the neighbourhood, would you mind if I stopped in?'

I hesitate a bit before answering. 'Yes, that would be fine.'

When he hangs up, I sit on the couch deep in thought. Why would he want to see me? What does he want? I'm hardly the belle of the ball, dressed as I am in old clothing with spots on it, with sleep-deprived eyes and long unkempt hair. What's the attraction? Does he feel sorry for me? Is that what this is about? Sympathy? I really don't need it, thank you.

A week later he drops by in early evening. 'I was doing a story nearby and thought I'd see how you were,' he says with a warm smile. I am nervous and wish he'd given me warning, at least enough time for some emergency repairs.

'You look like you could use a break. I'll tell you what: it's near sunset – how about a walk on Bondi Beach to see the colours? It's not far, and my crew's in the van. They wouldn't mind watching Scott for an hour.'

Of course it's out of the question. I can't leave Scott. We're both bone-tired after another exhausting day. With his crew? Impossible. But I find myself saying yes. Strangely, I feel feminine.

We deposit our shoes and socks in his TV van, and walk the warm sand as the sun slinks behind the Sydney skyline. He is a gentle man who quickly puts me at ease with his unpretentious charm and whimsical laugh. I talk of my experiences growing up in Wales, my life in America, and now here I am in Sydney. I share the story of my crazy days in Berserkley, and how Ron Kovic inspired me to take my boys to a sit-in protest against the Vietnam War. Walter tells me of his military experience in Vietnam, and that he speaks Vietnamese. He never mentions what he did. I suspect he was in intelligence but I don't ask. I do sense Walter saw a lot in the war, to which I credit the compassion in his eyes.

When we return home, Walter's crew is entertaining Scott with wild stories of filming life on the streets. It has been a relaxing and needed break, and I have enjoyed myself more than I want to admit. 'I'll call again,' Walter says, as he slips out the door. I half hope he does and half hope he doesn't. Where could this possibly lead? He meets beautiful women every day. Why bother with me? It makes no sense. I live on the edge with little to offer. He can't be serious.

About three weeks later, Walter calls again to invite me to dinner, and I agree. 'Where would you like to go?' he asks.

I laugh out loud. 'Me, how should I know? I never leave this place.'

Walter escorts me to an elegant Asian restaurant with a view of the twinkling harbour lights and the soft reflected glow of the Sydney Opera House. I have dressed as nicely as I'm able, tamed my hair and added a little make-up, and Walter, bless his heart, flatters me to death. But I am uncomfortable thinking of Scott. Shirley is with him and I trust her, and I left the phone number of the restaurant, but his condition is fragile and anything could happen. As I gaze at Walter across the candlelit table, I am unable to shake a nagging thought: I'm the mother of three young men including a brain-damaged invalid. What's the point of this?

In early December, Walter calls with an offer to spend Christmas (our second in Australia) at his family home in Byron Bay, a resort area a few hundred miles up the coast, where the beach is secluded and never-ending, and people swim with dolphins. The invitation is for Scott as well, and I am tempted. But after anguished thought, I say no. The trip would be long and difficult for Scott. Also, he fears sleeping in another's bed, as he needs so much attention and is frequently incontinent. After that refusal Walter continues to call, but with less frequency. He still enquires about Scott's health, and how I feel, but no longer asks me out. I wonder, if only my destiny had been different.

The Ray Martin crew returns often to our small home for follow-up stories. After they air, the expected happens: phone calls from potential volunteers, and more offers of marriage. During my last months in Sydney, I appear in eleven different TV programmes, including a feature on Australian *60 Minutes* which I am told will be picked up by its American counterpart. My most memorable TV appearance, however, is on *Probe*, an investigative programme. The subject is the follow-on care of head injuries and the reluctance of government and insurance companies to pay for treatment. I am seated at a round table, ringed by the dark curtains of a TV studio. The moderator, an intensely serious-looking young woman whom I like, is seated on my left. A head-injury survivor is on my right, and directly across is my old nemesis, Dr Rosen from Coorabel. Fortunately, the commotion caused by technicians laying cables, moving cameras and targeting lights spares Dr Rosen and me those awkward moments of silence.

The moderator begins my story. I relate my experiences with Scott over the past year, interspersed with filmed scenes of our home and the volunteers, showing some of the progress he has made since he left Dr Rosen's care. I tell how St Vincent's, with its wonderful doctors, and the taxpayers of Australia have invested vast sums of time, energy and money into nurturing my son back to life from his coma, only to cast him into the dismal swamp of rehabilitation hell where all progress ceased. I am shocked, I say, to see so much money spent on saving people, only to have them ignored after the emergency passes.

The other guest tells the story of her never-ending, discouraging struggle to find services, how her insurance company refused payment, and how finally with only the aid and support of neighbours and family has she been able, after several years, to resume a somewhat normal life.

Finally, the moderator turns his attention to Dr Rosen, with a curt question. 'Are these allegations true, Dr Rosen? Is head-injury rehab the dismal swamp Mrs Carl claims?'

Dr Rosen's face turns a light shade of red under the hot lights as he gamely defends the honour of his hospital and the state. On the defensive, much of the arrogance I had earlier encountered is now missing. Slowly, under the moderator's pointed prodding, Dr Rosen gives ground on one issue after another. The live programme lasts a full hour.

Afterwards, as Dr Rosen and I exit the studio, I stop him in the hall. He still seems shaken from the on-camera grilling. I ask him gently, 'Dr Rosen, why were you so uncaring about Scott? Why did you try to take my hope away?'

He looks into my face, then down and away, and says contritely, 'Mrs Carl, I am deeply sympathetic about your son. But I have a budget to follow. I could rehabilitate ten people so they can return to a working life. Or I could easily spend the same money on a year of intensive therapy for your son so that he just might – and I say might – be lucky enough to get out of a wheelchair.'

For the first time I feel compassion for him. 'Why didn't you tell me the truth? Why didn't you tell me there was no money available? I would have accepted that fact. Instead you made me discouraged and angry.'

He sighs. 'I know and I'm sorry. But few relatives would hear that and accept it. Few have your understanding.'

Following the attention drawn to head-injury rehab by *The Ray Martin Show*, Walter Pearson's coverage, my hour on *Probe*, the *60 Minutes* segment, and the hundreds of letters from volunteers and well-wishers, along with the vocal advocacy of many others, the

Australian Parliament launches an investigation into the care and treatment of coma and head-injury patients, which eventually results in additional resources being devoted to this long-neglected area of medicine.

When I am forced again to explain my illegal status to Immigration I bring along a box overflowing with 350 letters and several newspaper clippings. 'Here,' I say to my case officer just a tad smugly, 'my friends have written you letters.' He looks at the form I have filled in. This time in the section where it asks why I want to stay in Australia, instead of writing again about Scott's condition, I have written, 'I love the sunshine sunshine sunshine sunshine,' and added at the bottom, 'see previous requests.'

After shuffling through and reading several of the handwritten letters, he places them back in the box and appraises me guardedly. 'How do you know all these people? You've only been here a short while. How do you make so many friends? I thought you were housebound. How did you get on those television programmes?'

I just smile sweetly. He runs his tongue across his lips in consternation, and with a deep professional sigh of resignation, says, 'You know our phones have been ringing day and night. You've caused quite a stir. I still don't see how you did it.' He leans back in his chair and runs a tired hand through his thinning hair. 'Okay, this is what I can do.' He picks up my passport and waves it about. 'I can issue a short temporary visa so you can take care of your son. However, there is one condition.'

I knew it, there's always a condition. My stomach tightens as I wait for the axe to fall. These people have so much power. He controls everything.

'As soon as possible you must arrange for a rehabilitation hospital in England or America and I will need an acceptance letter from them before I can release him.'

'And if I can't find a hospital?' I ask, my blood turning cold with fear.

'Then we will find a place for your son here, most likely a convalescent home, and you will have to leave. If he gets better you can return for him. If he doesn't, well . . .' The officer pauses and looks down, then resumes quietly, 'It's better you go on with your life, Mrs Carl.'

I clasp my hands in my lap in an iron grip to keep them from shaking as I guess the consequences of his plan. They will cut Scott's tendons. They will water him like a vegetable until he wilts, and they will turn him under the soil. I won't stand for that, I want to scream. But I can't. I dare not. I won't give this man the pleasure of knowing how desperate I am.

Where would I take Scott? In America medical care is better but very expensive, and I have no insurance. In Britain, Scott qualifies for the National Health Service. So I will take him to England. I have no choice.

Finally the officer slides my passport across the desk. 'I have given you a ten-day special return visa effective when you leave the country, so you can travel and find a facility. When you return, you must bring me the letter, and I will extend your stay until an immigration doctor checks on your son to determine when he can travel. I'm afraid this is the best we can do.'

Returning home, I call Shirley, who took over while I was out, into the kitchen, and tell her of my meeting. As soon as possible, I tell her, I must leave for England and find a hospital. Shirley studies my face, and sees my worry. She also sees what I haven't told her, that I have no money for a ticket. She gives me a warm hug. 'Let's calm down. This will work out just fine,' she says with welcome confidence.

Less than a week later, Shirley slips an envelope into my hand. 'An early Christmas present from your friends. This should get you to England and cover your stay.'

'I can't take this from you,' I tell her, shaking my head as tears well up in my eyes.

'Oh, it's not from me,' she says with a warm smile. 'My present is that I will take charge of Scott while you're gone. The money is a gift from the Sai Baba people, who have spent days collecting it.'

The Sai Baba people, followers of an Indian guru by that name, are dedicated to doing 'seva' – an Indian word that translates into service, or giving of oneself. Many of them make pilgrimages to hear his teachings. They tell me his message is, 'Do not follow me, but go out into the world and do seva with my blessings.' His organization has a huge hospital in India for all kinds of injuries and sickness. It is staffed completely by volunteer doctors and nurses. How I wish I could get Scott there, but I can't. Instead some twenty members of the Sydney Sai Baba network are among Scott's corps of volunteers. There is an architect, a musician, Chris, whose wife is training to be a doctor, and there is an Egyptian who gives Scott moxa treatments. It is mainly the Sai Baba crew who staff my stall at the Paddington Market, which is open every other weekend.

One time when a pair of them went to India, they invited Scott to write a letter that they would carry to the great man himself, and as it turned out, Sai Baba did select that letter from among the many that were held up in his presence, and he read it. So perhaps there was a blessing there. Scott showed me the letter, and what it mainly said was he would appreciate it if some of his pain could be taken away – that's all, nothing about a cure or a normal life. They all took Scott on as their seva project. Think of it – to come up with the airfare for me to go to London! They were incredible. They were always joyous, just calm and quiet and joyous.

Scott's nurse, Stephen from St Vincent's, who has become quite a regular in our lives, offers to stay day and night with Scott so I can depart for England.

As I sit in the British Airways departure lounge, waiting for the boarding call, I am in turmoil. Scott takes so much care, day and night. Then I remember how Stephen took such good care of Scotty while he was in the coma, and knows more than me about health issues. Of course he is quite safe.

And what about me, with only ten days to travel halfway round the world, find a hospital, obtain a letter, and return. Is that enough time? What if I can't find a hospital? What if I can't get a letter? What if I leave Australia and they don't let me back in? So much can go wrong, but I must have faith. What else can I do? When my flight is called, I collapse into my seat in nervous exhaustion.

Jonathan has flown in from Denmark to meet me at Heathrow. In a rented car he whisks me to the small London hotel where we will stay. 'Mom, I've been doing some research on rehab hospitals,' he says, sifting through his notes, while I unpack what little I have brought. 'Not particularly good news, I'm afraid. I've only found five, and they're pretty small. There's one in Oxford, one in Scotland, one in Bristol, and two in London. That's it.'

Bone-tired from the flight, I can barely digest the implications. So few hospitals. I hadn't realized. Could my task be impossible? No, I can't think that way. 'Which is the best?' I ask. 'The Rehab

Centre in Wimbledon gets the highest marks.' Jonathan skims his notes. 'The man you need to see is Dr Rhys.'

'Let's go,' I say.

'Mom, you just got in. It's still morning.'

'Let's go!'

The Rehab Centre in London is a long, single-storey building of red brick with a grey roof, surrounded by park-like green lawns and mature trees. Jonathan parks in the circular drive and we enter to the receptionist's desk.

'I'd like to speak with Dr Rhys, please,' I tell a conservatively dressed woman in her fifties with tightly curled salt-and-pepper hair. She looks up at me over the rim of her reading glasses with the thin smile of someone who controls a vast kingdom. 'Do you have an appointment?'

'No, I don't, but you see I've just flown in from Australia.'

'Without an appointment I'm afraid it's impossible.'

'Can I make an appointment? But I must tell you I have only a few days.'

'The waiting list for appointments is three months. There's nothing I can do.'

'Is Dr Rhys here? Couldn't I just ask him one question? All I need is a letter . . .'

The receptionist tightens her lips in exasperation. 'Dr Rhys is here today, but his schedule is full. He covers several hospitals and when he's here his schedule is tightly controlled, so for all purposes, he's not here.'

'Can I wait?' The receptionist shoots me a look that says, can't you see I'm busy, and without answering returns to her work.

I sit on a hard chair beside Jonathan in silent discouragement.

My mind races. Now what? Do I try another hospital? Which one? The receptionist's phone rings and she turns away, talking more loudly than necessary. 'Dr Rhys is in consultation now in his office, but will be leaving for lunch at half past.'

I check the office clock. It's ten past twelve. Grabbing Jonathan's hand, I whisper, 'Let's go. We have twenty minutes.' I drag him down the hall to a wall directory where I find Dr Rhys's office number. A few moments later I park myself outside his office. Soon the door opens and a patient leaves. Before the door closes, I slip inside. A startled man in a white coat looks up from an open brown file. 'How in the world did you get in?'

Surprised at his heavy Welsh accent, I decide in a flash to gamble. In rusty Welsh I blurt, 'Bore da,' and continue quickly: 'Dr Rhys, my family's from Haverford West and I grew up in Cardiff and I've just arrived this morning from Australia where I'm caring for my son who was in a coma from a terrible accident and has a brain injury, and I desperately need a letter from you.'

I inhale deeply and wait before babbling on. Dr Rhys's face looks as if it's been blown out to sea by a cyclone. Quickly recovering his composure, and with eyes now crinkling with amusement, he slowly stands and extends a hand towards a chair. He is in his mid-fifties with silver hair and light brown eyes, about five foot ten, a bit heavy around the middle. As I sit he studies me for a few moments, then gives his head a slight shake and breaks into a quiet chuckle.

'Haverford West, is it? I know that area; I grew up very near there. Now what's this about a letter?' Ever so slightly, I relax, deeply relieved. Had he not known I was Welsh I'd most likely be out the door.

I quickly relate Scott's story. Born in Britain, raised in America, how he came to Australia, the accident, the coma, my volunteers, and my long vigil of rescue. 'So you see, Dr Rhys, we're not Australian citizens and they want us out, but they won't release my son until I have a letter from a rehabilitation hospital in Britain saying they will take him.'

'But we can't take him, not now,' Dr Rhys says. 'We only have twenty-eight beds at the Rehab Centre, and the wait to be admitted is one to three years.'

'But they don't need to know that, do they? Couldn't you give me a letter saying he will be admitted, but not when?'

'But I can't promise he will be.'

'But at some point he could be, couldn't he? Even if it's three years or five years or whenever, it is possible. Just don't give a timeframe.'

Dr Rhys begins to laugh, not out loud, but internally, so his frame shakes. 'I must say you are an interesting woman. You've worked hard for your son. His name is Scott, you say? And didn't you say he played rugby? I played rugby. Now that's a man's game.' He heaves an audible sigh, and wipes at his chin with a hand. 'I suppose I do have to help a fellow Welshman, but you do understand I can't promise?'

'I understand, no promises, just say in a letter that you'll let him in.'

Dr Rhys laughs again and shakes his head. 'I'll have a letter for you this afternoon.'

I slip out of the doorway into the hall and give Jonathan an ecstatic hug. 'I've got the letter,' I say in an excited whisper, 'by this afternoon. Let's get coffee.'

A week later, fresh from my flight, I walk into the Australian

143

Immigration building and hand-deliver Dr Rhys's letter to my case officer. He unfolds it and studies the contents, carefully scrutinizing each line. Finally he raises his eyes.

'The letter says your son will be admitted to the Rehab Centre, but it doesn't say when.'

'I couldn't tell Dr Rhys when, because I wasn't told when I would be leaving Australia. But Dr Rhys assured me the Rehab Centre will take him.' The officer reads the letter again, chews on his lip, then slides it into my folder. 'I will arrange for the Immigration doctor to visit you soon.'

Our apartment is as crazy as ever, like a train station, with volunteers coming and going from morning to night. Steve and Shirley have done a masterly job of coordinating Scott's care, and after the break in England I am able to evaluate his progress with new eyes. I am amazed at how far he has come. He is now able to sit upright in a wheelchair, move both legs on command and walk on his knees with help. His back is much straighter, although the untreated left shoulder is still crooked. He can place his right heel on the ground when he is standing with help. His right arm and hand are very powerful and sometimes he can lift himself from the floor onto the couch by getting on his right knee, placing his right hand on the couch and swinging himself around. He is also much more alert, drawing and painting with good and increasingly long periods of concentration. His speech has improved greatly and he is able to string together longer sentences. And he looks very healthy.

He is so aware by now that whenever anyone takes him out he insists on carrying his wallet, a leather pouch on a string he wears round his neck. Inside is a piece of paper with his name, address and telephone number, and a little money. It makes him feel independent and in control, although I find it quite amusing as I can't imagine him having enough energy or mobility to get himself lost.

As before the phone is constantly ringing. Walter calls to welcome me back, and asks if I might consider having dinner. Surprised, I tell him perhaps a farewell dinner might be in order, as I've been told I have only a few days left in Sydney.

The Ray Martin Show wants Scott and me to do a final programme. The next afternoon we are on live television. Ray asks how Scott is progressing, comments on the differences he has noticed from a few months before, and asks about my recent trip to England. Then before I grasp what he's doing, Ray picks up the phone and calls the Australian prime minister. To my surprise he gets through.

'Mr Prime Minister,' Ray asks, 'the Australian government is deporting Mrs Carl. Isn't there something you can do to stop this? After all this time, she's as good as Australian. I'm putting Mrs Carl on the open line with you now.'

I turn several shades of red as I listen to the prime minister, caught off guard and groping for an appropriate response. Ray prompts me with looks. I jump in, stammering, 'Mr Prime Minister, I want to tell you how good Australia has been to me and my son, and how grateful I feel for your generosity. But I do think it's time we return to Britain, where my son was born, and receive better rehabilitation than I can provide.' Ray Martin intercedes to thank the prime minister and quickly hangs up.

I am so embarrassed I can barely look at him, and the programme quickly winds down. I thank him for the several shows he has devoted to our plight. Through him I have garnered many wonderful volunteers, and Scott's and my days in Australia have been eased by their spirit of generosity.

Finally the day I have dreaded arrives. The Immigration doctor, the same one I dealt with at St Vincent's, with a harrumphing voice, walks through our door. After a time observing Scott and the volunteers about him, the doctor turns my way. 'I believe your son is fit to travel. That's what I will put in my report to Immigration. I suggest you make the necessary arrangements.'

'How much time do I have?'

'One, two, maybe three weeks. You will receive a letter.'

When the doctor leaves, I walk into the kitchen to be alone and gaze out my kitchen window into my garden of dying blooms, and beyond towards the coast. I see in my mind's eye Scott's old flat on Potts Point. It's now April, a year and eleven months since I set foot on Australian soil and visited the scene of Scott's tragedy. He arrived a picture of health and youth, with a ravenous appetite for life, but will leave this glowing land of opportunity a severe cripple in a wheelchair. The thought flashes that perhaps Immigration will again forget and we can stay longer, but my instinct tells me no, the end is here. When I board that plane I will have come full circle. I will have achieved my mission to rescue my son, and now I must leave. But then what?

True to the doctor's word, the official letter arrives. I have two weeks to leave.

Eight

I'm haunted by the cost of flying Scott and myself to England. It will run into the thousands. For nearly two years I've been living on pennies and the generosity of friends and strangers. I have only days left. How will I raise that kind of money?

Once again Shirley steps into the breach and takes control. She creates several fundraising committees staffed with volunteers. A jazz saxophonist named Chris offers to organize concerts, and is quickly joined by many others – David the guitarist, the African djembe drummers, the high-school violinist, an amateur opera singer, a professional clarinettist, and several more. The Waverly Philharmonic Society agrees to sponsor a benefit concert, and a group of jazz musicians offer to hold a fundraising jam in a church hall.

Another group of volunteers comes together to promote an art auction. They mobilize other artists and tap into the whole Australian art scene, making dozens of phone calls to ask for donated work. Within days, 148 artists from across the country, many well-known, donate original works of art. What starts as a trickle soon becomes a flood. Strangers walk in carrying all sorts of artwork: large canvases stretched over pine frames, sculptures and objects of all sizes, small packages in brown paper, sealed wood boxes, cardboard sleeves. Pried open, unwrapped and peeled back, they contain a menagerie of artistic inspiration: watercolour seascapes, acrylics of the Blue Mountains, pastels of garden flowers, cubist renditions of nudes, oil abstractions in bold, brassy colours, ceramic vases in muted browns and yellows, bronze sculptures of animals and children, even intricate Calder-like mobiles, and a few pieces of folk art. Within days my apartment is choked with little room to walk let alone host volunteers.

Each art piece comes with a notation attesting to its estimated value and signed by its creator. The note on an oil painting, in a hasty scrawl says, 'In my gallery this would sell for $4000, but you can sell it for whatever you wish.' Another on a pastel reads, 'I have no idea what this is worth because I refused to sell it. To me it's priceless. But I don't mind donating it to Scott.' Reading through all the notes and short letters I am deeply moved by the selfless generosity of these strangers, people who may only have heard of Scott's struggle from a single phone call, yet have responded as if he were a member of their family.

Donald Friend, whose art hangs in museums around the world, writes me a poignant letter to say he is recovering from a debilitating stroke and has read about Scott in a magazine article and seen a photo of him painting. He encloses a cheque for $5000.

The Sai Baba people step forward to organize one last blowout sale at the Paddington Flea Market. Usually their Saturday store is a modest ten-by-ten with white canvas sides and two steel tables. For this Saturday, anticipating an increase in donations, they double the size to ten-by-twenty, with five tables and double the volunteers, but their expectations prove modest. They and the other volunteers have organized a phone bank, with each person calling several friends and each friend calling their friends. The multiplier works, and as the week draws to an end, nearly 400 people have emptied their closets, sheds and garages, donating every conceivable kind of object, from souvenirs of the Great Barrier Reef to used clothing, kitchen items and garden tools, books, tapes, sports equipment, lamps, furniture, radios and an old TV. 'Aid pours in to help Scott,' announces the headline of an article in the *Sydney Morning Herald*.

With the apartment already stuffed and overflowing with art, I must now make room for an extra cornucopia of goods destined for the flea market. Come Saturday morning the Sai Baba people will haul it all away, but in the meantime my front and back gardens resemble the aftermath of a hurricane. I cross my fingers for dry weather. A torrential spring rain could well destroy it all.

During that first week my phone rings constantly. Volunteers calling to help, calls for instructions, calls offering support, calls from the curious and calls from cranks. One call is especially memorable. 'Mrs Carl, my name is Stewart Thomas,' the voice says, measured and hard-edged. 'I'm an attorney with one of the largest law firms in Sydney. I've been reading about your son and how the government is trying to kick you out of the country. I want to represent you in a suit against the government.'

Caught off guard, and surrounded by a sea of confusion with people coming and going, I hardly know what to say. 'You want to represent me? Why?'

'Don't misunderstand me, Mrs Carl. I'm not doing this for you, I'm doing this for my career. But I can help you. I can get the government off your back so you can stay in the country and continue treatment for your son. All you have to do is sign a few papers. The rest is up to me. What do you say? Should I come over?'

I take a couple of breaths.

I've already moved beyond the idea of staying in Sydney. I've come to terms with my fate and although Scott is sad to be leaving his friends I know he is excited at being able to get the rehabilitation he needs in England. Now this. Could we really stay? Is it possible? Now my head is really swirling. Sydney is our home, this is our life. These are our friends. 'Can you really do that?' I hear myself ask.

'Absolutely. I can file the papers in the morning and I'm sure you won't hear from the government again. And you can continue Scott's medical treatment.'

The reality sets in. I can't do it. Scott needs help, medical help, and he won't get it here. Plans have already been made. What do I say? The pause grows longer. I have to say something.

'I'm sorry, Mr Thomas. It won't work. We're on our own with no insurance. Even if the government leaves us alone, even if Scott is eligible for treatment, there aren't any services available. There are no services and no money for head-injury patients. The government would just put him away somewhere. Thank you for your offer, but there's really nothing you can do for us.' It is the most difficult no-thank-you I've ever said.

The Saturday flea market is a huge success. I'm amazed at the crowd and what sells. Every piece of donated treasure seems to find a smiling buyer and a new home. What little is left over the Sai Babas donate to another charity, and our Paddington store is closed for good.

On Sunday afternoon, with Richard Neville as auctioneer, nearly

Hold My Hand

150 people gather for a sit-down auction in a cavernous space – now art gallery – donated by a civic group. As each art piece is presented, Richard reads a description and announces the suggested value stated by the donor. The auction proceeds briskly until every item is sold! Many pieces from some of Australia's most recognized artists are scooped up for pennies on the market-value dollar. Each time a piece sells, Scott, seated near the front, gives a thumbs-up and then bangs the arm of his wheelchair with his good hand.

That night, the Philharmonic Society holds a benefit concert in the auditorium of Cranbrook School, with the premier of a new work, 'Sagittarius' by Sydney composer Graham Major. And a few nights later, the improvised jazz concert is held in a suburban church hall before an enthusiastic audience with donations accepted.

In five days of intense activity, the flea-market, art auction and concerts raise $28,000, sufficient to purchase the five airline seats (three for Scott, plus Jonathan and me), with seed money left over for our new life in England.

Jonathan arrives from Denmark to help me pack and move Scott to England. The flat, now empty of art and flea-market treasures, seems larger than I remember. It is certainly quieter. Two or three volunteers stop by to help us pack, but I say no, thank you, packing will not be difficult. We will leave with little more than we brought.

I am gazing with great nostalgia out of the front window when the phone rings again. 'Is this Mrs Carl?' an older woman asks in a strained manner.

I am instantly curious about this conflicted voice that sounds on the edge of tears. 'Yes, this is Glenys Carl.'

'My name is Ann Meadows and I badly need your help.'

'How can I help?'

'Like you, I have a son with a head injury. He's twenty years old. I can't get him any medical help. I have nowhere to turn, and I can't do it alone. I'm desperate.' She breaks down in muffled sobs. My heart goes out to her. Tears come to my eyes. I know the desperation she feels. That hollow, lonely feeling that no amount of consolation will fill.

'What do you need?' I ask.

The woman struggles to regain control. 'Next week I'm going to chain myself to the gate in front of the parliament building and go on a hunger strike, and I need you to be there with me.'

'But why me?'

Without missing a beat she replies, 'Because you get all the publicity. If I do it alone, no one will care. If you're there, everyone will care. The TV will come, the newspapers will come, the world will know. Will you help me, please?'

I am stunned. How can I help this woman? What can I possibly say? How many are there like her who are suffering in silence? How many mothers of head-injured children are leading lives of quiet desperation? Do I deserve all this attention? Is Scott's story any different from this woman's? Any different from hundreds, maybe thousands of others?

'I'm so sorry, Ann. I wish I could help you, but we're leaving Australia in two days. Our visas have expired and we have to go. We have no choice.' Except for the quiet sobs, the line is silent. 'Let me give you a few names,' I offer, searching for a modicum of solace. 'These people have worked with Scott and understand your needs. They may be able to help.'

I hang up feeling empty and disconsolate. Tragedy is part of life.

I know that. How else will we recognize happiness but to be reminded so often? This abandonment of head-injury victims is a problem that must be fixed. Governments, insurance companies, families, they all pay out huge sums on emergency care, employing the latest technology to save lives in the face of overwhelming odds. Then what? When the emergency is over, when the patient is declared fit to live, everyone walks away, refusing to pay for rehabilitation, deserting the very people they have struggled to save. It's all so crazy, so inhumane, and so callous.

On the final day I softly close the front door to my flat in Five Corners. It is empty now of everything but the spirits of the hundreds of volunteers who lent their energy, enthusiasm, laughter and compassion to help my son Scott, a stranger, struggle to achieve his dream to lead a full and rich life again.

The neighbourhood is strangely quiet as Tim, the same pony-tailed young man who drove us from Coorabel the first time, loads our suitcases into the boot of his cab. With all the publicity he knew when we were leaving, and he volunteers my final ride to the airport as a parting gift. He and Jonathan position Scott in the back seat while I collapse the borrowed wheelchair and lay it in the boot. Tim will return it to the hospital, he tells me with a grin.

On the ride to the airport I think of nothing else but the joy and support I have found in the people of Australia. I arrived a solitary stranger, and leave with a vast network of dear friends. So many people have given so much. I am humbled by my inability to respond. The word 'grateful' rings hollow next to the debt I owe so many.

Tim takes us to the international terminal. He arranges an airline wheelchair for Scott, checks our luggage, and gives me a long hug.

Jonathan wheels Scott to the ticket counter to check in. Then we turn for the departure gate at the end of a long concourse. We wheel past throngs of excited families welcoming and saying goodbye to loved ones. I hear the public address system paging passengers with exotic names and announcing departing flights. The reality sets in. I am leaving for good, and a hollowness seeps into my stomach. I feel very much alone.

I turn the last corner to my gate and find a mass of people blocking the way. They are an oddly boisterous group wearing party hats, some with musical instruments, others with balloons. Someone shouts, 'There's Glenys! There's Scotty and Jonathan!' And they surge forward to mob us.

I am stopped in my tracks. I see Julie Clarke and her mother Johnnie, and there's Rollie and Robin, and the fifth Beatle strumming his guitar, and Maori James, and Rick and David in all their glory, and nurse Jenny beside Dr Croches.

Robert, the medical school dropout, gives me a warm hug, with Billy the Magic Man right behind, and there's Second Hand Rose next to the black and white boxes. A group of Sai Baba people blow us kisses. Haiki, the Israeli medic, layers Scott's face with lipstick. Beyond the three housewives, who are openly crying, Keith the osteopath gives me a high five sign, and Brendan the physiotherapist lifts a bouquet of coloured balloons.

Walter gives me a long, warm hug that I am reluctant to break. We never had that farewell dinner, and I feel guilty. Then I am in the arms of my dear friend Shirley. We are both in tears as we hug in silence. To the side, a film crew catches it all.

There are fathers with children perched on their shoulders, mothers with babies, strangers attracted by the crowd, and neighbours. It seems every person I have ever known in Australia has come to say goodbye. There must be a hundred. For nearly an hour, the kissing, hugging and tears continue until our flight is called. Many are so distraught they cannot speak, choosing to push money into my pockets instead, or pile floppy Australian bush hats on our heads.

My last view as we wheel Scott into the jetway for the plane is of Walter and Shirley standing behind the beautiful brown-haired high-school girl with her violin tucked under her chin. The ghostly quality of her soaring strings lingers in my mind like sweet incense on soft summer air.

With Scott stretched and propped across his seats, I watch with tearful eyes as the gorgeous city of Sydney slips beneath our silver wings. Already I mourn the loss of my dear friends and am gnawed by fear of the unknown, but I have no choice. Destiny has brought me to Australia, and destiny propels me onward towards Britain, a country I have not known for twenty years.

Nine

Eyes closed, I'm praying for sleep. While my body's drained, my brain's going wild, spinning off into strange places, as if I'm cross-wired. An hour in the air, twenty-one to go, and I'm caged like a hamster, running in small circles, and now I'm off again across the globe, continents away. Will it never end?

I look out of the plane window. Stringy grey clouds are tinged with the burnt red of sunset. We are flying west into the dying sun, retracing my route of two years before: Singapore, Dubai and London. Odd, but I'm wearing the same silk blouse I arrived in. I didn't deliberately put it on. I have other blouses, not many but enough for a variety, yet when I dressed this morning I reached instinctively for yellow – comfort, cheeriness in a sea of departing sadness.

Oh God, here I go again. Playing mind games over and over. Let it go, Glennie, let it go before you cross that line into never-ending self-pity. Isn't it also sad for Scott? He's left so many friends who have become his hands and legs. He was so accepted in his injured state. How will he be welcomed now in England?

Scott murmurs and I turn in his direction. He's lying at my feet, asleep on a blanket, stretched on the floor between the two rows of seats. The row I purchased for him is empty. Even with the armrests up they're lumpy, and Scott couldn't find comfort, so Jonathan and I made a bed for him on the floor. His eyes open, and he looks up at me with an expression I know by heart. I catch Jonathan's attention across the aisle and mouth the word *bathroom*. Jonathan edges his brother out from between the rows, lifts him across a broad shoulder, and works his way down the narrow aisle towards the lavatory. Those claustrophobic cubicles are scarcely large enough for my small body, let alone one man struggling with another. I watch them disappear, but can't picture how Jonathan is coping, and something in me wishes not to know.

The closing lavatory door takes me back to another closing door years earlier, when Sammy, Jonathan, and four-year-old Scotty walked out the front door of our compact Berkeley home in search of a food market. We had just moved in, and the boys were eager to explore their neighbourhood.

∾

'Send us to the store,' Jonathan pleaded, 'we need food, don't we?'

'Yes, yes,' Scotty chimed in, pulling on my hand, jumping up and down like a baby kangaroo. 'I'll get some milk. No candy, I promise. Please, Mom, please, please!'

I resisted at first, still a stranger in this neighbourhood. I had yet to fully scout the streets to confirm their safety, but the boys were cooped up, and I wanted a little quiet to finish unpacking. Against my better judgement, I finally relented. 'When you go down the front steps,' I instructed the eldest, Sammy, 'turn left. The main street is three blocks away. There's a small supermarket on the corner. Here's some money; bring me back half a gallon of milk. You can buy an ice-cream if you want, but come straight back – it's close to dinner. Do you boys understand?' Wide-eyed and bursting with giggles, they nodded in unison.

I watched the front door close behind them and mentally crossed my fingers, hoping I'd done the right thing. I turned to my chores but when an hour had passed I became concerned. At an hour and a half I hastened to the supermarket, but they were nowhere to be seen. I dashed back home in an increased state of alarm, my heart pumping. Two hours had now passed since the front door closed. I called the police and a patrol car arrived within minutes. The sergeant, a calm older man, took down their descriptions. I gave him a picture of the three boys taken a few months earlier in Detroit, and he promised to find them.

After two more hours of frantic pacing, as the streetlights were popping on, the patrol car drove up and my three boys sprang from the back seat.

'Wow, Mom,' Sammy gushed, 'you ever been in a police car?'

'Here's the milk,' Scotty announced, holding up a carton.

The sergeant stood over them with a warm smile. 'They're safe and sound,' he told me. 'They've an interesting story to tell, so I'll leave you alone. But if I were you, Mom, I'd keep a string on 'em.' With a nod the sergeant climbed back into his car and drove off.

Sternly I herded the boys inside and lined them up against the kitchen wall. Their smiles had gone, but not the giggles in their eyes. Scott's shirt had a dribble of chocolate ice-cream on it.

'Okay, someone here owes me an explanation,' I began in my best tough-Mom voice. 'I gave you strict orders, up and back with no side trips. So what happened?' The three glanced at each other with looks only a mother could decipher, and I suspected they'd already rehearsed a new version of reality.

'We did just as you said, Mom,' Sammy volunteered. 'We walked three blocks up to the corner and bought the milk.'

'But when we came out,' Jonathan said, 'we forgot the way home.'

'That's right,' Sammy agreed. 'We looked every way and it all looked the same. So we picked a street and walked up it for three blocks, but that wasn't the right way, so we walked down another street, and that wasn't the right way either.'

'We got lost,' Scott said, emphasizing the obvious.

'It was starting to get dark,' Jonathan said.

'And remember how you always told us,' Sammy added, 'if we ever got lost, to just stay in one place so people could find us. We knew we had to go back to the supermarket, but it was getting late. So we decided to do it in the morning.'

'We went to the hospital,' Scotty jumped in with a grin.

'The hospital?' I whispered, a chill sweeping my body. 'Are you hurt?'

'Oh no, Mom,' Sammy said. 'It was getting dark and we knew we had to find someplace to sleep. Then in the morning we'd go back to the supermarket so you could find us. The hospital was Scotty's idea.' I could only stare at my youngest with incredulity.

'That's right, Mom,' Scotty said. 'I saw on TV about a hospital, and I remembered hospitals have lots of beds. So I told Sammy and Jonathan, "Hospitals have beds." So we asked someone where the hospital was.'

'When we found it,' Jonathan said, 'we walked in and went to the desk, and Sammy told this woman that we needed a place to sleep for the night.'

'I told her we needed three beds,' Scotty said firmly, his arms crossed.

'She had us sit in some chairs,' Sammy explained, 'and pretty soon this policeman comes and brings us home.'

'And we brought the milk,' Scotty finished, 'just like we promised.'

Dumbstruck, I could only stare at my three boys, lined up in order of age, their faces a cascading series of innocent smiles. Could I ever put strings on these clever kids? 'I think your dinner's cold,' was all I could muster, giving each a hug.

෴

I take my eye off the white lavatory door at the end of the aisle, as a smiling stewardess passes by handing out small white pillows and dark-blue British Airways blankets. I tuck the thin blanket about my neck and let it drape over my folded legs, now drawn up and pressed against my body, and turn once again to gaze out the window. The orange sun is balanced on the horizon, deciding what to do. Is it setting or rising? Except for my own sense of time, I wouldn't have a clue. What would I prefer? I muse absently. So many have worked so hard to get Scott this far, but for what? Are we returning home to Britain for his sun to set, or to rise?

I close my eyes for just a moment, and when I open them again, the sky is a charcoal grey edged with black. The sun has gone down, vanished. Someone else, it seems, has made the decision, but not for me. For me Scott's sun is rising. I am sure we are flying home to heal.

The cabin has also darkened, broken only by the spotty glow of reading lights and the muted hum of far-off voices. Scott is asleep at my feet and Jonathan is a curled shadow across the way. I rearrange my blanket, crimping it even closer, and close my eyes.

As a little girl, it was in the dark of night that I felt most lonely, even tucked into my bed within the sturdy four walls of my room. With Dad off fishing the North Atlantic for weeks on end, Mum and I would make do alone. Nanna, at some of these times, would be staying with her other daughter. Even when he returned from the sea, Dad was rarely there to put me to bed. Snuggled under my quilt, I would wait in the dark for the sound of the front door banging shut as he returned from an evening at The Moorland, then his heavy boots pounding the stairs and the creak of my door swinging open, knowing that his great bulk would soon be leaning over me to plant a whisky-soaked kiss on my cheek as he growled his bedtime prayer: 'Sleep tight, my little Glennie, you sleep tight.' It was difficult for me to sleep until he came home, and after his kiss, when I could finally drift off, there was the lingering perfume of his breath.

Those days are far off now, receding into memory just as with every mile my sun-filled days in Sydney are passing towards time's scrapbook. But I can't let those moments die, not yet. I have to hold on to something. Such dear friends. In my mind, I see Dr Croches and feel his compassion. He would never talk to me without reaching out to touch my arm. And Shirley with her wise eyes, and Walter Pearson, such a dear man, and Nurse Jenny, Richard, Julie, Johnnie, so many others. Will I ever find such good friends again?

I wipe at the tears welling in my eyes, and pull the blanket closer and tighter, but they keep coming. My eyes blur and I blink hard to stem the trickle, which becomes a running stream. Helpless to staunch the flow, I pull the blanket up to cover my eyes and muffle my sobs. No one must know how I feel, especially not Jonathan or Scott. But my control slips away until my emotional dam, riven with fractures, is finally breached. I pull the blanket right over my head, and curling into a tight ball, start sobbing uncontrollably. My body shudders with spasms. I cry with abandon as it all gushes forth, every throttled emotion. I cry until my eyes, like a desert spring, go dry, and I lie limp with exhaustion. Then a great stillness settles upon me.

With the fear drained, my emotional reservoir starts to fill with hope. Gathering strength, I wobble towards the lavatory. Locked in, I stare at the gaunt, red-eyed, pasty face in the mirror. Filling the stainless-steel sink with cold water, I plunge my face into the bowl – my little shock therapy – wash my eyes, then pat myself dry with paper towels. Again I confront the mirror.

Breathing deep and long, I'm steadier now, and colour has returned to my cheeks. Narrowing my eyes, I reproach the other set staring back: Okay Glenys, you've had your pity time. Now let's get a grip. You've miles to go before you sleep, and lots of promises to keep. This is no time to go wobbly, not now. Not when Scott's come so far. Not when we're going home. Think of the future, think of the joy in the world, and give thanks for what you have. Now clear the decks, and go for it!

Touching up my lips, with a little blush on my cheeks for camouflage, I exit the lavatory with renewed determination. Some time after Dubai, Jonathan again takes Scott to the lavatory. I watch them emerge and see the sadness etched in Jonathan's face. With Scott repositioned on the floor at my feet, Jonathan settles in next to me and we make small talk. We talk of everything but what's important – Scott's true condition and his chances of full recovery. There are things a parent never shares with a child: the great fears of death, failure, loneliness, destitution.

He's reserved a small hotel in Wimbledon, he tells me for the second or third time, and after Scott and I settle in he must return to Copenhagen for school. 'You know, Mom, I'll be just a short flight away,' Jonathan whispers to calm me. 'I can be in London in just a few hours.' I smile his way to ease his guilt, and lay a hand of reassurance on his. Jonathan must lead his own life unburdened by his mother's cares. But I'm thinking how soon that will be, just hours away, and how when he does leave, I will be alone again, to face the harsh realities of another impersonal city.

After twenty years in other lands, my childhood English friends have drifted off. Even my Welsh relatives, cousins mostly, have become distant. My brother John is living in Canada. Mother has moved to Lytham St Anne's in northern England and Dad, bless his tortured soul, has passed away. Jonathan carries on with suggestions about where I should live, as if I will have a choice, and we discuss the prospect of finding a rehab hospital for Scott. In spite of Dr Rhys's letter of promise, which he provided under my velvet duress and which committed him to nothing, I brace myself for the likely battle with the National Health Service.

The pilot's voice comes over the intercom to say the plane is on final approach into Heathrow. London weather is low clouds, limited visibility, fifteen degrees Celsius with light winds and heavy rain, he tells us. 'A perfect spring day in London,' he adds with dry British humour. On cue, bullets of rain splatter against the window as we descend through layers of lead-grey clouds. Instinctively, my body shivers with memories of Cardiff and Marble Hall Farm. Memories of a little girl staring from her upstairs window into the same oppressive low-hanging clouds and wind-driven rain, wondering if it would ever end, wondering if I would ever see the sun again. Memories of rolling my baby brother in his black and white Silver Cross pram back and forth across our small front porch while rain cascaded in never-ending sheets from the roof over my head. I was a small child, and as I think back, I realize that despite the wool sweaters, mittens and coal fires, I was rarely warm. In my mind I can still smell the coal dust and feel the bone-numbing chill of the air.

Tucking the blanket around my neck, I unconsciously run my right hand up and down my left arm to calm the goose bumps. After sunny Sydney, I'd forgotten about the unreliable English weather. How long will this rain last? Will it be too cold for Scott? His immune system is so weak. Has bringing him home been a mistake? Pneumonia crosses my mind, but I shake that evil thought away.

With the plane at the gate, we wait for others to depart before gathering our few belongings to set foot onto our new, old land. Entering the waiting lounge, I pause midway, stirred by feelings of familiarity. We have disembarked at the same gate that I departed from so long ago. There is the counter I threatened to climb on to bully the stubborn BA agent to let me on the Sydney-bound flight. And there across the way is the wall I slumped against in despondency, this yellow silk blouse plastered to my back from fear of being stranded and never reaching my son in time. I have come full circle.

A black cab takes us to a small and charming three-storey hotel in a quiet part of Wimbledon. I register at the ornate, brass-on-old-wood front desk, with Jonathan behind me supporting Scott. Our room is two floors up. The deskman pushes the key across the counter, taking in Scott with a passive eye, no doubt wondering if he might be intoxicated and trouble might be looming.

With Scott over Jonathan's shoulder, we move down the wood-

panelled hall towards the lift with its sliding black metal gate, typical
of an old English hotel, another reminder that life has changed. It
will be too small for a wheelchair. Jonathan places his brother on
the floor, shuts the gate, they disappear upward and soon the lift
returns for the folded chair and me. Our room is small, with dark
bedding, yellow and brown wallpaper, and a single wood-cased
window overlooking the street. Mentally I lay out sleeping arrangements. A bed on the floor for Scott, while Jonathan and I take the
two single beds. We are exhausted, but first a little shopping.

Leaving Jonathan to care for his brother, I borrow an umbrella
from the deskman and head into the street. At a corner chemist,
I am given the phone number of a supplier of wheelchairs. From
a delicatessen I purchase bread and cold meat, and from a small
greengrocers' a few pieces of fruit. We make sandwiches on a towel
spread across a bed, and as night falls, Jonathan gives Scott a bath
before we all collapse into fitful jet-lagged sleep.

The next morning I am up early. Pulling open the curtains, I face
a dismal grey day. It's still raining, and my heart sinks just a little. In
Sydney I might have walked into this rain to let it wet my hair,
stream off my face and drench my clothes, knowing that even as it
refreshed me it was also bringing life to my flower garden and the
land would burst with joyous green. But this isn't Sydney, this is
cold England, and spring in this northern land emerges slowly. It's
best I forget about Sydney and get used to where I am.

For breakfast we have cold sandwiches with fruit and a cup of
coffee, and after Scott is settled I again leave Jonathan in charge
while I go out for a newspaper to check the rental listings. With
Jonathan leaving for Denmark in late afternoon, I have little time to
waste. Ordering coffee at a small cafe, I spread open the *Guardian* in

search of a place to rent, but my eyes are drawn to the narrow street, to the anonymous black umbrellas that bob along the pavement above darkly cloaked bodies, and to the cars that roll by, their wipers slapping, spinning tyres sending out thin sheets of cold spray. For all those years away, this is still home, isn't it? And for all the strangeness, it does feel good, doesn't it, like old postcards pulled from a long-forgotten chest of memories. My thoughts drift to that cherrywood chest containing the baby photos that I left with Stefan. Last Christmas in Sydney, he promised the chest was safely in storage and he would send it when I was ready. One of these days I will ask for it, but not yet. One of these days, when I'm ready.

I scan the rental ads, but they make little sense. I don't recognize the street names, and I have no car to chase leads. If Dr Rhys admits Scott, long shot that it is, I must live as close as possible to the hospital. I close the paper, drain my cup, place it silently on the saucer, and with an inward sigh think, what now? Leaving the cafe, I choose a direction almost at random, and set off on my quest for inspiration. Perhaps I'll find a bookshop with a bulletin board, or a rental notice tacked to a pole, or a small sign hidden in the corner of a window, as I might have in Sydney. After an hour of wandering, I pause before the bay window of an estate agent to view a handful of photos of homes for sale. This is the closest I've come to finding a rental. With nothing to lose, I walk in.

The office is narrow and long with a row of wood desks against one wall, and two or three private enclosed offices along the opposite wall. I approach the receptionist's desk, occupied by a woman in her mid-twenties. Deep in a phone conversation, she looks up and raises her eyebrow in a may-I-help-you arch.

'I'm looking for a rental, and I thought—' But before I can

complete my thought she gives her head an emphatic sideways shake, dislodging tight blonde curls. 'Sorry, luv,' she says quickly, a hand over the mouthpiece, anxious to return to more important business. 'Suggest you try adverts in the papers. Only listings for sale here.'

Behind her a man emerges from one of the private offices. Spying me, he moves to the front. 'May I help you?' he asks, flashing a nice professional smile. Afraid of being cut off again, I blurt out my needs all at once. 'I'm looking for a rental in the Wimbledon area where I can live while my son is in a rehab hospital, but it must be near public transport and shops, because I don't have a car and can only push the wheelchair two or three miles. And it must have a wide front door with no steps so I can get a wheelchair through. And the rent has to be reasonable.' I take a breath. 'Very reasonable,' I add quietly.

Surprised at the urgent rush of my outburst, the agent draws back a bit, then purses his lips in thought. 'Well, let me think . . . Yes. I do have an ideal situation, and it does meet all your specifications.'

I hold my breath, thinking: but there's a problem, isn't there?

'But there is one small knot,' the agent resumes slowly. I exhale disappointment. 'The house I'm thinking of is for sale, and will surely sell within the next few months. But I can ring up the owners to see if they would rent it to you in the meantime at a reasonable rate.'

With that he slips into his office, only to reappear in a couple of minutes, a broad smile on his face. 'Well, I must say you are the lucky one. The owners have agreed and you can have it for a third of the normal rent, that is until it sells.'

'Would you please drive me over to look at it?' I ask, and briefly explain my situation with Scott and the hotel and Jonathan leaving. The agent stops his car in front of a lovely cottage in Northview, a cul-de-sac across from Wimbledon Common. There are no steps. The front door is large enough for the wheelchair. There is a large bay window for views and light. And the street is quiet.

As we drive away the agent says, 'If you come round tomorrow with the first month's rent, I'll hand you the keys and you can move in.' Giddy with delight I almost burst out laughing. Move in? What a quaint concept. Move what in? I own nothing but an old suitcase of old clothes. Not even a teacup, let alone a bed or a chair. But I do have a roof, the beginnings of stability, and that alone is worth gold.

When the agent drops me in front of the hotel, I rush upstairs and burst into the room fairly shouting, 'The gods are with us! I have found the most beautiful little cottage you could imagine.'

Scott lets out a loud hooray, and I notice for the first time he's sitting in the wheelchair I ordered the night before. It's gloriously black with shiny chrome wheels, not beat-up like the one we borrowed from Coorabel.

I also notice Jonathan's bag by the door, small, black and tightly packed for a trip, so little for such a strong, healthy young man. I look into his eyes. How much longer do you have? my face asks.

'I'm so glad you're back,' Jonathan says with relief. 'I was getting worried. The taxi will be here in half an hour, and I delayed leaving as long as I could.'

Again we make small talk. 'Stay in touch, Mom. Call me if you need anything. Scott's in good hands.' I keep a weak smile pasted on my face. Parting will be hard enough without my showing the strain. I glance at Scott. He is looking down and trying not to show his sorrow. When the time comes, I go with Jonathan into the hall, wrap my small arms about him and hold tight – too long and too tight, I fear. We exchange love and he vanishes into the lift with tears in his eyes.

The next morning I call Dr Rhys. Fortunately another receptionist answers, not his own office lady, and I'm quickly put through. Dr Rhys answers.

'Dr Rhys, this is Glenys Carl calling. I spoke to you several weeks ago about my son Scott in Australia. You gave me a letter. Do you remember?' I hear a low chuckle.

'Ah, Mrs Carl,' he says, his thick Welsh voice light with humour. 'How could I ever forget what you did to our poor Welsh language? How could I ever forget the woman who persuaded me to do more for her in ten minutes than most people accomplish in a year? And where are you now?'

'I'm in a hotel in Wimbledon Village. I've managed to find a cottage near the common. But I'm alone and don't know anyone in the area. Could I possibly drop Scott off for the day while I move in?' I wait with bated breath.

'So you're really here, after all. I was wondering if that letter would get you anywhere. You're not one to be stopped, are you?' I hear him chuckle again, a rumble in his throat. 'Why don't you bring your son over a little after lunch, say about two? You can leave him for a month. We'll start rehabilitation right away, provided you take him home each Friday for the weekend. Is that agreeable? We can see to all the paperwork later.'

Agreeable? I'm stunned. I try to answer, to say of course it's agreeable, but how can I speak when I can't even breathe?

'Mrs Carl?'

'Of course, Dr Rhys,' I finally manage. 'About two then. And thank you, thank you.' I turn to Scott. 'Dr Rhys is admitting you this afternoon.'

Scott says nothing, but his shifting eyes reveal apprehension. I hug him for reassurance. 'The hospital has a wonderful reputation, Scott. Better than Coorabel. You'll like Dr Rhys, I promise. And I'll be there for you. I can visit as much as I want, even during your therapy sessions.'

After lunch I repack Scott's suitcase for the hospital. But how can I possibly get him into the lift, and into a taxi? I will need volunteers.

Stepping into the hall, I spot one of the staff doing maintenance. He is stout, with a short haircut and rather large arms. 'You seem like a strong young man,' I say with a friendly smile.

His face lights up. 'Well I do lift weights, luv. Press about a hundred kilos.'

'That's very impressive,' I say, wondering exactly what he means, but then he wouldn't be bragging if it was a mediocre feat. 'Do you think you could lift my son? He's in a wheelchair and I need help getting him downstairs to a taxi.' The man blinks several times and gives a shrug. I smile to myself in silent triumph. I've just recruited my first volunteer.

In the lobby I ask the deskman to order a taxi and to tell the dispatcher one of the passengers is an invalid with a wheelchair and will need assistance. It's not fair to spring this kind of surprise on an unsuspecting driver. I never felt it necessary to warn a driver in Sydney, but I know the rules are different in London. I stand by the glass front doors, waiting. Cars stream by, their wipers in soundless motion. It's still raining; I gnaw on the inside of my lip. Won't this rain ever stop? When the taxi arrives, the driver and my new volunteer deposit Scott into the back seat. I fold his wheelchair and leave it with the deskman with a promise to return.

Scott has a lovely room, with off-white walls and a large window overlooking a verdant lawn with a clump of budding roses. His roommate is another head-injured young man named Thomas who had suffered a severe car accident in Zimbabwe, leaving him with useless legs. Thomas watches with vacant eyes as two orderlies in crisp white medical trousers and shirts lift Scott into his steel-frame bed while I unpack a few belongings. Placing his compact stereo on a side table I try to plug it in, but the plugs are different and I will have to buy an adapter. Another reminder that life has changed.

I sit on Scott's narrow bed and hold his hand. To settle his apprehension I read for over an hour from a slim volume of mystery stories. Finally I tell Scott I must run out to pay for our cottage and do some shopping, but I will return early the next morning.

His eyes look down and away, and when I try to remove my hand he grips it more tightly. Scott won't complain, he never does, but I know he's frightened of the unknown, as are we all. Rehab will begin soon and he knows pain will follow. Like me, he misses the hustle and bustle of people in and out of our apartment in Sydney, and like me he's terribly lonely for his friends. We're both starting over again.

A taxi drops me at the hotel. I retrieve Australian dollars from my suitcase and walk to the nearest bank. With British pounds in hand I hurry to the estate agent where I nervously count out a month's rent. The receptionist jots down the address, thrusts the key across the counter, and before anyone can change their mind I bolt through the door and disappear down a side street quickly enough to elude any pursuer. I have found a home.

Our new cottage is about two miles away on the other side of Wimbledon Common. The rain has stopped and the dark rolling clouds have lightened into a translucent glow from an afternoon sun. I set off on a rapid walk through the picturesque village of brick and cobbled streets. It is dotted with charming old red brick houses, some of them imposing with three storeys and several chimneys and roofs of charcoal slate. Tucked between are smaller cottages, a few with single chimneys thrusting above roofs of thick thatch. I pass quaint teashops, a pharmacy, pubs, and formal lawyers' offices with the mellow patina of the Oliver Twist era. I gaze through windows into cramped bookstores, and shops that make hot pasties, steak and kidney pies and homemade soups and offer fifty varieties of cheese. I pass a butcher, a fishmonger, a little post office, a bank, and myriad gift shops, all with classic English charm.

As I walk and absorb this history, I feel a gentle settling of my spirit, and begin to consider that after the rambunctious disorder of Australia, with its unbridled energy and passion, perhaps what Scott and I require now is the deeply rooted stability of our mother country.

Crossing from the village, I enter the rolling green tranquillity of the common. Thanks to the rains I have been cursing, spring has taken hold with a vengeance. The grass is lush, and the woods glow with the yellow-green of budding leaves in a green meadow. A young woman impeccably dressed in an English riding habit passes, her speckled mare snorting and tossing its head. I pause to trace her disappearance into a deep patch of wood. How very English, I muse, how very civilized. Even after twenty years, how little has changed. And a great warmth flows through me, a river of content.

Leaving the common I walk to the cul-de-sac and stand before our rented cottage. From the agent's car window my view was fleeting. But now from outside the front gate I take full measure of our new home.

It is detached with two storeys of old brick with a grey slate roof and a single brick chimney rising from the right side. From the black metal gate a walk of cobbles runs about twelve feet to a front door of cream and white. Each cobble is separated by curly thyme, and the length is bordered by low green shrubs and red and purple early spring flowers. To my right a large bay window, also trimmed in white, lends the cottage a spacious air. Attached to the left side of the house is a single-car garage, also of brick with a shed roof, which must be for storage as the drive has been absorbed into the garden. Upstairs, a bank of white-trimmed windows, most likely bedrooms, are shrouded with white lace curtains.

The cottage is fronted by a three-foot brick wall that runs along the pavement. On the other side is a patch of clipped dark green grass, pockets of rose bushes and gay colours of tulips. Fences of wood about four feet high run past the sides of the house into the back garden. Bookending my cottage are a pair of larger and more substantial dark brick homes, each of three storeys with grey slate roofs, set in manicured gardens.

At that moment something miraculous happens. As I'm reaching to open the gate, the front of the cottage takes on a shimmering luminescence. The dull brick glimmers with life and the white trim radiates. A yellow shaft of sunlight has broken through the walls of clouds and ignited the front of my home. No doubt other homes also enjoy this sunshine, but to me the message is personal, simple and unmistakable. This house is now my home, and it will be a home of healing. Accept it and live to the fullest, I think to myself.

I have this overpowering feeling of spiritual connection. Scott and I will live here for a long time. That ray of sunshine heralds a four-month splurge of sunny weather that breaks records in southern England.

Turning the key, I walk inside. Before me wood stairs run from the front door straight up to the first floor. Moving to the right I enter a living room of brown carpet and off-white walls. Against the wall is a gas-log fireplace enclosed in glass with no mantle. I slide open lace curtains at the bay window to view the open spaces and dark woods of the common and, off to one side, the trimmed greens of a private golf course. Small figures in red sweaters – apparently the uniform of the members – are pulling carts of clubs. Volunteers, I say to myself, and make a mental note. Turning my back to the bay window I face the conservatory, a rounded room with windows looking over the back garden. A very small kitchen runs off the conservatory, too small even for a little table. It has a white porcelain sink under a window, a small gas stove, a white refrigerator and an under-the-counter washing machine, a luxury I covet. In Sydney, a lot of volunteers did our never-ending laundry. Here I will be proudly self-sufficient. A rear door exits into a back garden of lawn, a tidy flower garden of snapdragons, yellow tea roses, pink and white Chinese daisies, and a single tree covered with red buds, a flame tree, all surrounded by a wood fence.

Upstairs are two bedrooms, one large and one small, both looking over the common. At the rear is the only bathroom, small and clean with a mirror over a porcelain sink and a bathtub at one end, all fed from old plumbing. I pause in the doorway to consider the problem of where to place Scott. The bath is upstairs, but for convenience of cooking, treatment and access to the volunteers I will have to recruit, and to avoid carrying Scott up and down several times a day, his bed should be downstairs. That will be a problem, but then, isn't the beauty of a rose guarded by a thorn?

Another problem is the absence of furniture. The cottage is ghostly empty. I plan to sleep here this evening, and Scott will be home for the weekend in two days' time. Already it's late afternoon. At the least I will need bedding, if not a proper bed. Where shall I begin? Time to meet my new neighbours.

Girded by that quaint American attitude of egalitarianism that I acquired after nearly twenty years in the United States, where no one is above or beneath you and no one is a stranger, I walk next door and boldly knock on the front door. After several minutes it cracks open to reveal a bowed and balding man in his seventies, wearing a brown wool pullover and dark trousers, leaning heavily on a stick with an ivory crook. His hands are arthritic. He looks at me in puzzlement through wire-rimmed glasses. I introduce myself, explain I am his new neighbour, tell of Scott, and that I need help in acquiring a few things, bedding and such, and could he point the way to a supermarket and perhaps a place to buy used furniture.

A bit unsure, he calls in a patrician voice, 'Miss Potts, Miss Potts, would you come here?'

A lady soon appears behind him wearing a dark dress with small flowers embroidered on a white collar. She is about his age with white hair and red lipstick. 'Yes, what is it, Mr Potts?' she asks with a touch of impatience. Looking over his shoulder at me, her face softens.

'Miss Potts, this is Mrs Carl. She's our new neighbour and is in a bit of a bind. See if you can help her.'

I explain my situation again, saying that I wish to spend the night in the cottage but lack a few necessities, and I need to buy a few things before the shops close.

'I'm not sure that's possible, my dear,' Miss Potts says sympathetically. 'I'm afraid you're a bit too late.' She turns to the gentleman. 'Mr Potts, don't we have a few things in storage in the attic?'

He furrows his forehead in thought. 'Yes, I do believe you're right, Miss Potts. That would be jolly good, wouldn't it? Why don't you have a look?'

As Miss Potts hurries off, he stands aside, invites me in, and with a twinkle in his eyes says matter-of-factly, 'Miss Potts is a widow and I'm a widower. My wife died quite suddenly several years ago, and shortly afterwards her husband died as well. We're brother and sister, you see. So we decided to move in together to keep each other company. She has a married name of course, but I prefer her maiden name. To keep a certain distance it's best to adhere to certain formalities, don't you think? You know how brothers and sisters love to fight,' he adds with a mischievous smile. I instantly fall in love with this man.

Miss Potts returns, her face a beacon of success. 'Mrs Carl, I have discovered a small bed, a little chest of drawers and two floor lamps, which we will happily lend you until you're settled. And I have some extra bedding, towels and crockery, that sort of thing, that you are more than welcome to use. But I think we will need some help. The stairs are dreadful, don't you think, Mr Potts?' With that she hurries off. I hear her in the next room on the phone and then she's back. 'I phoned Harold. He's a neighbour. He's coming to help,' she says.

With some effort, the furniture and accessories are transferred to the living room of my cottage. Afterwards Miss Potts calls a taxi and

I return to the hotel to gather the wheelchair and my luggage. Then I stop at a supermarket to pick up a basket of food and an inexpensive alarm clock. I'm due at the hospital the next morning at nine, but as I am drugged by jet lag, my internal clock in shambles, I fear I might sleep through the day.

That evening I position my freshly made bed with its brown headboard in the bay window and sit cross-legged upon it with a cup of steaming milk – my security blanket – between my hands, watching the sun's setting rays throw the spring woods of the common into deep Robin Hood shadows. When the ceremony ends with the onset of darkness, I snuggle between white sheets, and fall into a deep sleep.

Ten

The rude clatter of my six a.m. alarm jolts me from dreams of happier times. I sit bolt upright in bed, fearing something terrible has befallen Scott. Disorientated by my new and strange environment, my mind struggles to recalibrate. Where am I? How did I get here?

Sweeping the empty living room, I discover I've woken alone on my bed in the bay window, having never closed the curtains the previous night. I'm now exposed to the world, like a sleepwear mannequin in a department store window. Remembering that Scott's tucked safely away in rehab, my panic passes and I breathe more easily. The streetlights still emit their warm moist glow, and dawn's first blush reveals no one about. Even if someone were parked outside peering into my sanctuary, I would not alter my aversion to closed curtains. Walls are walls after all, even if made of fabric and not stone, wood or steel. Nature nourishes my soul, and I refuse to shut it out, even if cloistered England encourages otherwise.

Barefoot and pushing back stringy hair, I pad into the kitchen to heat water in a small aluminium pot for coffee. Adding hot milk, I pad back to my perch in the window. Staring into my coffee cup, I begin my morning meditation. Curling my feet under, I sit cross-legged on the rumpled bed as I did the evening before, and in stillness take in the woods of the common, and how their spring-leafed crowns are just capturing the sun's earliest rays.

Nothing is more precious than these moments of silence I award myself. Nothing is more important to Scott's progress than for me to stay centred within my universe. All my life the big, stupid things – cars, television sets, and expensive clothes – have never been important. Only the small stupid things: a rose bud in a glass vase, a twisted stick covered with green moss, a fluorescent sunset, the curl of a perfect wave on a deserted beach, the crystal silence of dawn, a wry smile, a furtive kiss, a hug. My small rituals multiplied by the years become anchors in a tempestuous sea.

With the world's awakening comes my own. Scott will be home tomorrow evening and I am not yet prepared. My bed will become his, so I will need another. Everything I have borrowed, with the possible exception of the furniture, I must replace: linens, towels, pots, cutlery. I can't even call a taxi, so getting a phone is a priority. I will also need at least a week's food, and I promised Scott I would join him for breakfast and wheel him into rehab at 8.30 – in two hours' time. So much to do, so little time. Stay calm, I caution myself, let the sun rise, relish the stillness, let the world yawn itself awake. There's always time to act. Still, the concern that most burdens my mind is the volunteers Scott and I will require.

Unlike in Australia, I am strangely handicapped by coming home. There I was a stranger, unconstrained by the social mores and conventions, ignorant of their rules. I was free to break them, and no doubt unwittingly did so on numerous occasions. My Australian friends, knowing I was an alien, were quick to smile and forgive behaviour they may well have frowned upon coming from a fellow citizen. But I am back in Britain now, and can no longer plead innocence abroad. I've been here only a week, and already the firm hand of English tradition – the reticence, circumspection, privacy and slowness to open – weighs upon my thoughts and actions. Yet I have no choice but to act. Without volunteers, I cannot manage.

With half my life spent in the United States, am I not also an American? My speech is full of Americanisms, and so are my actions. Perhaps that's my salvation: I'm an innocent American abroad. That's what the English think anyway, I muse with an inner smile. In the States they know I'm British as soon as I open my mouth, yet now when I return to Britain, people immediately enquire where I come from. They don't expect it's anywhere nearby.

After bathing and dressing in a summer skirt and a mauve cotton pullover I knitted for myself in Sydney, I walk the two and a half miles through the common, into the village and beyond towards the rehab hospital, enjoying the rustling of the leaves that set a rhythm for my steps, even as I hurry.

In Scott's room orderlies are dressing him for breakfast in the cafeteria, with rehab scheduled afterward. Heartened by their sense of competent compassion, I stand aside to observe, and remain quiet. In the next bed Thomas is also being prepared, and I wonder vaguely, being from Zimbabwe, does he have family nearby? I make a mental note to ask, and if he's alone to include him in my daily activities with Scott.

As the orderlies finish, Dr Rhys enters the room. 'I'm off to another hospital in a few minutes, but wanted to officially welcome you and your son,' he tells me before turning to Scott, whom he is meeting for the first time. 'Well, Mr Carl, your mother's informed me you're a hell of a rugby player,' the doctor says with a disarming smile. 'My favourite sport. Played rugby myself a few years back. Always glad to share the company of a co-conspirator.'

Scott's eyes light up, and his mouth wrinkles into that familiar half-grin. 'I haven't played myself for a little while,' he answers in his slow and slurred speech. 'In Australia, I played flyback. In a few months, when I'm better, I'll challenge you to a scrum.'

Dr Rhys smiles amicably. 'I suspect it'd be dangerous to take on a young man like you.' Turning my way, he says, 'Mrs Carl, I'm sure you'll find our staff very supportive. If there's anything you need, please let me know.' His amused eyes convey a knowing look. 'And I'm sure you will.'

The rooms of the small hospital slip quickly past as I wheel Scott down a central corridor towards the cafeteria for breakfast. Several times we are stopped by staff who enquire if we are new. They ask Scott where he's from, and he replies with a laugh to every query, 'From another world. I'm here to check on humans,' which inspires equal joviality.

'Be kind to us,' a nurse responds lightly, 'we are only human you know.'

'So we've been discovered,' quips another, giggling.

Let the circus begin. All welcome us with open and friendly smiles, and I sense Scott's comfort grow. At the same time we both understand that after breakfast comes rehab with its unknown amounts of pain. As we move from the cafeteria towards the rehab room, I notice how Scott's good right hand grips the wheelchair arm more firmly than usual, his pale knuckles a sign of his apprehension.

I roll him through two large swinging doors into the large rehab room, fifty or sixty square feet, painted a medical off-white. Along one wall is a bank of windows that overlook an inner garden of waxy green shrubs and beds of roses, while the three other walls are bare except for a few charts and mirrors. An oak handrail runs under the windows around the perimeter, crossing in front of the mirrors, the kind of rail you see in a ballet studio. A dozen heavy wood therapy tables covered with black Naugahyde are to one side, while in a far corner are six mechanized tilt tables, now flat and empty, arranged in a circle. Under one of the windows is a large plastic bin of coloured exercise balls, some the size of volleyballs and others at least three feet in diameter, used to lie on and stretch. There are smaller ones as well, the size of baseballs, of hard rubber for squeezing to build hand and wrist strength.

A young man attired in the crisp whites of a physiotherapist takes over, and wheels Scott toward one of the black massage and stretch tables. Another therapist, an older woman, comes my way. 'Mrs Carl, I'm Wendy,' she says in a resonant voice. 'I'm in charge of physiotherapy and will be monitoring Scott's progress.' Wendy is in her fifties with short dark hair, soft eyes and a trim figure tucked into a pale-blue uniform. I will soon learn that she is recently divorced and has two grown children, both in the medical field, and that her patients come a close second to her first love, gardening.

I take several minutes to explain Scott's history: the coma, his months in Australia, the volunteers, his allergic reaction to most medicines, the techniques I have used, progress made, and Scott's limitations. I also relate my hopes for his future. 'If we can just get him standing,' I tell Wendy, 'maybe even taking a few steps, I will be overjoyed.'

Wendy listens intently and asks numerous pointed questions that affirm my confidence in her dedication and the competence of the staff here. 'You've done wonders on your own,' she tells me, 'and I predict Scott will make substantial progress here.'

Drinking in the words I so desperately wish to hear, I take a chair against the wall and watch as two therapists set to work on Scott, bending, stretching, massaging, toning. Since his last therapy session in Sydney he has lost some flexibility and some of his progress. It happens very quickly if one is sedentary most of the day and can't walk; it is an ongoing battle. But his wit and spirit have not diminished. If anything, in spite of travel and eating on the run, he's added weight and colour. I bask in the fact that we've come light years from Coorabel, and I'm full of excitement at the possibility of Scott's continued recovery. But I'm also sobered by the ever-present thought that Dr Rhys's, commitment is for only four weeks. After that I will be on my own.

Towards midday, after informing Scott I must finish preparations for his return home and promising to fetch him late the next afternoon, I slip away and catch a taxi into the village. Roaming through used furniture stores and junk shops, I accumulate a single bed frame, a mattress set, a wooden end table and cobalt-blue table lamp, a small white chest for my clothes, additional linens, and kitchen utensils. I chance upon a box of used music tapes, two for a pound, and pick out a dozen: reggae, jazz, Sinatra, Louis Armstrong, and others I know Scott will like. Next to the tapes is a used TV set at a reasonable price, and I pause before it. I'd been given a small set in Sydney that I rarely had time to watch, so absorbed was I with managing the flow of volunteers and with Scott's constant needs. Our private time was so rare, our quiet moments together so special, that television seemed an obscenity, and in Sydney the outdoors was always an alluring option. But here in London, with its cold and wet weather, Scott will be housebound, perhaps for weeks at a time.

With some reluctance I pay for the TV and, having promised all the shops to return the next morning and collect my purchases, I walk home through the common to lose myself, if only briefly, in the regenerative stillness of nature. Along the way I collect souvenirs of nature's art: feathers, contorted twigs, weeds, pods and budding flowers to decorate our cottage for Scott's homecoming.

The next morning, at the request of Miss Potts, Harold arrives at the wheel of an ancient Land Rover, and we set off to the village and retrieve my things. He helps me to carry the chest, mattresses and bed frames upstairs, and to set everything up. I make American tuna salad sandwiches, which we eat sitting on Scott's bed in the window. Harold, a short and spry man with little eyes and a receding hairline, talks the entire time of his days in the army. He never married, he tells me wistfully with a far-off look, as if he senses he's missed something but isn't quite sure what. Maybe the camaraderie of soldiers in intense war builds lifelong bonds. It is a shame that sometimes it takes such tragedy and desperation for people to find deep connections, but soldiers seem able to do this. Aside from his nearly thirty years in the Royal Fusiliers, Harold seems not to have had any durable relationship. But his heart is gold, and as time goes on Harold will stop by on one pretext or another to work in the garden or sweep my path so I might listen to his lonely stories of past glory, and reward him with American-style tuna salad sandwiches.

I rearrange the living-room furniture, shoving Scott's bed to the rear next to the stairs, with one of Miss Potts's paisley-patterned brown floor lamps at the side and the chest of drawers at the foot, to clear space for our future, still imaginary volunteers.

Then I return to the hospital to pick up Scott for his first weekend home. The receptionist rings for a cab and we wait on the kerb. Soon a four-door sedan arrives, a dark green Rover, and the driver slides out, a heavyset man with an overhanging girth, about sixty, with burly arms, a square jaw and a tweed cap. Seeing Scott in the wheelchair, he comes over.

''Ere, love, lemme give ya an 'and.' Without hesitation he lifts Scott, and easily deposits him beside the driver's seat, while I struggle to comprehend what he is saying. It's been years since I've heard a Cockney accent and my ear is rusty. After putting the wheelchair inside, I climb into the rear seat. 'Where to, love?' the cabby calls out. I give him our address and he pushes off into the traffic.

'Where ya from, love? I can 'ear yer not from round 'ere,' the cabby says, eyeing me in his rearview mirror. Still wrestling with his accent, I answer: 'Wales, America, Australia, and now we've returned home to England for medical treatment.' The cabby nods his head. He seems to understand me better than I do him. Perhaps he's honed an ear for tourists.

''at's what I'd do, love. Best treatment's 'ome if ya ask me. Wife and me adopted a son a few years back. Anything 'appen to 'im, I'd want to be at 'ome.'

Parking in front of our cottage, the cabby hoists Scott and takes him inside to the wheelchair. When I pay, he tips his cap and hands me a card. 'Me name's Luther. 'ere's me number. You call day or night. Even if I'm off I'll come fer ya.'

I look into Luther's thoughtful, tired eyes. His invitation is genuine, and in the weeks ahead he will often arrive unannounced to sit with Scott while I run errands, or to take us on outings. Scott and Luther become great friends. Somehow they understand each other, and I think Luther becomes a surrogate grandfather for Scott. I often hear Luther reminisce about London in the old days when he was growing up. He never talks down to Scott and his simple humanity shines through in the way he handles him.

Now, thanking Luther, I close the front door and turn round to see Scott working the right wheel of the chair with his good hand, trying with little success to propel himself forward into the bay window. He's acquired considerable strength in that arm, but with his left arm still disabled by the broken clavicle, his efforts are mostly futile, a source of deep frustration for him. I push Scott to the window so he can observe the street and the woods beyond and retreat to the kitchen doorway to watch him and contemplate my predicament.

Even knowing in advance the difficulties I would face caring for Scott alone, I have nevertheless seriously misjudged the full impact of even a weekend without help. I cannot possibly leave the house for any length of time, not for a walk, not for groceries, certainly not to the village, without someone to care for him. I cannot possibly get him up the stairs and into the bathroom, let alone into the tub. Only with the greatest effort will I even be able to transfer him from his chair to his bed at night or back again in the morning. We are prisoners of each other, even if chained only by love. So this is my wake-up call. Next weekend I will be better prepared.

We do manage to make it through this day. I help him into bed for an afternoon nap, and afterwards I push him up and down the neighbourhood streets for some fresh air. I realize my skill at pushing him in his chair must be improving as he rates me as high as a 'plus nine' going down kerbs, though still a 'minus five' on certain corners and bends. I smile to myself at his good humour and perseverance. By this time, the muscles of my legs, arms and torso have become strong from many hours of manoevring Scott in the wheelchair.

On our return, I wheel Scott by the Potts residence for an introduction. I leave Scott at the gate in his wheelchair while I knock on the door. Miss Potts hurriedly appears, dashes straight down the path, thrusts a little sponge cake with lemon icing into Scott's hand, says hello, then quickly retires into her abode. As sweet as she is, I recognize the sort of awkwardness I have often noticed when one first meets an invalid.

That night, as he lies in bed, I massage his legs with lavender oil and read to him until his eyes flutter closed. Upstairs I fall asleep at once, until I am jarred awake at midnight by the clanging alarm clock so I might check on Scott and change his position in the bed. Back upstairs I reset the alarm for three and, under the pall of another routinely rude awakening, drop into a fitful sleep.

On Sunday morning, to vary our routine, I announce we will journey into the village for hot chocolate and croissants, which is greeted with a loud hurrah from Scott. First we must clean up, I tell him, and dress our best. This will be our first English Sunday, and in England Sundays are for promenading. I cover the kitchen floor with black rubbish bags. We remove most of the pillows from the wheelchair and position the chair with Scott in it over the plastic. I help him slowly shed his clothes and proceed to shower him with a watering can full of warm water.

'First time I've gone swimming in a wheelchair.' He laughs.

'Forgot my flippers, Mom,' he splutters as I lather him with soap and shampoo his hair. 'By the time we're finished, I'll be certified in scuba,' he jokes, as I repeat the shower until his skin has the smell and shine of a baby.

I manoeuvre the wheelchair back into the living room, where I proceed to lay towels on the floor, and we execute our well-practised routine to get Scott down from the chair. I pull his torso up until he can balance with some of his weight on one leg for a few moments. (The natural move for most people would be to lift him from under the arms, but with his poorly healed clavicle that would be disastrous.) Then I get down on one knee and put my other knee under his other leg, and we gradually roll and slide his body from the chair to the floor, ending with a little bump as I cradle his head on my upper arm and roll down with him. Then I swaddle him with the towels until he's dry, and help him slowly to dress. The whole bathing and dressing operation takes over an hour, as does almost any chore involving my son. But time flies, as he's always ready with laughter and frequent comments on my performance. What begins as a chore turns into wisecracks and often hilarity. Finally, his hair combed and in his best trousers and a white shirt, Scott is ready to promenade.

Almost from the start in Wimbledon, friends and volunteers become an occasional part of our routines. Some show up on their own, and some are drafted by a desperate and now somewhat crafty mother, availing herself of the squads of golfers moving along the manicured lawns across the road. One day when I am running over to the golf course to find a helper, I am stopped by a policeman. Firmly and suspiciously he demands to know what I am doing, why I am talking to these men, and whether I plan to ask them into my home. Evidently he has noticed me for some time already, and thinks I am soliciting men for sex. The officer doesn't believe my story about an invalid son, so I invite him over to see for himself. Once he meets Scott, Constable Riggs becomes our friend and an avid volunteer.

It seems such an idyllic life in some ways. I have a pretty cottage, the common, beautiful, interesting friends and volunteers, lots of music that has been given to me. If only I could make Scott better. But I can't change things. We can only keep trying so that eventually he might walk, and Scott is game for anything.

Eleven

On our second weekend together in the cottage we really celebrate. Our grey clouds are fading, our sun is breaking through, and our skies are turning blue. Scott is making so much progress that his smile rarely leaves his face, and I'm overjoyed with all he's accomplished in two short weeks of intensive therapy. We've found a home and gathered friends. It was only a few months ago in Sydney after he walked on his knees that I first entertained the unimaginable: Scott might actually learn to walk. Now he can stand, with help. Imagine what a few more weeks might bring.

Early Saturday morning I wheel Scott back to Annabel's for breakfast, but while I'm in the ladies' he orders hot chocolate and a heap of ice-cream instead. It's an overdose of sugar for his body, considering the blandness of his hospital diet, but Scott ploughs through it unfazed and would eat more if I didn't intercede.

Along the path home, Jonathan springs from behind a hedgerow and showers us with hugs and kisses. Scott lets out such a yelp of elation it would wake the neighbours were it not mid-morning. Struck dumb with surprise, I can do little but cling to him.

Jonathan has travelled for twenty-four hours on a dilapidated bus that regularly plies the road and ferry routes between Scandinavia and London. It was slow but cheap. He can only stay until Monday morning, two days later, when he has to board the return bus to Copenhagen for school. I am amazed at his dedication and endurance: an hour of bus time for each hour with us. But I'm also saddened by the shortness of his visit. A few hours with your children are never sufficient, especially when they're old enough to be good company. But Scott is ecstatic, and soon the brothers are huddled together making secret plans.

'Mom, you've got the day off!' Jonathan announces. Then, with a teasing grin, 'Remember your curfew, now. Be home by ten or I'll send the police after you.' Curfews were a big issue when the boys were younger, and later when I was dating Stefan they turned the tables on me.

∾

I returned home a little after midnight to find the boys waiting in the living room with all the lights blazing.

'We wanted to go to bed, Mom,' Sammy said with great gravity. 'But we didn't feel comfortable until we knew you were safely home.'

'That's right,' Jonathan put in. 'We were about to call the police to report you missing in action. But they'd want a picture of you and this was the only one we could find!' He held up a grainy photo and I felt my face burn. It was a horrible picture, one I thought I'd torn up, of me in an ill-fitting bathing suit, with wild hair and a big smirk, taken on the beach. 'We weren't sure you'd want the police to have this,' he added with mock concern, waving it in the air. 'What if this got into the newspapers?' I snatched the photo from his hand.

Scotty all the while had been sitting to the side making a theatrical display of staring into the face of an old alarm clock. He shook it then held it up to his ear and shook it again in overacted disbelief. 'This says 12.30, Mom, but I can't tell, is it after noon or after midnight?'

I shut their drama down by turning off all the lights.

∾

I haven't had an entire day off without any responsibility for months, it seems, and the question of how to use this gift throws me into confusion. Finally, after repeated assurances from Jonathan that he and Scott will survive just fine, I head out the door to Covent Garden for a day of bliss.

Slowly and methodically, unwilling to miss the smallest detail, I weave through the bustling market, poking into each artist's stall, vintage clothing shop, and every one of the nearly endless antique and junk shops. I have little money, but that doesn't matter. What I crave is artistic stimulation, and muses to spark my imagination. As the day wears on my creativity is rekindled. With mostly bare walls at home, my mind churns with endless possibilities. I purchase a sketchpad, a box of charcoal pencils, some acrylics, and a variety of pastels. I also select several skeins of blue and brown Scottish wool yarn for knitting sweaters, socks for Scott, perhaps even a shawl for me. I'm having so much fun that I fail to notice the setting sun, and would have continued my wandering had the shops not begun to lock their doors.

Rushing home, I slip into a darkened cottage to find the two brothers, arms wrapped about each other, in deep sleep on Scott's bed. I remember Jonathan telling me once that Scott was like his shadow. 'He would always follow me around,' Jonathan said, 'but I didn't mind. I never wanted to get rid of him like so many older brothers try to do.' My mind slips back to their childhood, when I would often peek into the boys' bedroom to find baby Scott bundled with one of his brothers, and I would feel wonderfully at peace. Few things warm a parent's heart more than knowing their children love and support each other. If only Sammy were here, I would truly be content. Sammy, as a little boy, had this infectious laugh that always set off the others.

Slipping into the kitchen, I quietly make phone calls to the Potts, our other neighbours, Harold, Constable Riggs, Luther and several of the hospital staff, with an invitation for Sunday tea the next day. Some are not home and I leave messages. While my effort is last-minute and may ultimately meet with little success, I have this joyous compulsion to celebrate Scott's good progress with others and introduce Jonathan to our new friends.

The next morning I send Jonathan off to the patisserie for cake and scones while I arrange freshly clipped flowers from my garden in the kitchen pots and tall glasses that serve as my vases, and randomly place them about the room. Scott's chest of drawers, covered by a bed sheet, becomes our side table, and disposable picnic plates and cups are substituted for the fine white china I do not own.

Standing back, I take in the scene. It is hardly glamorous, which is why I rely on flowers. I am always amazed how small fragments of nature contain such power of change, how in a blink our simple brown existence is transformed by these dainty explosions of reds, yellows and whites into a visual feast. Of course, at the moment, the mystery ingredient of all social success is missing: our guests. People are each other's diversions, each other's foils, sources of amusement and inspiration – if they come.

That afternoon, with us all dressed in our Sunday finery, our guests begin to arrive. I hope for the best, and soon find our small living room brimming with friends. Mr and Miss Potts, beautifully dressed, take over the front door, welcoming guests as if my home were theirs. Luther arrives with his wife and their adopted son. Harold, with a military decoration on his lapel, struts as though commanding a column of troops, making formal statements as he's introduced to Jonathan and the others. Constable Riggs, in uniform and on duty but accompanied by his wife, drops in for a short stay before returning to his rounds. Some of Scott's nurses join us too, along with Sister Bendall, the head of his ward.

Surprisingly, Dr Rhys makes an entrance. I had left a message at his office, more a courtesy than an expectation, and never dreamt he would find the time, but he has detoured while crossing town between hospitals, and I'm very moved by his thoughtfulness. I pour him tea and he accepts it absentmindedly, like grabbing a cup of coffee on the run from the hospital cafeteria. He moves to the fireplace and studies an intricate mantle wreath I have woven of twigs, reeds, dry grass, a bird's nest, pine branches and other fragments of nature's art I've gathered on my walks.

'Where did you get this?' he asks.

'From over there,' I say with a nod toward the bay window. Dr Rhys looks past me out the window. All he sees is open space, and his face clouds over in confusion. I sense he's looking for a shop.

'From the common,' I say, 'from what I collect. I walk there most every evening.'

Dr Rhys studies my art piece quietly. 'I think I'm beginning to understand you,' he says thoughtfully.

Susan, a nurse from the rehab hospital who lives just down the street, arrives with her husband and her two teenage daughters, Claire and Holly. Both are immediately drawn to Scott, but it is Claire, tall and slim, with long dark hair and flashing eyes, about to finish school, who dominates Scott's attention.

'Claire is quite interested in social service,' Susan whispers pointedly in my ear, perhaps feeling compelled to justify her daughter's obvious behaviour.

'She's an attractive young lady,' I whisper back. 'I'm sure she will be quite successful.' Inside, I'm tickled. So were the young ladies in Sydney, I want to inform Susan, but keep that thought to myself.

In the coming weeks, Claire often turns up when Scott is home, as if guided by some sixth sense, with offers to run errands for him or wheel him about the village. Sometimes she brings girlfriends and the three or four of them, taking turns pushing Scott, move down the pavement in a ball of commotion like a gaggle of squawking geese. For some time, I wonder how Claire knows when to appear. It occurs to me that Scott loves to sit in the garage, in his chair or propped up on the table, with the door rolled up so he can watch the traffic and socialize with passing neighbours. Rolling up the door is probably the signal that he is home and open for business.

On Monday morning Jonathan and I return Scott to the hospital for his next round of rehabilitation. As the brothers hug, Jonathan promises Scott, 'When this is over I'll come back, and Ulla and I will take you fishing. I know this great place in Wales that's loaded with trout. We'll catch a bucketful, guaranteed.' After a tearful goodbye Jonathan heads back into the city to board the ratty old bus that will deliver him to Copenhagen.

A few minutes later, Susan swishes into the room, grabs the handles on the wheelchair and moves Scott towards the door. 'We're taking you to the plaster room, Scott,' she says directly to him. 'One more time may do the trick. We'll include your left arm this time to see if we can get that working a bit more.'

They are gone before I can react, but then what could I say that would make a difference? My instinct is to protect Scott from pain, but that's impossible, and I can't interfere anyway. In the two hours Scott is gone, I straighten up his room, which is little more than shifting things round, squaring the stack of books on the side table, fluffing the pillow, adjusting the window blinds, incidental actions designed to give me some sliver of control. I hang a geometric mobile of coloured bits of glass I've purchased at Covent Garden. A gentle breeze makes them dance on their threads, casting refracted light along the ceiling and walls. I place a few more of nature's objects on the windowsill, and roll a cluster of freshly cut flowers from home out of their newspaper sheath, snip the stems and arrange them in a blue plastic vase. With nothing more to do, I slump into a chair and stare vacantly out the window, feeling empty and useless.

Scott is rolled back into his room on a trolley, both his legs and his left arm encased in plaster. As the orderlies transfer him to his bed, I ask myself: Is this progress? If he's getting better, why does he look worse? Perhaps it's just me. Our Sunday tea party was such a high – I felt so connected and alive. Then comes Monday morning: Jonathan leaves, and now this. I go to Scott's bed and reach out to comfort him, but he is groggy from the sedative and unaware of my presence.

'It will be a couple of hours until he recovers,' Susan says, entering the room. 'He may well sleep the rest of the day. With this much casting we'll most likely keep him over the weekend because he'll need more attention.'

I catch a bus home, aimlessly putter around sweeping and dusting, sit on Scott's bed with a cup of hot milk as the sun dies, and toss all night. I return each day and sit with Scott, who is mostly confined to his bed. He is in considerable pain, especially his arm. Through two years of neglect it has healed awkwardly and fallen into disuse, and now the ligaments and muscles are crying out in protest. There's nothing I can do but talk to him, read aloud, and ask questions to distract his mind. I encourage him to focus on the fishing trip.

'Let's write down a list of what you'll need for fishing,' I suggest.

'I'll have to pack a bag.'

'What clothes should you take? Tell me what music I should pack. How about snacks?' As Scott talks I jot down several lists. Soon we have settled all of the trivia, and there's no more to be said.

In the afternoon he's given a sedative and I leave for home. That weekend the house is empty and quiet. The garage door remains down and Claire does not appear. So that's it, the garage door is the key, I conclude. But then it dawns on me that her mother is Scott's nurse! Claire has only to ask her mother about Scott's schedule, or more likely, her mother has only to tell Claire; the garage door is meaningless. And why am I even thinking of this?

Life returns to normal the following weekend; normal for us, that is. Scott's casts are off, and the improvements are satisfying. With help he can now stand with both legs straight and feet flat on the ground. With great effort, stabilized by two therapists, he can walk by shifting his legs, rocking from right to left. I watch as he thrusts one foot forward, then the other, and I am filled with hope and swelling pride. I can see too that after the intense struggle of each session, Scott is happy and proud of his progress.

The left arm is straighter, and the therapists devote extra time exercising those muscles and developing hand-eye coordination. Dr Rhys extends Scott's hospital treatment by another two months and I continue the therapy at home on the weekends, massaging and stretching. I place a hard rubber ball in his hand and count one-two, one-two, as he squeezes and releases. It takes exhausting concentration on his part to link his will to a muscle response. The nerve pathways in the arm have shut down, so the electrical impulses from the brain hit roadblocks or simply dissipate, eliciting little or no response. It will take time to progress, it will be slow, but it's worth the struggle. Once the left arm and hand are strong enough, Scott can graduate to walking the length of the parallel bars, supporting himself as he goes. From there, all things seem possible.

∾

The days fly by until I am once again facing the last week of the additional weeks of therapy approved by Dr Rhys. I know he's done all he can, and I am very grateful. I know better than to even broach the subject of additional time. It would be unconscionable. Beds are in short supply and the waiting list is long.

As Luther helps Scott into the front seat of his Rover for our Monday morning trip to the hospital, I realize I must focus my attention in earnest on recruiting more volunteers. Jonathan and Ulla will be arriving on Friday for the long-promised fishing trip, and after that Scott will be home full time. We will be on our own, and in spite of his progress, I am still incapable of handling him alone. Faced with the facts, a sense of urgency finally takes hold of me.

In front of the hospital, Luther helps Scott into a wheelchair, and I take him straight away into rehab, where Wendy takes over. I watch for a few minutes, and then head for Dr Rhys's office. He warily eyes me as I take the wood chair in front of his desk, fearful perhaps that I will ask for more than he can give.

'I know this is our last week,' I begin, 'and I'm making arrangements to treat Scott at home. I've had a gym built in my garage, and I have lists of volunteers to call upon for assistance, so I believe we will do just fine.'

Dr Rhys's posture relaxes almost imperceptibly, and he smiles. 'Scott has made so much progress it breaks my heart to turn him out, but we are so underfunded and there are so many in need.' He shakes his head in resignation.

'When we arrived in the spring,' I say, 'I would not have believed Scott would be so much better. Your staff have worked miracles, and I'm deeply grateful. But I need your advice on something. At the end of the week his brother is coming from Denmark to take Scott fishing. They plan to be gone for several days. Do you think it's safe for Scott to go?'

The doctor rocks back, his face furrowed in thought. 'Glenys, you know I've been quite taken with your son. I broke a few rules to admit him and he has not let me down. I can't recall another patient with his determination. He's progressed far beyond my expectations. But to answer your question, I've been monitoring his file, and I've talked to our staff, and I know his overall health is good. He seems stable, so I don't see any reason why he can't go.'

I leave Dr Rhys's office greatly relieved. Still, it will be the first time Scott has been off on his own. Even if Jonathan and Ulla are with him, I can't shake the feeling that something might happen. But then, I always worry about that, don't I?

I use the rest of the week to gather items for the trip, and at night I outline a plan for recruiting volunteers once Scott returns. All along I've been collecting phone numbers from the men I pull off the golf course. They will be a good place to begin. I'll encourage the volunteers to recruit others, like I did in Sydney, and I will also put up flyers. Perhaps the hospital staff will help. They've become attached to Scott and are always offering suggestions. When I fall asleep each night, it's with a pad in my lap and a pencil in my hand.

Jonathan and Ulla fly down Friday morning from Copenhagen and arrive at my front door in a rental car. After lunch we drive to the hospital to collect Scott. When we walk into the rehab room, Jonathan stops in his tracks. Across the way, his brother is standing between parallel bars with the help of a physiotherapist, while another coaxes him to take halting, awkward steps. I find nothing unusual about the scene, as Scott has now been working on the bars for two weeks. But Jonathan, his image of Scott's abilities still fixed in Sydney, has never seen his progress. Rushing over to him, Jonathan throws his arms about his brother in a long hug. When they separate, their faces are flushed and eyes moist even as they break into oversize grins. Even Ulla has a handkerchief out, and I find myself fumbling for tissues.

That night we share an intimate family meal, using Scott's chest of drawers as our dining table. Afterwards Jonathan carries Scott upstairs for a bath, and by eight, exhausted by an intense week of therapy, he is sound asleep on his bed in the living room. An hour later I slide blissfully between my own cotton sheets, a contented mother at peace with the world, and drift into dreamland to the muffled conversation and laughter of Ulla and Jonathan as they plan tomorrow's trip. In the morning, bags, wheelchair and fishing gear are loaded in the boot, and with Jonathan at the wheel, excited Scott in the other front seat and Ulla in the back, we blow each other kisses and the great fishing adventure begins.

As I turn back to the front door, I realize what a milestone this trip is for Scott. While I long to join them, I know I can't and it's better I don't. This outing is more than simply going fishing. It is Scott's re-emergence into the larger world, into the mainstream of life. In the process, psychologically, he's letting go of me, just as a child must eventually break the bonds with his parents to thrive.

Years back, after Jonathan's high school graduation, he and Scott had pestered me to let them drive cross-country from Westport to Santa Cruz. Scott was fifteen at the time, but in my eyes barely out of the crib. I stalled, throwing one obstacle after another in their way. It was too far, nearly 3,000 miles. Jonathan's car, a used and faded red Fiat convertible he had received as a graduation gift, was mechanically risky. 'What if you break down?' I asked. 'How would you get help? How will you pay for it? Where will you sleep?' But the boys were deaf and blind to all potential pitfalls.

This trip had nothing to do with mechanical safety. It had everything to do with the psychological imperative in children to establish their identity, breaking from their childhood. Eventually I saw the light and relented, but only after promising to fly out and meet them in Santa Cruz. The boys completed their trip a week late after breaking down several times and running out of gas. Each time their needs were met by the generosity of strangers, and they arrived safely and in great spirits. Parents are there for guidance, but sometimes they shepherd too much.

At the door of the cottage, my mind returns to the present as I turn to catch a fleeting view of the rental car leaving Northview to be absorbed in the stream of traffic. Scott is letting go of me, I remind myself. But, I wonder vaguely, will I ever be able to let go of him?

I putter aimlessly around the empty house, thinking up things to do, then find myself restless but not wanting to do anything. In late afternoon I set out for a long walk, crossing into the common, into parts that I have yet to explore. I stumble across an old cemetery with weathered headstones from centuries past. It is deeply quiet with thick green grass and ancient trees that must have seen so much.

From nowhere, a light breeze rustles the topmost branches, a faint whisper of vibrating leaves that gives me an odd premonition that I am being called. By whom and why? Unsettled, I move on, and after a brisk walk emerge in the village.

I pause for coffee at a cafe, but find I cannot sit long. Agitated, I walk the teeming streets, peering in shop windows but focusing on nothing. The boys should be arriving soon. Their destination is a fishing stream in Wales about 200 miles away. They plan to camp by the stream. The banks are gentle, and will provide easy access for Scott. The weather is stable, mellow in the mornings with warm afternoons. We've thought of everything. So why am I concerned? I don't know. I try to push these nagging thoughts from my mind.

I'm just doing a number on myself, I think. My real fear is my own loss of purpose. Or is it?

I arrive home late and sleep fitfully with dreams of Stefan and his brothers rowing me about on the River Neckar. I see flashes of myself looking in the mirror at the bluish bruise about my eye. Stefan dismissed it as an insect bite, but it wasn't. Pieces of Germany flip through my subconscious. Baby pictures and visits to the Hellers and piles of freshly ironed pyjamas.

I awake early, exhausted. Lighting candles, I put on the Bruch violin concertos given me by Robert, the dropout med student in Sydney, and spend my early Sunday hours in meditation, scribbling thoughts in a journal, and reading articles on head injuries from the hospital's medical library. Mid-morning the phone rings. I answer it with a bit of irritation, as my tranquillity has been disturbed.

'Mom?' It's Jonathan calling to check in, and my spirits lift. But then I catch myself. There's something about his voice.

'What is it?' I say quietly.

'Mom, Scott's had a seizure. He's in a coma. You'd better hurry.' My body turns cold, and I begin to shake uncontrollably, until I can barely hang on to the phone. I feel faint, unable to think. I suck in deep breaths, fighting to clear my head and regain control.

'Where are you?'

'Still in England, at a cottage hospital near Kidderminster. Take the train. I'll meet you at the station in Kidderminster. Better hurry.'

With tremulous fingers, I dial Harold. Luckily he's home. I explain about Scott and ask for a ride to the train station. I throw on clothes, stuff a few things in an overnight bag, crush money into my purse, and wait on the steps. Harold is at the kerb a few minutes later in his old Land Rover and we're off to Euston station. But this is Sunday with reduced schedules, and there is no express run. I pace the station for an hour, and once aboard twitch in my seat, impatient and increasingly agitated at every lazy and unnecessary local stop.

A seizure. How did it happen? He's been stable for a year. There were no signs. What happened? Over and over, as the iron wheels hypnotically click along the steel tracks, I pound myself with the same question. Why did I let him go? How did I let this happen? Finally in late afternoon, with the sun throwing deep shadows across the rolling green landscape with its leafy hedgerows, I step off the train in Kidderminster.

Jonathan drives me to the small, rural hospital. I pause in the doorway to Scott's room. He's lying in a white bed, at peace, as if he's slipped upstairs for an afternoon nap. Drip tubes snake out from under the top sheet, up to several bottles hanging on a stand. Ulla, her face ashen, rises from a chair by the bed. I hug her in silence before moving to inspect the drip bottles. One is a saline solution, but the two others are medicines I know cause allergic reactions. Alarmed, I ask Jonathan to find the doctor. When he appears, a kindly grey-haired man, I briefly explain Scott's history with medicine, and ask that everything but the saline solution be stopped. He is sceptical, but complies.

When the doctor leaves, I suggest to Jonathan that they may wish to take a walk. 'I know you've been here for hours,' I say quietly. 'And I'd like to have a few minutes with Scott.' Sensing my request is really an order, they slip out for coffee.

In the silent room I sit at Scott's side and hold his hand. I'm wondering if he has come this far only to find that he wants to pass on to the other side. Has he finally given up? As soon as I generate that thought, I know it's defeatist, and I shake it free.

With eyes closed, I seek a connection with his energy. Machines are too clumsy to tell me all I need to know. I've been told by doctors of Oriental medicine that they can monitor the entire body and its organs through the rhythm and pressure of the pulses alone. While I know little of that, I do know I enjoy an unusual psychic connection with Scott, and through his energy I can intuitively sense the wellness of his body. I find his pulse weak, but not fatally so. It's more the pulse of a peaceful rest. I fail to detect organ infections, although the drip medicines have caused an allergic reaction, as I note by a slight swelling of the glands in his throat. What I'm searching for, what I'm desperate to know, however, is the severity of this coma.

I can't be sure, but I do sense this is not the deep, traumatic coma of Sydney, but one where he's hovering just under the surface of consciousness. The coma might in fact have been medically induced. I sense it will not last long. Scott is telling me this is not the time to give up. His message is strong. I don't know where it comes from, nor could I explain how I'm picking it up, but the message is unmistakable, and I trust.

Later I am shocked to learn from the doctor that Scott has suffered a grand mal seizure. When he was brought into the emergency room, the doctor on duty, unaware of the earlier coma and allergies, had prescribed a massive dose of Valium, standard procedure to relax the body and prevent further seizures. The Valium may well have pitched Scott over the edge from simply being unconscious into a coma. But it may not have been the medicine at all. I will never know. This is a small hospital in a small town. Had they known Scott's history, would it have made a difference? Most doctors practise a lifetime without encountering a patient like Scott and they can't be blamed. My job is to deal with the here and now. I can spare little emotional energy speculating on the what-ifs.

Working in shifts, Jonathan, Ulla and I spend a week in the hospital at Scott's side. I hold his hand and talk to him as if he were wide awake. Sometimes I sing to him while I massage his hands and arms. Frequently, I ask him to squeeze my hand and pause to see if he understands and responds. Most of the time there is nothing, but sometimes there is. I know what to look for; a twitch of a finger, the slightest pressure of a thumb. These are sufficient for me to believe in my diagnosis. This coma is temporary, I tell the doctor. Scott will awaken soon. The doctor gives me an unbelieving look. But I'm not bothered, I know what I know.

At the end of the week the doctor arranges for Scott to be taken by ambulance, accompanied by a doctor and a nurse, to St George's Hospital in London, so he might recover near home. I ride back with Jonathan and Ulla. Once Scott is settled, they will return to Denmark, and dreading that moment, I spend a good part of the trip in silence, looking out at the passing fields, my mind a thousand miles away, wondering how it happened.

There was no warning, not a clue. What was the trigger? I ask Jonathan to tell me again about their fishing trip, hoping in the retelling to discover an answer. They left Wimbledon on a leisurely drive through the country, staying on the narrow lanes and byways that reveal a country's character and charm but that those in a hurry

206

choose to avoid. Just over the Welsh border Jonathan had glanced over to see his brother's body in a shaking spasm. Quickly pulling to a stop, he lowered Scott's seat to a reclining position, and turned his head to the side so he wouldn't choke on anything regurgitated. His body soon relaxed and the seizure seemed to pass. But then he had another one, longer and more violent. Growing more concerned, Jonathan pulled Scott from the car and laid him on the ground, but the seizure didn't stop. His temperature rose and his lips began to turn blue. Leaving Ulla in charge, Jonathan jogged twenty minutes to the nearest farmhouse for help. The farmer led them back across the border to the little hospital outside Kidderminster. Jonathan had tried to call me from the hospital and tried again several times that night, but I wasn't home. Not wanting to leave a message, feeling it was important to tell me directly, he did not call again until Sunday morning.

Still I'm baffled. What caused the seizure? Was it the constant vibration of the car ride? Or the strobe-like glare of sunlight as it flashed through the trees? That particular day was one of the hottest on record. Was heat the culprit? Perhaps Scott was dehydrated. Perhaps all these conditions came together to trigger a reaction that none alone would have produced.

The thoughts ricochet like loose marbles through my mind. But I keep them to myself. Jonathan already carries a heavy burden of guilt and I won't add to the weight. At St George's, Scott is placed in isolation with round-the-clock care. I am also there day and night, as I was in Sydney, sleeping where and when I can. Sometimes he does respond when I ask him to squeeze my hand – only small responses, but enough to boost my hopes a bit. He remains in that coma-like state for another two weeks, during which I never leave his side. I just keep talking, touching, singing to him, as if he is wide awake.

I am convinced Scott will recover, but my lingering doubts prompt a call to Sammy in Connecticut with the news. I ask him to come quickly just in case. He arrives a few days later in the same brown suit he wore nearly two years earlier in Sydney, but without the spare-no-expense-I'll-pay-for-everything bravado. This time he stands in silence next to his brother, his shoulders sagging, his face deeply etched in pain. It hurts me deeply that Sammy would come so far only to once again find his brother in the stone-cold silence of a coma. I am sad that they are denied the camaraderie and good cheer they knew as children.

Though Sammy and Scott have too long been separated, they maintain strong brotherly bonds, calling often and exchanging letters. When they were younger, in the Santa Cruz Mountains, Sammy was the big brother, always looking out for baby Scotty. Before heading off to school, Sammy would make sure Scotty's shoes were tied and he was properly bundled for the weather. Sammy would dote on his brother to the exclusion of himself. Too often he left the house with his own untied shoestrings dragging in the dirt and his coat unbuttoned.

Ulla stays two more days then departs for home. Sammy leaves soon after, and after another week so does Jonathan. Once again, I search for the strength to forge ahead.

I notify Dr Rhys, and he comes to the hospital. After reviewing Scott's charts he turns to me. 'This has surprised us all, Glenys,' he says in his thick Welsh accent. 'You can't be hard on yourself. He's never had a seizure like this. Even if we knew he might, they are hard to predict, and with his allergies, we have so few tools at our disposal.'

I can only nod in agreement. I am trying not to be hard on myself, but it's not easy. A mother can never completely distance herself from guilt. Didn't my body produce this person?

Dr Rhys comes to sit on the bed with me. 'I hope you understand,' he says. 'I'm not going to do any heroics for your son. If he's meant to make it he will. It has to be his decision.'

I smile weakly. I understand. With Scott, it's always been his own decision.

Dr Rhys stops by several times a week to monitor Scott's progress. His presence is a rock for me, even if little is spoken. I believe he secretly admires my dedication to my son, and I adore his dedication to this larger family of patients. I often wonder how he can remain so pleasant and upbeat when on a daily basis he encounters so much grief and sadness. So many of his patients die, and of those who live, so many are damaged for life. God only knows what he thinks in the dark of the night. I deeply respect his courage, and I am eternally grateful he is my friend.

Over the next two weeks, Scott gradually emerges from his coma. Indeed this coma is not as serious as the one in Sydney, and his recuperation is less spectacular and more rapid. Lying in bed he will open his eyes and look up at me as if he knows exactly who I am, then slowly his eyes will shift to scan the room with a stranger's wondrous expression at exploring a new world, before he drifts off into a long nap. Soon I am propping his back with pillows. He knows what I am doing, and makes an effort to shift his weight to help, though he is unable to do so. But I'm heartened at his alertness.

To further his responsiveness I lay four items in front of him, including his toothbrush and comb, and instruct: 'If you can understand me, pick up one of these objects and show me how it is used.' Clumsily, Scott grabs the toothbrush and manages to stick it in his mouth, though he is unable as yet to make the motion of brushing. I'm ecstatic. It is another small miracle, the beginning of yet another recovery.

Meanwhile, he contracts septicaemia and golden staph, the same hospital infections he suffered in Sydney. Once again, without medication and to the considerable amazement of the hospital staff, his body shakes them off. Even I am amazed at my son's resilience. Time and again he bounces back, as if he's teaching us something. I can only wonder what.

As word of Scott's hospitalization spreads, our new friends and neighbours begin to visit. In addition to Dr Rhys, who includes us on his twice-weekly rounds, Wendy appears often to assess Scott's health and to suggest a new regime of therapy I can try at home. Susan and Ronnie bring their daughters on Saturday morning, and while Claire and Holly tease Scott, Susan monitors his medical charts with a critical eye. It makes little difference that he is no longer in her charge; once a patient, always a patient.

The Potts, Harold, Constable Riggs and others put in appearances, some with flowers, others with chocolates, and Scott's face ignites in appreciation. Therapists from the rehab centre drop in, and this in turn attracts ward nurses and orderlies curious over the commotion. Often I glance up to see half a dozen people milling about the room, some sitting on Scott's bed, their heads bent next to his in conspiratorial whispers, others engaged in chatty teatime conversation, with frequent bouts of laughter. Once again Scott's room becomes a centre, and I have this warm sense of contentment and gratitude that so many people care. They are the silver lining that rings the black cloud of Scott's ongoing struggle.

In the fourth week at St George's, Dr Rhys strides into the room, his white coat flapping open, a black stethoscope dangling from his neck. Scott is asleep, and he stands quietly at the foot of his bed, engrossed in the medical chart. I come to his side. Finally lowering the chart, Dr Rhys studies Scott's peaceful face, shakes his head in wonder and says quietly, 'I must tell you, Glenys, I'm amazed. That boy just never gives up. He never quits, does he? Septicaemia, golden staph, and no antibiotics. How does he do it? It's like everything we're taught in medical school is wrong. I'm ready to release him. He's doing fine. Take him home for a week, and then bring him back to the rehab centre. He's such a fighter. I think he deserves another try.'

Twelve

Once again Dr Rhys proves to be a godsend, but in my excitement I've glossed over the small detail that the next round of rehabilitation is still a week away – more than that, almost ten days – and I'll be caring for Scott at home, by myself. As I struggle to settle him into his bed in the living room, it becomes even clearer that the seizure and the weeks of recovery at St George's have not been without a price. While his overall health is good, Scott is much weaker and has lost more weight, more muscle tone than I imagined, and he will not be as physically able as I hoped. Once again, I will be setting my alarm clock to three-hour intervals to help him turn over at night.

But more than his strength, which I know will return with exercise, I'm concerned his speech has been permanently damaged. While he comprehends what I say and responds to my questions, his ability to speak has been impaired. The little nerve centre buried deep in his brain that synchronizes all the parts of speaking, from the forced expulsion of air by the diaphragm to the coordination of the muscles of the voice box, seems not to be fully organized. The result is halting. Sometimes in his hurry and frustration to get a word out there is no speech at all. Fortunately, speech therapy is part of Scott's rehab programme, but I suspect that won't be enough and that eventually I will again assume the role of speech therapist as I did in Sydney, coaxing Scott to practise sounds, shape his lips and coordinate breathing.

While I'm saddened to think that over two years of progress and the love and labour of so many could be in jeopardy, I dare not reveal my thoughts to Scott, and keep up a cheerful patter. If he shares my discouragement, he fails to show it. What I see in his eyes is that old spark of fight, and I suddenly feel ashamed that I am always the one who seems to give way to despondency first. Time and time again, it's Scott who provides the strength for both of us.

∾

Years later, what I feel most ashamed of is what happened about a week after leaving St George's. When he left the hospital, Scott still had an open wound in his chest where a central line had been inserted, connected to an artery. The line was for the emergency injection of medication, a port that serves as a backup to the saline drip system, a standard procedure for patients in critical condition. A few days prior to Scott's release, a nurse or perhaps an assistant had removed the line and covered the incision with a bandage. The day before I was to pick him up, someone had removed the bandage to let the incision finish healing in open air.

I wasn't aware of the damage until after Luther had carried Scott in from the taxi and positioned him in his bed. Noticing that he seemed frantic to scratch his chest, I opened his shirt and was dumbstruck to find the incision an oozing mess. The skin around the incision was raw, and Scott's scratching had opened up the wound. It was swelling with infection. It was only later that I learned what had happened. When the bandage had been removed, the tape had left adhesive on Scott's skin. Wishing to tidy him up, that same someone had resorted to nail-polish remover as a cleaner. She or he might as well have poured gasoline on his wound.

For two and a half years I'd nursed Scott, following him from one hospital to another, and in the process encountered almost every degree of medical care imaginable, from the heroism of the doctors at St Vincent's and the compassion of Dr Rhys, to the negligence of Scott being allowed to fall in the shower. But this? Perhaps I was overly tired, or tired of the struggle, but the sight of this festering open wound struck at the very core of my being.

Quickly I took off his shirt and set about cleaning it. Unable to use antibiotics, I'd come to rely heavily on herbal medicines. I remembered from when I was a young girl how Nanna would prescribe lavender, honey and a tincture of arnica root (from the aster family of flowers) to the locals who would appear at her back door for help with wounds. And I'd always kept my own herbal first-aid kit for just such emergencies. After cleansing Scott's wound, I smeared it with raw honey, one of nature's great medicines. Body heat melts honey so it flows and seals the wound and keeps it moist. Then I placed a loose bandage over the incision to protect it from Scott's clothing. Over the next few days Scott kept scratching the inflamed wound until eventually I taped socks over his hands to protect it from his nails.

About a week after his return from hospital, sometime after midnight, as I lay on my bed on the living room floor, I awoke suddenly to low moans, and an agitated sound of rubbing. Turning on the lamp near his bed, I recoiled in horror. His clothes and sheets were soaked in blood. In his sleep, Scott had used his teeth to tear off the socks and clawed at the bandage on his chest, ripping it off and gouging the incision, which was now oozing blood.

I must have cracked. I was on the edge anyway and it wouldn't have taken much. Groggy from lack of sleep, physically and mentally exhausted, after years of heartache and frustration, I must have gone crazy. Grabbing a mirror off the wall, I held it above him so he could see the full extent of his self-inflicted damage.

'Look what you've done to yourself!' I shouted, tears streaming down my face. 'Do you want it to get infected? Do you want to go back to the hospital, and maybe die? Is that what you want? Look! Look at yourself!' I was shaking with anger and fear.

The picture of Scott's frozen face is still etched in my mind. Unable to defend himself, he was at the mercy of a mother out of control.

'Jon, Jon!' he cried out in his broken voice.

That hit me hard. Was I so far gone that my son must plead for his brother's protection? Awakening to what I had done, I collapsed on him, sobbing. 'I'm sorry, I'm sorry,' I said through my tears, and begged his forgiveness. He didn't speak but started stroking my hair, then picked up my hand and kissed it, and tried to give me a one-armed hug.

I knew Scott had no control over his condition. He wasn't accountable for his behaviour. I'm the mother, I thought, I'm the parent; it's my job to be strong, to carry the weight. Why am I not able? Why am I so weak? In the dead of night, in grim determination, I dried my tears of rage and self-pity and set about making it right.

Again I cleaned his wound, and this time rubbed the area around the incision with arnica ointment before adding a fresh bandage. After changing his shirt and sheets, and taping clean socks on his hands, I turned out the light and sat on his bed in darkness, clutching his hand in mine, unable to let go until I heard his breathing slow to the gentle rhythm of sleep.

∾

By the time Scott returns to rehab he has fought off the infection and the incision has begun to heal, but it will be another month before only the redness of a fresh scar remains. We are lucky it heals so well.

During those ten days, as Scott continues to recuperate in bed, I find myself nabbing golfers off the course. It seems easier this time, and the volunteers I recruit early in the week often return a day or two later accompanied by friends who also volunteer. From relative silence, now my phone rings more often. The Potts call, as does Harold, to ask if I need more help than usual. I receive calls from strangers, people who have never volunteered, asking in their awkward way if they might bring food or stop by to lend a hand. Luther and Constable Riggs swing by almost every day, a considerable increase on their usual pattern. And Claire arrives with fresh baked biscuits, filling the cottage with a calming fragrance of homemade love. Somehow or other, by the grace of God, we make it through a very long week.

Back during our early days in Sydney, whenever Scott's condition turned for the worse and our need for volunteers increased, they seemed to materialize from the blue, and when his condition would improve, they'd mysteriously fade away. It's a pattern that has played itself out over and over.

Now it's happening again. How do these people know of our need? Who is spreading the word? Luther? Susan, Claire or Holly? Is Scott sending messages into the cosmos?

At about this time, two men appear in my life. They both become stalwarts and very good friends. I open my front door one afternoon to find a tall, handsome man with fine blondish hair, in the process of folding a black umbrella that glistens with light rain. He is dark-eyed and impeccably dressed in a dark-blue suit that bespeaks someone important. 'Are you Mrs Carl?' he asks politely in a confident voice.

I nod with some hesitation, wondering what I might have done to warrant this attention.

'My name is Howard Pinter, Mrs Carl. I understand your son is an invalid, and that you depend on volunteers for part of his care. Am I correct?'

Again I nod. 'Yes, my son is brain injured, but he's at the rehab hospital right now. When he's home, I do have volunteers who assist. They help a great deal.'

Suddenly realizing the poor man is still standing in the grey mist and my door is wide open to the elements, I invite him in, although I'm slightly self-conscious about opening my simple home to someone who is obviously used to more. But he is oblivious as he follows me into the living room, and when I offer tea he follows me with an easy grace into my cramped kitchen. As I put the kettle on, he apologizes for the intrusion and goes on to explain that he's a lawyer with Chase Manhattan Bank and travels frequently between London, New York, Hong Kong, and most recently Moscow. The more I listen, the more I find myself falling under the spell of his gentle-manly charm. I steep loose black tea and pour it into two pottery cups, and lead him back into the living room towards the only two chairs I own.

'I'm a little confused,' I tell him. 'What is it that I can do for you? And how did you find me?'

'Ah, yes,' he murmurs, searching the pockets inside his coat. 'I read about you in the Wimbledon *Guardian*. Here's the clip.' And he hands it over.

I'm embarrassed and speechless. A week ago a reporter cornered me and took Scott's photo. I had no idea it had been published. Now here it is, a head and shoulder shot of Scott in a striped shirt, with his curled left hand in plain view. And under the bold heading 'Stubborn Mother' there is a description of Scott, his history and plight, and how he relies on volunteers for therapy. I am quoted extensively. The mystery is solved. Here is the reason for the increase in volunteers.

'I haven't seen this,' I say, as my eyes plough through it. 'When did it come out?'

'A few days ago, actually. I clipped it and stuck it in my pocket, but I've been so busy I haven't had the time to follow it up.'

He asks me many questions about Scott and for the hundredth time I relate the story. But Howard is so interested, and his eyes show such intensity of compassion and purpose, that I find myself going beyond my usual explanation, to talk about my childhood in Wales and stories about my life in America and personal vignettes I rarely share with strangers. Suddenly, two hours have slipped away and Howard, after darting a quick look at his watch, rises to leave.

'I look forward to meeting Scott in a few days' time. For some reason, I was attracted to Scott's story,' he says with a smile, then grows a bit serious. 'Perhaps it was about the struggle, about not giving up. I've experienced that in my own life. I know a bit about carving one's way through life's jungle.' He pauses. 'Usually I wouldn't respond to this type of article,' he finally adds. 'Don't generally do this sort of thing, come by like this without calling. I would like to be one of Scott's volunteers, Glenys, but I fear with my travel schedule you couldn't count on me. I will come when I can, if that's acceptable.' And that's how he leaves it.

During the next few months, Howard appears in random spurts, several times in one week, then once in several weeks, depending on his travels. Scott increasingly looks forward to his coming, for Howard is a man of considerable intelligence and sophistication who also manages to be thoughtful and generous, and he instils in Scott not only great self-respect, but also high expectation. Whenever Howard comes through the door, Scott lets out a cheer and extends his good arm for a hug, as if he were greeting his long-lost father.

Howard wheels Scott through the neighbourhood, or puts him in his expensive car and goes for a drive in the country. I remember Howard saying at the end of one visit how he loves Scott's company, and is especially fond of those one-armed hugs. Months later, he confides in me that aside from his girlfriend, parents and twin brother, he has never learned to love another human being fully until he met Scott. How hard it is for some people to reach out, though there is so much to be gained.

Dr Rhys stops me in the hall one day, a week or two after Scott is readmitted. 'Glenys, do you recall a man at St George's named Arnold? His son Justin was a patient there with Scott. A few rooms down your hall, if I remember. Does he come to mind?'

I shake my head. 'No, he's not familiar, but then I was so occupied with Scott that I paid little attention to the others.'

'I think you would recognize him,' Dr Rhys insists. 'His son is recovering from a drug-induced coma, and there is brain damage. He's been transferred here for rehabilitation. I just came from his room. It's right down there,' he nods towards the end of the hall, 'on the right. Arnold is there with him now. Poor man's beside himself with grief, blames himself it seems. The boy is only seventeen. Please go and talk to him, Glenys. He needs a little support.'

As I enter the room I see the boy sleeping and a man in a chair near his side, leaning forward, his elbows on his knees, hands clasped as if in prayer, and head hanging low. I make a noise and the man slowly turns about and rises. I introduce myself and tell him I have a son in rehab like his. Arnold moves a few steps closer, and indeed I do recognize him from St George's. We would pass in the hall, but even when he was close he seemed so far away. I remember having the unsettled feeling of having brushed sleeves with a ghost. He is still quite distant, but I resolve to engage him. 'I'm on my way for coffee, and thought you might like to come along. I could use the company.'

Arnold glances at his sleeping son, unsure how to respond. Finally he gives a small nod and we make our way to the cafeteria. Settled at the table, I mention that we've seen each other before.

'Yes, I do remember you from St George's,' Arnold says with a nod. It's the first complete sentence he's spoken, enough for me to catch his accent.

'You're Welsh,' I say. 'So am I, from Pembrokeshire, but grew up in Cardiff.'

'A bit of American in you, too, if I'm not mistaken,' he responds, and I know he is paying attention. I smile and explain my life in the States, and when I come to the time in California, Arnold's face lights up.

'I've always wanted to live in California,' he says with a yearning look. 'It's been in my dreams. Life's so hard in Wales and then this with my son . . . In the long days since his accident'—Arnold would never mention drugs or overdose or coma, but speak only of his son's accident—'I close my eyes and dream of being in California. I've never been, mind you, but some day I will.'

Arnold is the single parent of three children: Justin, the youngest, and two daughters. He used to be a salesman, he tells me, but over the last few months he has spent so much time with his son he's lost that job, and now earns money working at his hobby, repairing and refinishing furniture. As he talks, I see his body relax and the walls between us tumble. A quick, gentle smile flits across his haggard face. In the few times he looks straight at me, I see in his sad eyes a deep pain.

'How did it happen?' I ask. 'Tell me about your son's accident.'

'He'd gone out to a party,' he begins in a voice threaded with guilt. 'It was Saturday night and he came home late. Usually on Sunday he sleeps in anyway, to ten or ten thirty, so when it came to eleven I knocked on his door for him to get up. When he didn't answer I looked in, and he was dead to the world. I thought he must have had a rough time the night before and probably needed his sleep. When it got to be about two in the afternoon, I finally went in to wake him. But I couldn't; he wouldn't wake up. So I called an ambulance.'

I place my hand on his shoulder and lean closer. 'You can't blame yourself for that, Arnold,' I say softly. 'You were doing what you thought best. You thought he needed his sleep and you were being considerate, just like a dad. How could you have known?'

Arnold turns his face away and wipes at his eyes. 'I had no idea he was into that stuff. He always seemed so normal. I should have woken him up earlier, when he usually gets up, instead of letting him sleep. It's those extra hours that did it. This wouldn't have happened if I'd done what I was supposed to. Now the doctors say he's ruined for life. It's his legs. He'll always be in a wheelchair, that's what they're telling me.'

'My son also had a terrible accident,' I begin, a hard edge in my voice. 'Nearly three years ago now. I was repeatedly told he would never recover. Every doctor in every hospital told me they couldn't help, that he would probably die. They told me to go back to America and leave him. But I said, "No, miracles happen." I refused to believe them, and I fought back. Today my son can almost stand. He can almost take steps, with help. One day he will walk.'

I lean a little further across the table. 'You have to fight back, Arnold. Don't let anyone take your hope away. Justin can do it. You always have to try. He's young. He can stand too, maybe. But he needs you, he needs your strength and your determination more than ever. Don't let anyone tell you no. Don't let anyone take your hope away. Never, never give up, do you hear me? Never.'

Arnold is watching me intently, but I can't tell what he's thinking. It's hard to know if people are really listening, or if the spirit is already too far gone.

We share coffee nearly every day at the hospital, and as time goes on Arnold and I become close, bonded by the situation of our sons, who need us more now than they did as children. On weekends when both boys are at home, Arnold and Justin often come by.

Arnold lifts his son onto Scott's table in the garage, and with the door rolled up and the red and gold autumn leaves swirling before the winds on the common, I show him the exercises and massage techniques I use on Scott.

On week nights when the boys are in the hospital, Arnold sometimes knocks on my door, and we light the gas fire under my fake log and entertain each other with stories of Wales. Arnold sings old Welsh songs in a pure, sweet voice. I miss having a piano so much that I just close my eyes and pretend to be playing along. Or we read aloud to each other from A. J. Cronin, Arthur Conan Doyle or mystery stories. Arnold loves to recite the poetry of Dylan Thomas, much of which he knows by heart. Sometimes Harold joins us and we talk of music and art, or the best flea markets for antiques, and share homemade soup or stew in front of the fire. It is so soothing to have an understanding companion.

After a night of song and verse and conversation, when I'm curled in my bed, my thoughts drift to how life might have been if my destiny were of another kind. I might have found happiness with Arnold, as I might have with Walter in an earlier time, but I'm not in that place. My job remains unfinished, and I'm not ready for any kind of relationship, so Arnold and I remain the best of friends.

Our long, hot summer has drifted into autumn, and the lush green leaves in the common have turned to a kaleidoscope of blazing colours. Early November brings a great rain, stripping the trees of their dead leaves. They stand suddenly stark naked against a damp, grey sky. I watch the transformation from my bay window, just as I watch the days slowly become squeezed between the late rising and early setting of a shrouded sun. Now when I walk the common I dress warmly with boots and a wool hat and scarf, and scrunch through banks of fallen leaves. And when Scott and I go to Annabel's for our Saturday morning hot chocolate, it is often through a light rain or a veil of mist, with Scott holding a black umbrella the size of a circus tent, and me with my nose running because of the cold, hunched under it as I push. We must be quite a sight rolling down the pavement, little me pushing my oversized black toadstool on wheels.

The thought of the impending winter is sobering. It's the time you regret not making all the repairs you should have made when the sun was out and it was warm. I have been giving Scott baths in the back garden with a jerry-rigged shower, but I always knew we would be forced inside when it turned cold and I would need to devise an alternative. With Scott in rehab during the week, the need has not been urgent. We get by with sponge baths on the weekends. But rehab will end soon and I'd best give bathing some thought. At least we have a fire to warm the towels to wrap him in.

On a chilly afternoon I begin my hunt for a small tub that can be placed in the kitchen and filled with a hose from the sink. After darting in and out of numerous old furniture stores and junk shops with my new friend and neighbour Ingrid, I run across the perfect solution. It's an oval tub of galvanized steel, buried under an eclectic pile of castoffs at the rear of a shop filled with used saddles, bridles and other riding equipment. The owner drags the old tub out, wipes off the dust, and I stand to one side imagining what it would look like on my kitchen floor, and what Scott might look like as he sat in it. My vision is ludicrous. I begin to laugh and the owner gives me a perplexed look. It isn't like a normal tin bath; it has a rounded back sticking up on one side. In an instant I get past my amusement and see that Scott could put his legs over the low end and it would be quite comfortable for him. Best of all it would be therapeutic. My search is over.

'I was just thinking of a Western movie I saw once,' I tell the shopkeeper. 'There was a grizzled old cowboy taking a bath in a tub like this. He's in the middle of nowhere, hunched over in his tub with his big cowboy hat on to protect his head from the sun, and his horse is drinking from the other end . . .' The shopkeeper fails to see the humour. I do, but that's not unusual. And my imagination has at the same time gone further, to see that this could be turned into a comfortable chair for Scott.

I ask the price and we start to bargain. Gradually the price drops close to what I can afford, and after I tell him the purpose, that it's not for a horse but for my invalid son, the price drops further. I buy it for about ten pounds, and he agrees to deliver it to my house.

I store the tub in the garage and spend several afternoons painting the outside an antique golden yellow, and adding a number of leaves freehand. It will be a breath of spring during those winter days, a great pot of leaves that will never die or have to be watered. I'm so happy with my great find that as soon as the paint dries I drag it into the living room. When Scott comes home I help him sit in it, propped up by cushions, with his back against the high end and his legs extended. As I had visualized, his feet reach the floor and gravity provides a natural stretch for his calves and the backs of his thighs.

It is a perfect fit, and we never use it as a bathtub. As Scott settles in, his arms rest on the sides a bit below shoulder height, ideal for the bad arm. I add a couple of cushions to keep his legs open, adjust the ones behind to bring his hips down and legs up and his knees fold over the edge to plant his feet easily on the floor. This is a wonderful static exercise. Scott can relax completely, and I can sit on a pillow in front of the fireplace and do reflexology on his feet. It's the ideal chair, and when he isn't in it, it looks – to me, anyway – like a pretty piece of furniture. We seem on cloud nine, listening to Louis Armstrong sing one of Scott's favourite tunes, 'It's a Wonderful World'.

Once again I have recognized a piece of rehabilitation equipment in disguise. I begin taking it back with him on Mondays to the hospital. Everyone thinks it is a great idea, and some other mothers go on a hunt for similar tubs.

The cold weather also forces me to face another issue: my financial situation. In Sydney I came to rely on earnings from the Paddington flea market for daily expenses. When I left Australia I carried with me enough money to provide for some months. Now it is nearly exhausted, and I apply for government benefits. Scott is eligible for an immobility allowance and I for a caretaker allowance, and we're both entitled to a small stipend for rent. But the payments vary greatly, depending on how many days Scott is sleeping at home. I need to consider something else to supplement our income and balance the budget. With the extra bedroom upstairs, I begin to wonder if taking in a boarder isn't the answer. How will I go about this? I ponder.

It comes as a complete surprise a few days later when I hear a rapping on my door and find a young lady on my step, with long dark hair and sparkling grey-blue eyes. Her face breaks immediately into an endearing smile, revealing beautiful white teeth. 'My name is Siobhan,' she begins in an Irish lilt, 'and I'm looking for a room to rent for a few months. One of your neighbours suggested I ask you.'

I can do nothing but stare at this charming girl. I have not said a word to our neighbours. I have in fact done nothing more than kick the idea around in my mind. How could anyone know? And what brings this young lady to me at this particular moment and not a week earlier or later? I have no answer. I can only be glad that I am careful in what I ask for, since it so often soon begins to happen.

Interpreting my astonishment as uncertainty, Siobhan quickly goes on. 'I'm a student at the College of Music, and I will need the room until I graduate in a few months.' When she mentions the magic word music, my heart melts and I quickly invite her in.

'How soon do you need to move?' I ask.

'Actually as soon as possible. I have only my clothes, a few books and my instruments.' She pauses for a moment. 'And if possible, I have a budgie.' How nice, I think, she has a pet that can sing. Then: 'And I will need to practise every evening, usually about two hours, in my room. Music doesn't bother you, does it?' What a funny question, I think to myself. How could music possibly bother anyone?

'Of course not,' I reply. 'I play the piano although I don't have one now. Scott and I love music. First, let me give you a tour and show you your room. Then you can decide if it's what you want.'

I take her upstairs to my room. 'You can have this bed. I sleep downstairs with my son.' I explain about the injury and the hospital, how Scott is home on weekends but soon will be here full time. Siobhan listens intently. I see how her eyes soften, and know for certain this will be a fine arrangement.

Siobhan's time with us is memorable. She is an accomplished flautist, and on weekend nights as Scott and I lie on the floor before the fire, we hear her practising above us. The muted notes fly higher and higher as she climbs the scale, then down, down, down she goes. Up and down her fingers fly for about twenty minutes before launching into the most wonderful pieces of music. We keep a contented silence during those concerts.

Siobhan is also an excellent cook, specializing in exotic dishes. We agree to prepare at least one unusual meal each week for each other, and on those nights when we try to out-cook each other, our cottage is filled with the richest of aromas from around the world: saffron, cardamom, curry, ginger, cumin. When Scott is home she massages his back, arms and fingers and asks about his life growing up in America. Scott in turn asks about her childhood in Ireland. She seems not to mind that he speaks slowly and sometimes not at all, and offers steady encouragement, sometimes laughing aloud at his stories.

Sometimes we try to get Scott to sing, to see if this will assist in his breathing. I know that a person with a stutter is often able to sing without stuttering, and I want to see if the same principle will work on Scott, even though his situation is different. Stuttering has to do with the brain's control of the mouth muscles, and with Scott it is the breath and throat that need to come under control. In the end it doesn't seem to help, except that Scott, as always, relishes the effort and laughs at himself, even as he strains to perform and never really succeeds. Siobhan and I join in his merriment.

At times I catch a glimpse of Siobhan at the bay window peering out across the soggy common. She seems lost within some private moment of sadness. I wonder about her deeper story, but I don't press and she never volunteers. Sometimes that's what friendship is all about; listening without asking, understanding without judging, feeling safe in separate, private worlds.

In the mornings she often comes tearing down the stairs, calling out, 'I'm late, I'm late, I'll miss my bus!' before disappearing from view. It brings back long-forgotten memories of my boys flying out our front door in the Santa Cruz Mountains, yelling the same thing. Having Siobhan with us is like reclaiming part of my younger years, and I know when she finally departs the void she leaves will be hard to fill.

∾

I pick up the phone one late afternoon and Stefan is on the line. 'I've just flown in from Stuttgart for a meeting in London. Would you like to join me for dinner?'

'Tonight?'

'Yes, of course, tonight, in about three hours. I'll come get you and we can find a quiet place to eat, somewhere near you.' His voice is light and gay and for a few moments I'm transported back to our happiness in Westport. I hesitate, nonetheless.

'Do you need someone to stay with Scott?'

'No, he's at the hospital on week nights.'

'Then why the hesitation? Afraid of having too much fun?'

'Of course not,' I answer too quickly, and wonder if I'm being overly defensive.

Stefan leaves his car in front of my house and we walk to the village in the chilly darkness. He is full of humour and banter and talks of old times in Westport, in a voice laden with nostalgia. He never mentions Germany and it dawns on me how unhappy he must be. In America he was very happy, and when he visited me in Australia he was happy like the Stefan I used to know. And he's happy again tonight in London. Poor man, happy anywhere but home.

As the evening progresses the conversation subtly changes to us, how if we came back together he would find a job in London, or in the States, or you name it. He is soft and affectionate, and I begin to understand how much our relationship has meant to him, maybe more to him than to me. He never talks of what brought him to London, and I suspect it was a charade to spend some time with me.

But I know our situation is hopeless. Too much water has passed under our old bridge for us to ever get back together. Still, I enjoy the evening and admit to being captivated by the Stefan of old. As he escorts me home and we snuggle against the light drizzle, a part of me wishes it had all been different. Had we stayed in Westport, maybe got married, and never gone to Stuttgart . . . But alas, that's only a part of me speaking. The other part, the greater part, believes something else. For my journey with Scott over the past two and a half years has made me realize how very precious life is, and the struggle just makes it more so, a hard-won self-knowledge the prize.

I look up and November is gone. The days continue to shorten and the cold nights to lengthen. My routine with Scott continues. The days collapse into one another with little notice and the weeks fly by like the windblown rain outside my window. Scott has recovered much of his strength and is back at the parallel bars, taking halting but hopeful little steps under the close eye of two therapists. His speech is improved only a little, and I'm beginning to worry the damage is permanent. But then, I tell myself, it's better not to expect too much, too soon. Stimulation is the key. The brain must be engaged for it to thrive as it takes time for it to rewire.

When the hospital speech therapist finishes for the day, I take over with flash cards, prompting Scott to repeat after me. We follow that with word games where I ask him to list his favourite things: songs, books, artists, musicians, authors, sports, birds and so on, until I run out of categories and energy. While I tell myself I need patience, I'm nevertheless in a hurry. The year is drawing to an end and with it, I fear, Scott's professional care.

When Dr Rhys asks to see me early one December morning, I enter his office with deliberate calm. The meeting is brief and to the point. Come mid-December Scott will be released for the Christmas holidays, and with the new year his place in the hospital will be assigned to another.

'I know we've been down this path before, Glenys,' the doctor says softly as he escorts me to the door, a hand on my shoulder. 'I've told you it's over, but then there's a reprieve. I wouldn't count on it this time if I were you. We've done all we can. The rest is up to you, and Scott of course. But he's in very good hands – your hands.'

Dr Rhys opens the door and looks at me, a sparkle of amusement in his eyes. 'Sometimes I think you know more about this business than we do. I've often thought, Glenys, that if more parents were as involved as you, I'd find myself with little to do. I might even have to consider a new line of work,' he adds with a wry smile.

Of course I know he's flattering me. I am far from a professional. I know what works for my own son, and little more. It's just that I'm not afraid of going into the unknown, letting my instincts take over. Yet his charm has worked, and I leave his office with a light step, feeling good. Isn't it interesting how some people can say no in such a generous and thoughtful manner that you thank them anyway? I so admire this man.

On the way back to Scott's room I encounter Susan in the hallway, conversing with a white-coated orderly. She breaks away as I approach. 'How did your meeting with Dr Rhys go?' she asks.

'Fine,' I say, then look her in the eye. 'How did you know I just spoke with him?'

Susan laughs. 'I didn't, but knew it was coming, could tell by your face. What's the verdict?'

'Two more weeks, more or less. Then we're on our own. I knew it was coming too. This time it's for real, I'm afraid. Everyone's been so wonderful, so supportive. It's hard to let go, but it's time, I guess. A season for everything.'

'How about your volunteers?' she asks, concerned. 'Do you have enough?'

'No, but I will when the time comes. Somehow it always works out.'

Susan fishes in her uniform for a scrap of paper, jots something down and hands it to me. 'You should talk to Robin. He's the headmaster at King's College School and a wonderful man. All his students are required to perform community service. Too late this term I'm afraid, but something might be worked out for next year. He's a friend of the family. When you're ready we can call him and set something up.'

In late November, while taking morning coffee at Annabel's, I had met a striking man, an architect with a prominent London firm. Seated at the next table, he introduced himself, and we fell into conversation. Scott wasn't with me at the time, as I would often stop in for coffee on my way to the hospital, so Ben knew nothing of him until I mentioned where I was going and why. He listened intently, offered a few carefully chosen words of consolation, and our conversation moved on.

As November slips into December I often see Ben at Annabel's. He must like me, as he seems always to be there when I stop by. Soon he's paying for my coffee and croissant, and our lingering conversations often cause me to arrive at the hospital a little later than usual. Eventually, Ben asks if I would like to see a play in the West End. We go, and have dinner beforehand at a quaint French restaurant. What a treat it is for me. He makes me laugh, which is good for my soul. A few days before Scott is to be released, I'm again having coffee with Ben, and with a flirtatious glint in his devilish green eyes, he says, 'My firm is having a New Year's Eve party and I would be delighted if you would accompany me. We've secured an elegant restaurant near the city, so it will be a formal affair.' Of course I want to go; what girl wouldn't? But I'm not just any girl – I have a small problem.

'Why yes,' I tell him, 'but my Scott will be home then and I can't leave him alone. He will need a nurse.' Ben gives a dismissive wave. 'A nurse shouldn't be an issue. I will be happy to make the arrangements, and so it's done.'

'I'm having a small gathering at my house on Christmas Day,' I blurt out. 'Mostly a few friends and hospital people who have cared for my son. If you are available I would love to invite you. You can meet Scott.' Ben accepts with a disarming smile and that too is agreed.

I'm going to a gala New Year's Eve party! It's something I haven't done in years. But what in heaven's name will I wear? At the first chance, I start looking in the second-hand stores and find a beautiful black velvet dress, very plain, which I think will do the trick. It's very large on me, so I re-cut the velvet into a brand new dress.

Scott is released from the hospital a week before Christmas. It will be my first in Britain in over twenty years, and Scott's third Christmas since the accident. I want to make it festive and grand. Neither Sammy nor Jonathan and Ulla will be able to join us, but we will celebrate with the neighbours and friends who have become our shadow family.

Five days before Christmas, with Scott as artistic director orchestrating from his chair with hand movements, I string lights and hang coloured balls and bows. His motions direct me lower, sideways, or over to another wall. There is little satisfying him. I purchase a five-foot Scotch pine and place it in our bay window. For decorations I begin by setting the oven to 150 degrees. When I was growing up in Wales, our family always made our own decorations, and with Scott's support I am doing the same.

I cut a sheet of white muslin into foot-long strips, dip each one in a flour batter, tie it in a bow, and carefully lay it on a metal biscuit sheet. I put the sheet into the oven for ten minutes and when they are still only half baked, I extract the sheet, adjust the pliable bows into more perfect shapes, and slide them back in the oven for another ten minutes. With the bows fully cooked and rigid, I set them aside to cool before spraying them with gold paint. When the paint dries, I clip each bow to a red candle holder, and clip the red and gold ornaments to the tree with a candle stabilized by each clip. There are about fifty of them, each the size of a small hand.

The day before Christmas is spent baking custard pudding, trifle and sweets. Weeks earlier I have already made a plump fruitcake full of nuts and berries. I make a large batch of biscuits shaped like Santa and a pan of rich chocolate fudge. Scott serves as official taster and chief biscuit decorator. Every time he decorates one 'wrong', say if he doesn't get the eyes in the right place – which seems to happen half the time – he eats the spoiled biscuit. At the end of his work I feel guilty. His face looks a little pale from all the sugar, and if everyone shows up we may not have enough biscuits for them all. It's a good thing he only has sugar once a week.

On Christmas Eve, Arnold visits with Justin. With our sons bundled in the back seat of his car, we tour the bright holiday lights of London. It is reassuring to have so much male energy around, and for a few hours that evening my whole being relaxes and I slip into a quiet, almost surreal peacefulness. We are the perfect family on a wholesome family outing like those old-fashioned scenes on Christmas cards or the covers of housekeeping magazines. Back at my cottage, we have only been inside about ten minutes when the young girls and boys of the neighbourhood start singing carols outside the door – a very British tradition, reminding me of my time in Wales.

Sammy calls from America and I watch Scott's face light up. He made a Christmas card for his brother weeks before. I'm aware that secretly Scott was hoping Sammy could be here.

I call Ben to ask if he might arrive on Christmas afternoon before the others to help me hang a few difficult decorations, and help me put up a shelf above Scott's bed. True to his word, about an hour before the guests arrive I open the door to Ben, smiling and smartly dressed, with a toolbox in one hand. After I show him about, he asks, 'Where's Scott? I've been looking forward to meeting him.'

'He's out for a walk. Claire, a neighbour's girl, is watching him so I can finish up all the details.' We finish our work quickly, and soon Claire wheels Scott in. I introduce Ben to Claire, then to Scott, who extends his right hand. As Ben tentatively reaches out, Scott tries to say, 'Nice to meet you,' his face a crooked half-grin. Ben takes my son's hand, but his face, from a confident smile, has gone a little ashen, and his lips are pursed in a tight line.

As the party begins, Ben excuses himself for family reasons and eases out the front door. I force myself to put his behaviour out of my mind. Our cottage is aglow with candles, coloured lights, ribbons, laughter and good cheer. Scott, his wheelchair decorated with red and green crepe paper, greets each guest at the door. Sandwiches, tea and desserts are served, this time more formally on my new plates. Scott puts on a laughing red Santa mask and amid his fractured ho-ho-hos, we exchange gifts. I give each guest one of the small Christmas ornaments Scott and I have made, a frame of twigs woven about one of the sparkling glass crystals I purchased from a New Age shop.

Later that day Jonathan and Ulla call. Scott listens avidly to what they are telling him on the phone and sends them a big kiss before hanging up.

In the evening, Scott and I lie alone on the floor in front of the fire, exhausted and overfed, but contented in our love for each other and for all our friends. In the quiet, we exchange our gifts. Scott leans into me and whispers his gift: a secret message of hope and love and gratitude, and as tears brim in my eyes he plants a kiss on my cheek. My gift will take a moment, I tell him, rising. I go quickly to the garage and back, and place on the floor a floppy-eared, sandy and white rabbit. As the rabbit lops about, sniffing out its new home, Scott's eyes burn bright with joy, then turn distant as he travels to a far-off place in the recesses of his memory.

I know exactly where he is. I'm there too. Back in time to our house in the redwoods with our red geraniums, old sheepdogs, hamsters, bunnies and a rat named Root Beer. Back to a time when life was simple, pure and full of youth, long before the leg splints, the pain and the infections.

'What will you name your rabbit?' I finally ask, hesitant to disrupt his reverie.

Scott is quiet for a long time. 'I think I'll name him Thumper.'

I start laughing. 'Scott, do you realize that at this very moment, in millions of homes around the world, every single Christmas rabbit is being named Thumper? Is that what you want?' I guess it is. So intent are Scott's eyes on Thumper as he hops around the room that he never answers. Oh well, what's in a name, anyway?

That night when I rise to check on Scott and make sure he's turned over, I find Thumper curled in a ball beside his bed, fast asleep. Already they are good friends. In the days ahead when Scott is in his wheelchair, Thumper will lope up and stand on his rear legs with a paw on Scott's leg, begging to be hoisted into his lap. I watch Scott reach down and with great gentleness scoop up the rabbit, who within moments burrows into his lap and under his tender strokes promptly falls asleep.

Cleaning up the next day I find Ben's toolbox stowed in a corner of the kitchen. I'm slightly confused. I knew he was uncomfortable, that was obvious, but did it mean anything? I'm not sure. The gala party is now less than a week away, so I throw myself into sewing my New Year's Eve gown. Since I haven't heard to the contrary, it's better to assume the best and set about making something any woman would like to own.

On New Year's Eve, Sammy phones from America to talk to

Scott and thank him for making such a lovely painting. Scott spent many hours on it with such love in his heart and we'd sent it as Sam's Christmas present. I see Scott's face crinkling into a smile at what Sam says to him, something secret I think. After he hangs up the phone, I stand before the mirror making last-minute adjustments to my gown. It is black and strapless, with a full-cut long black skirt. Down the left side of the skirt I have embroidered a chain of miniature leaves in gold thread. My hair is up, make-up applied, and I'm wearing a crystal necklace that belonged to my grandmother. The nurse has arrived, and is quite competent and cheerful, so I feel good about leaving Scott in her hands. Whatever the night brings, I am ready. But will he show up?

Three hours later, I decide he won't. The nurse and Scott keep looking at me without saying anything. I keep playing 'Over the Rainbow' over and over, and strutting up and down the stairs. Suddenly Scott takes my hand and starts kissing it to make me feel loved. Of course, I think to myself, it doesn't matter if Ben shows up – I have plenty of love right here at home. Finally I change to my nightgown, dismiss the nurse, tuck Scott in bed, put lavender oil on him, wish him a happy new year though it hasn't arrived yet, shut off the lights, and crawl into bed.

I shouldn't be surprised, I think as I lie in the darkness. The signs were certainly there. The gaunt face upon seeing Scott, his rapid exit. And he didn't call to reconfirm. But I was happy in my Cinderella dream. I should be angry, but I'm not. Ben's an only child from a well-to-do family and has been sheltered for so much of his life. In that regard he's no different from so many others. I haven't room in my heart to be upset with people just because they are unable to accept Scott. But then, I really never knew Ben, did I?

What if his life's been so filled with pain and suffering that he could bear no more? What if . . . I slip into sleep without finishing the thought.

About a month later, I receive a call. 'Glenys, this is Ben.' His voice is thin and nervous. 'I left my toolbox at your place on Christmas Day. Might I come by and collect it?'

'Of course,' I answer cheerily. 'It's right here waiting for you.'

'In about an hour?'

'An hour will be fine.' Hanging up, my mind is swirling with mischief. Why not have some fun? I run upstairs and change. When the knock comes, I throw open my door and watch Ben's eyes grow large. I'm dressed in my black, strapless gown, my hair up, face fully made up, my crystal necklace on.

'Happy New Year, Ben!' I say with a bright smile. 'You're a little late.' I hand him the toolbox. He is stunned and leaves without a word. I climb the stairs to change, and pause in front of the mirror, self-righteously smug, though the feeling soon fades. Maybe it wasn't the right thing to do; maybe I should have been more gentle. But I was disappointed. It was fun. I do feel better.

Thirteen

The blues of winter have set in. The holidays are behind us and spring is a distant dream. Outside my bay window, the trees on the common stand cold and bare, their life force retracted, while on the wet pavements of the village, black umbrellas have sprouted like mushrooms and the whole country has plunged into cold. It is my first British winter in half a lifetime.

Siobhan returns after spending the holidays with her family in Dublin, and once more our kitchen fills with exotic aromas as we cook up hearty food to keep our bodies and spirits fully charged. In the evenings, our Irish Pan retreats to her upstairs lair and our cottage is again filled with pixie-like melodies. Scott no longer sits in the garage with the door rolled up, waving to passers-by or listening to his music as he exercises his hand. It's too cold and damp and I have a nagging fear of pneumonia or some other virus attacking his weakened immune system. Claire and Holly still knock on our door, together or singly, not to push Scott on those meandering journeys of summer, but to sit with him in mostly one-sided conversation and tempt him with apple dumplings or cookies they have freshly baked. When they mentally tire, they take turns rubbing his back and arms without talking.

After eight months of professional care for Scott, I'm at a loss how to handle the full burden that now falls upon me. The series of reprieves from Dr Rhys that allowed Scott to continue his treatment have, unconsciously, filled me with false expectation. As I clean the house and cook, as I work with Scott on improving his speech and on the physical exercises necessary to maintain his strength, an almost unnoticed part of me is waiting for the phone to ring and for Dr Rhys to say, 'I have good news for you, Glenys. We've had a cancellation. A spot has opened for Scott. How soon can you bring him in?' But as the days slip by and there is no call, I come to terms fully with reality. Scott's continued development is my responsibility. Not the world's, but mine. So what am I going to do about it?

There's another problem. In many ways Scott's progress has put him beyond my ability to help. In Sydney his therapy was all about bringing him out of a deep coma and rescuing his atrophied muscles and ligaments. Massaging, stretching and working his muscles while he lay in bed were within my competence and that of my volunteers. In London, Scott's needs have changed. He's healthier and physically stronger, his legs are straighter and he has more mobility. He can stand with assistance, and take a few steps, awkward and halting though they may be, with someone on either side of him. Now continued improvement will require more sophisticated treatment than I can provide: water exercises, weight machines, parallel bars, staff to lift and balance him, and the services of a professional speech therapist, perhaps even an occupational therapist. Volunteers will still be critical so he doesn't lose ground, and to lift his spirits and keep him motivated, so I can't let up on that front.

Where will I find those machines and professionals? National Health hospitals are understaffed and overburdened, and with only five specialist hospitals in all of Great Britain, where will I search? I can't afford a private hospital. A conversation I overheard a few weeks back between hospital therapists comes to mind. They were discussing a small rehab hospital that has wonderful facilities and is underused, but they din't say where. I call Wendy to see if she knows of it.

'Yes I think I've heard of such a place,' she says after a pause. 'It might be a private hospital. It's a few miles out of Wimbledon, I believe, not sure where actually, but I'll look into it and give you a ring. And Glenys,' she adds, 'we do miss Scott at the hospital. I'm terribly sorry we can't accommodate him. We feel like we've lost a son.' I thank Wendy for her kind thoughts and hang up. If the hospital staff feel they've lost a son, then Scott and I have lost a family. We'd become so close over the months. But we haven't moved away, have we? This is our home and we can still visit.

Wendy calls back the same day with directions and later that week I'm driven by a friend to a small town thirty or forty minutes away and deposited at the gates of a large facility. It's not a private hospital, I quickly learn, but a military hospital, located on a military base. This is hardly what I'd anticipated, and I feel out of place, but if they can help Scott it will be worth the distance and discomfort.

Marching up to the uniformed security guard, I announce with all the authority I can muster, 'I'm looking for the person in charge of rehabilitation.'

'Yes, ma'am,' the guard responds, looking up from paperwork with a disinterested half-glance. 'Commander Jones.'

'Right, it's Commander Jones. I'm afraid I forgot his name since my last visit. He's in the building over there,' I add, looking vaguely in the direction of several single-storey structures.

The guard turns about to look, guiding me with his gaze. 'The far one beyond, actually, in the entrance and to your right.'

Thankfully the guard doesn't bother to ask my business, and I quickly march on, passing a large Georgian three-storey house of dark brick, and make a beeline toward the complex of low buildings as if I've every right to be there. Finding the commander's office, I march in, but a typist behind a desk blocks my way. Quickly I scan the room for another soul, but find only a case of books against a far wall. The other walls are filled with pictures of military men and the prime minister, and some certificates in black frames.

'I'm here to see Commander Jones,' I announce, and the typist springs off to find him. After some minutes he arrives, a dashing uniformed man with a stiff demeanour and a thin David Niven moustache. Seeing me, he raises a questioning brow.

'Commander Jones,' I begin, but not with the same bravado I felt earlier – the officer is a bit intimidating. 'My name is Glenys Carl. My son has suffered a head injury from a serious fall and is in need of advanced rehabilitation. I've been told your facility is possibly the finest in all England, and I wanted to visit you before deciding where to place him.' Hearing my praise, the commander's face lights up and he mumbles something about the reputation being well deserved. I resume: 'Would it be possible to take a short tour?'

'It's rather a small facility, actually,' he says crisply, 'but I'd be pleased to show you around a little, and let you see the pool.'

The tour doesn't take long. The weight room is impressive, as are the Olympic-size indoor pool and the beautifully outfitted physical therapy room, all mysteriously empty of patients at that particular moment. When we finish, back in his office, I'm complimentary. 'You have very modern and impressive equipment,' I say, 'much better than other hospitals I've visited.'

He waves a hand in modesty. 'This facility was built after the Falklands War to treat casualties. We are rather proud of it.'

'But you don't seem to have many patients,' I say. 'Why is it so empty? Is it because there's not a war on right now?' The commander's face darkens, but I press on. 'This would be perfect, nearly empty, with lots of personal attention. I'd like to bring my son here if that would be possible.'

'That might be arranged,' he says guardedly. 'What unit is he in?'

'Oh, my son's not in the military, he's a civilian. But he needs a really good rehab facility. Obviously you have that, and you do have plenty of room.'

The commander stares at me incredulously. Evidently he assumed my son was in military service, since I have got onto the base and into his office.

'How did you get in here?' he blurts out, his face an interesting shade of embarrassed red. I notice he seems to be having trouble breathing.

'Why, I asked for you at the gate. They pointed the way and gave me directions.'

'This is a military facility. We can't help your son here.'

'The government's already paying for his care,' I protest. 'Why couldn't you collect it? Wouldn't that be possible? Or if necessary I could pay myself. What's wrong with that idea?'

Commander Jones looks at me as if I am out of my mind, but I persist until he agrees to enquire about the possibility. Yet as I walk back towards the car, I know it won't happen. He's simply trying to get rid of me, and I'll hear nothing more, I suspect. And I'm right.

After my encounter with the commander, it's painfully clear I will have to stop grasping at straws and renew my focus on volunteers. They are, after all, the reason Scott's come this far. More importantly, their caring is rooted in compassion, love and commitment, not in salary, and that extra ingredient is a crucial part of the healing process. It is time to follow up with Susan's friend, the headmaster.

'I know you're going to like Robin very much,' Susan says when I call. 'Let me give him a ring and call you back.'

A few days later, with a volunteer watching Scott, I'm wrapped like an Eskimo and hiking across the windy common towards King's College School, a private school a shade over a mile away. I'm thrilled at the prospect of recruiting students. So many young people volunteered in Sydney and their enthusiasm, creativity and boundless energy were so infectious. They'd light up the darkest room.

Robin is about forty, of medium height, and casually dressed in a pullover, trousers and tweed jacket, all shades of grey. 'Susan speaks generously of you,' he says right off, as our footsteps echo on the hallway leading to his office. 'I'm quite interested in your story. Our school stresses community service; I believe Susan may have told you that.' His office, panelled in dark wood with a high ceiling and a row of imposing windows overlooking a courtyard, is cosy in spite of its size, and cluttered with books.

'I've invited a few of our student leaders to meet you,' Robin says, as four boys rise in unison from a table. They are in their mid-teens and dressed in the school uniform of navy-blue sweater, grey flannel trousers and maroon tie. After introductions we sit opposite the boys and I explain about Scott and our need for volunteers.

They are full of questions. Does Scott play sports? What was school like in America? If they come and help, mightn't they hurt him? Can he eat by himself? How does he go to the toilet? And on

245

and on. I answer as best I can, but soon realize that Scott's condition is an abstraction for these youngsters. They've most likely never met someone like him. To make this work I will have to become a teacher again. Still, I'm quite taken with them, with their Queen's English, the way they sit, their disciplined motions and infinite politeness. They're so proper and mature, so very British. I want to scoop them up and hug them all.

'They're just back from holiday, you understand,' Robin tells me as he escorts me out. 'Give them two or three weeks to settle in, then ring me up. I'm leaving it to the leaders but,' and he flashes a knowing smile, 'I'm sure something can be arranged.'

I'm so excited I fairly float across the common towards home. They're such perfect little gentlemen, little lawyers and accountants and doctors. Scott will love them. If only a few volunteer, we'll be the richer.

A couple of weeks into the new year, Claire appears with an unusually wide smile on her face. 'My mother sent something for you,' she says, then absently hands me an envelope as her attention is drawn to Scott in his wheelchair in front of the fireplace. I slit the envelope and a brass key falls into my hand. 'It's for the rehab room at the hospital,' Claire adds without glancing my way, intent on the chair she is pulling up next to Scott. 'Mum says if you go after four, you can have it all to yourself, and she says to tell you that Dr Rhys knows all about it so you don't have to worry.'

I turn the key over in my hand. Truly a key to the kingdom. It will be dry and warm with equipment. And a place to go to relieve the cabin fever of our cramped cottage. I can't help but think, where else would I be given a key without being a patient? Where else would they take the risk? I'm so happy they trust me. I'm so thankful there are still places in the world where the social fabric is whole enough to allow this trust. It's not long before I've rescheduled my volunteers to meet us once or twice a week in the rehab room of the hospital.

While the winter sun rarely shines in London, it doesn't rain all the time either, so I do take Scott for walks. As I push him through the village one afternoon, I'm approached by two strapping young men. 'Can we give you a hand?' one asks. 'Yes, please,' I say, exhausted by the thought of getting him all the way home by myself. Why was it so much easier to push him in the summer sun? Is it the winter boots slowing my feet, and the weight of our heavy clothing?

Nicholas, the taller of these two large fellows, is blond with Scandinavian features, and Justin is swarthy and has arms like logs. They've been on the British Olympic rowing team, they tell me as I walk comfortably between them towards home, Justin pushing Scott with only one arm, the other casually tucked in a pocket of his denim trousers.

'If you boys really want to help,' I say, 'I really need you in the evenings, getting Scott bathed and to bed. There's so much lifting. Not every night, of course, but every once in a while would be wonderful. You can have dinner with us if you wish.'

Dinner is an incentive I sometimes use to try to tip the balance with a prospective volunteer. It is the right strategy with these boys, almost too right. They accept my offer not just once but regularly, and I haven't even stopped to think what massive appetites these giant athletes have. They come nearly every Friday evening, always with girlfriends, or in Nicholas's case, girls – a different one each time. I begin to wonder if he is using the visits to Scott as a scheme to test their resilience and weed out the faint of heart; or, I wonder in less generous moments, is it to soften her heart and introduce the idea of physical contact into the evening's activities? But they are nothing less than wonderful, as volunteers and as friends. Upon arriving each Friday, either Nicholas or Justin picks Scott up, takes him upstairs for a bath, helps him dry off, dresses him and carries him back down to bed. The other one, along with the two girl-friends, will be in the kitchen, either cooking up a storm or else drinking beer while Siobhan or I do the cooking.

Our Friday meal started months ago as a quiet, end-of-the-week ritual with candles and music for Scott and myself. With Siobhan's arrival it became dinner for three with exotic recipes. Now with these fun-loving young men and their ladyfriends, it is dinner for seven, and those two strapping rowers eat enough for five or six ordinary bodies. My shopping budget is sorely strained.

Soon other volunteers learn of the Friday Olympic team dinners, and drop by to meet the boys and stay for food. As the circle grows, some bring cooked dishes and others pitch in as kitchen help, filling our cramped space with more hands than can be used. We eat cross-legged on the living room floor in front of the fire. Through the middle of it all lopes a fully grown Thumper, over and around and between our legs, sniffing out the food and causing great hilarity. Thank goodness these boisterous dinners don't happen every night. Scott and I still have plenty of the quiet time together that we both treasure. But once a week my home is again a salon filled with interesting people, their doings, conversation and love. How can I possibly complain?

Another volunteer I've grown fond of is Colin, an interior designer who works for a well-known company on the Kings Road.

He comes to our cottage after work or on Saturday morning, his arms full of fabrics left over from his business. Colin enjoys my design sense, and encourages me to try new ideas. With great enthusiasm, he spills forth one outlandish decorating idea after another, and I quickly turn his fabrics into all shapes and sizes of pillows, or weave them into wreaths, fabric hangings and other decorations. I love his *bon vivant* company and the creative stimulation he provides, as this in turn enables me to more creatively stimulate Scott.

Scott always joins my creative endeavours with enthusiasm. He helps to organize little bits of fabric, placing them together before I sew them to see which patterns complement each other. He looks intently at each pattern, tossing his rejects to the floor, using only one hand.

The small antiques I continue to collect in my forays with Ingrid – bells, candlesticks, picture frames, a birdcage – along with the pillows and fabric sculptures I've made, turn our cottage into an eclectic gallery with no rhyme and not very much order. But somehow the design sense works and it all hangs together.

When I call Robin back after a few weeks, he is enthusiastic. 'I believe the arrangements have been made. We've had a sign-up for those interested, and two dozen, perhaps more have enrolled, a rather good turnout I should say. When should they begin?'

'Next Monday,' I tell him.

'Very good, I'll pass the word. Monday after school. If this works, we'll make it part of our curriculum.'

On the appointed day, five nattily attired King's College boys are standing about Scott in my living room. There is apprehension in their young eyes, so I give a short educational talk on head injuries and comas, and what happens to the body. I tell them how it's important for someone with these injuries to stay active, because with the proper stimulation, the brain has a way of compensating for injury.

'Scott is a human being, just like your brothers or sisters or your friends at school,' I tell them. 'There's nothing to fear. You won't break him. Just don't pull on his bad arm and he'll be fine. Anything else you want to try, stretching his legs or his muscles and ligaments, or massaging his back or calves, will be welcome. And you can talk to him, he needs mental stimulation. He may not always answer, but he understands perfectly. His mind is very sharp.'

With the boys gathered around Scott on his bed, I demonstrate some of the simplest and most effective techniques I've found, gradually turning over the responsibility to their hesitant hands. In our culture it's hard for males to touch other males in a loving way. They may do well with their fathers or brothers, or a close friend, but with strangers it's a different matter. These boys have to learn to break that cultural taboo and feel comfortable about it.

When they return a few days later, they are more at ease and jump right in without prompting, and the new boys follow smoothly. During their second week, as I go about my household chores, I hear laughter coming from the living room. I look in to find them all gathered round a chessboard, coaching Scott in strategy, but mostly arguing loudly among themselves.

Or I'll find them trying to stand him up, egging him on with cheers and large helpings of adolescent laughter. When the weather clears, they have Scott in his wheelchair racing down the pavement as fast as they can push. The boys are always trying something new with my son and overflow with suggestions for techniques or devices to increase his flexibility and circulation. Though I'm mostly sceptical, I do listen appreciatively, and even try out a few of their ideas on occasion. It's a mistake to discredit creative young minds.

Over a month, two dozen boys churn through our cottage in chaotic fashion until finally they sort themselves into groups and settle on a schedule of three days a week. Sometimes on off days they drop scribbled little notes in my letterbox asking if they might come at the weekend, how I am doing, or if I need someone to run errands and do the shopping. I wonder whether they offer their own mothers this kind of help. By this time, I've fallen madly in love with them all. They're eager, boisterous and inspiring, and bring much joy into our home. They're always ravenous, consuming whatever treats I set out down to the last crumb. In so many ways, they remind me of my boys as teenagers and Scott eagerly awaits their thrice-weekly visits.

Perhaps it is the involvement of the schoolboys, or something else might have triggered the media, but I soon find myself talking to another reporter from the Wimbledon *Guardian*. She's following up on the story the paper ran before Christmas. 'Are there any changes in your son's condition?' asks the young reporter, all business, with an open notepad.

'Before, Scott was in rehabilitation in the hospital,' I say as her pencil flies, 'but as of the new year he's been discharged, and we no longer have access to professional help or facilities. I am like many other people. I have to rely on myself and volunteers now.' I go on about the lack of hospital beds for brain-injured patients, noting that great sums are allocated for saving lives in the emergency room, only to leave the patient vegetating for months or even years because of a shortage of long-term care. Therapy programmes are terribly underfunded and their staffs overworked, and the waiting list is two years or longer in this country, I tell the reporter, who has filled several pages with notes. 'Think of it, years of nothing until they receive professional help. But it's not just England. It's the same in Australia, the US, Germany and France. And these are the wealthiest countries in the world.'

A few days later a rather lengthy article about us appears in the *Guardian*. And I am surprised to see a separate article on the same page where Dr Rhys is quoted, pleading his case in very strong terms for more resources. I marvel at the man putting his reputation and future on the line in support of head-injured patients. What a huge heart he must have to take such a risk, I think to myself. Half-foreign though I may be, I know that employees of the health service in Great Britain, and especially a senior physician, are not seen to complain openly. It just isn't the done thing to make waves. But then, I have always found Dr Rhys to be an exceptional man.

I put the paper aside, not knowing what a storm it will generate. Within a few days I receive a call from Dr Rhys. 'Glenys, we're about to have a visit from Princess Diana. As you may remember, she's the patron of Headway, the charity institution for brain-injured children. She's also quite involved with our hospital. I was thinking you might wish to bring Scott in for her visit. He's been one of our star patients and might enjoy meeting her.'

'That's a lovely idea,' I say. 'I'm sure Scott will be thrilled. By the way, I read about you in the *Guardian*. I was surprised, actually.'

'Yes, well, so was I,' Dr Rhys says uncomfortably. 'This reporter pops in to say she's interviewed you about rehab conditions and funding and needs a few comments from me. I probably said too much. It needed saying, but still . . .' He drifts off and is silent for some seconds. When he speaks again his tone is quiet and measured. 'This visit has happened rather quickly. I think those articles may be responsible. Having Scott here might be useful.' There's more to be said, I sense, but after I thank him for the invitation we hang up.

When the day arrives, Luther bundles Scott into the taxi and we set off for the hospital. There is much hustle and bustle, with security squads roving around. Everything is especially shiny and orderly, and everyone is excited at the possibility of being introduced to the princess herself. The cafeteria has been converted to a large reception area, filled with masses of flowers, and all the staff and patients are dressed in their Sunday best. It is a big day for the hospital, something that rarely happens.

When Princess Diana arrives and enters the room, she acknowledges the nurses and spends ten or fifteen minutes talking to various patients in a warm manner, asking them questions, giving them encouragement, and flashing her famous smile. She speaks briefly with Dr Rhys, and with the MP for Wimbledon. After a half hour or so she is whisked away to another part of the building, and that is all we see of her. Neither Scott nor I have the opportunity to actually meet her.

After she leaves, everyone rushes to the main table for the special sweets that have been laid out – a sponge cream cake, a chocolate cake and fairy cakes – along with the typical cucumber sandwiches and lemonade. Before the Princess arrived I had been introduced briefly to our MP, Dr Goodson Wickes. Now he seeks me out, and we sit on a bench in the hallway and talk for some twenty minutes. I recount my experience in Australia, telling him the system is just as short-funded there. I point out how endless funds and pride seem to be invested in emergency care and intensive care, but then for the follow-through with so many head-injured patients, there is always a budget to be adhered to and it is all too limited.

Dr Goodson-Wickes was a physician in general practice before standing for his seat. He asks about the specifics of Scott's injury and how I find and train my volunteers and what they are able to do. He is especially interested in how effective my volunteers have been, as my experiences have been similar in two countries. He tells me he has children of his own, and I can feel his sincerity as he talks of what a tragedy head injury can be because of the lingering, multiple effects. A few years later I would learn that he took leave from Parliament during the Gulf War to go on active duty as a doctor in the war zone.

I felt that the MP had taken my points fully, but I am nevertheless surprised when he contacts me two weeks later to inform me of the specific initiatives he is taking to alleviate the plight of head-injured patients. He is working with the regional health officer and with Dr Rhys to press for funding to open additional beds. I am very impressed with the swiftness of his response and the direct plan of action. Dr Goodson-Wickes takes a personal interest in Scott's case, asking to be advised about his progress. Yet it is not just our own case that stands to benefit from my encounter with him that day, but also the many others with head injuries in London and across the UK.

Over the next few weeks, two other articles on the plight of the head-injured and the lack of resources appear in the Wimbledon *Guardian*. Though I haven't been interviewed further, Scott's situation is mentioned each time, and my points from the earlier article are paraphrased. I marvel at how the stories feed off each other in a continuing cycle. Each new round of publicity generates calls from complete strangers, people thinking of volunteering who want to know exactly what they'd be getting into, as well as cars moving slowly down our street trying to locate our cottage.

Another high-profile situation develops through one of my regular volunteers, Chris, who is a student at the British School of Osteopathy. He was introduced by another volunteer and after assessing Scott's situation, pitched right in. He is a studious young man, bright, alert, lacking in pretence and dedicated to his profession, with a special interest in cranial osteopathy. He visits every ten days, as if making a house call, to work with Scott and monitor his progress. One day he phones me.

'Glenys, I've got a favour to ask,' he says. 'You know that nerve machine I've been telling you about? Well, Princess Anne is visiting our college at the end of the week for a demonstration, and I thought with Scott in the newspapers lately, and since I do personally treat him, he might make the perfect subject. Would you help out?'

Chris has developed a scanning machine that can identify which of the cranial nerves are blocked and where, using a multicolour display. Several times he's brought Scott to the college to run tests with the machine, and he has spent considerable time explaining the results to me.

Of course I say yes. Princess Anne is the patron of the college, and while her visit might not help Scott medically, it could be a terrific boost to Chris's career. While I'm only mildly curious about meeting the princess, I'm happy to be able to return a favour to Chris, and as ever I'm ready to do anything for my son's sake.

The demonstration is set up in a large treatment room. Scott is in his wheelchair next to the machine, which stands on a stainless-steel cart. The row of doctors and staff standing along one side tenses visibly as Princess Anne enters the room. Being at this time rather an Americanized subject, I'm unsure what's expected of me, so I stay inconspicuously out of the way. The head doctor introduces Chris as the inventor of the nerve machine, and he in turn introduces Scott as the patient and me as his mother. The princess extends a white-gloved hand for a brief but firm handshake. Her gaze is level and steady and I sense that in spite of the numerous and no doubt tedious visits she's required to make all over the kingdom, she is a warm person, and genuinely interested in the advancement of medicine.

Chris removes Scott's shirt and attaches wires to his arms and chest and the demonstration begins. After fifteen minutes of explanations, with the screen flashing a variety of rainbows, it is over and Chris disconnects the wires. The princess says goodbye to Scott, then turns slightly towards me. After a formal farewell, she adds quietly, 'It's rather a nasty day outside. I would think your son would be warmer with his shirt on.' Then she turns and leaves to visit another part of the college. As I help Scott with his shirt, I sheepishly wonder how Her Highness recognized that Scott was cold before I did. I'm impressed with her thoughtfulness.

Chris phones again a couple of weeks later, bubbling with excitement. Thanks to the successful demonstration, he has received additional funding to continue development of his machine. I'm very happy for him.

The knocks on our door are now all too frequent, but one of them yields a long-lost face, wearing a huge grin. It is Niall, Scott's mate from his Burger King days in Copenhagen. I scream with delight and drag my fourth son inside for a long, joyful and tear-stained hug. He's filled out, but his Irish blue eyes are as quick and full of mischief as ever. When he and Scott shared a flat in Copenhagen, I flew over and spent several weeks with them. Later, after travelling through Europe, they came together to Westport to find their next jobs, and lived with me for a year, an idyllic time I've always cherished. When Scott set out for Australia, Niall accompanied him as far as London. That was over three years ago.

'How did you find us?' I gush, bursting with tearful happiness. He smiles his wicked smile, as if carrying a great secret. 'How about the phone book, Mom?' Then his smile fades. 'I hear Scott's had an accident. I've been living in Dublin but have just taken a job in London. This is the first chance I've had the time to look you up.'

From the entry hall where we have been clutching each other, I lead Niall into the living room where Scott is lying in front of the fire. He falls to his knees beside him. Scott's cheeks are wet with tears as he hooks the good arm firmly around his old friend's neck. When Niall finally looks up at me he is visibly shaken and struggles to hold back tears.

That night while he puts Scott to bed, I watch these two grown men with silent awe. Niall arranges Scott's covers and pyjamas, then tenderly brushes the hair from his eyes. He stays the night, and well into the next day, helping Scott through his dressing and morning exercises, before returning to the city.

These two have taken very different roads the past few years, but their friendship, forged seven years earlier while flipping hamburgers, remains deep and strong. Now each Sunday night, a time that we have kept outside the swirl of volunteers, Niall joins us for a simple dinner of soup and bread. And in the simplicity of that sharing, I always feel profoundly at peace with life, and richly blessed in our abundance of friendship.

Fourteen

With Scott home full time, I have few opportunities for morning coffee and paper at Annabel's. Not only must a volunteer be with him while I'm absent, but it must be someone trustworthy, someone with solid instincts, calm, collected and capable should something happen. So when the chance presents itself I'm off to the patisserie to sit in my favourite chair by the window.

I watch the people stream by, wondering who they are and where they're going and what their lives are like. And I wonder, when they return home, if there is someone to welcome them. I weave their life stories in my mind. Ever since childhood part of me has lived in this world of fantasy. I've often wondered why. Perhaps because it's safer, purer, untouched by human tragedy. I know it brings great comfort. As I observe life stream by, I sip my coffee slowly, savouring every drop as if it were life itself, until I'm left staring pensively into my empty cup. What I enjoy so much lasts so little time.

Then I gather my things and meander through the village towards home, dawdling in front of shop windows, studying the newest designs of clothes on plastic mannequins in one, eyeing an antique clock in another, a display of freshly baked breads and pastries in a third. Mostly I take the same route and stop before the same windows, and after a while I begin to wonder what I'm looking for

– the reassurance of sameness, or the possibility of change. When the mannequins change clothes I regret the passing of the old, yet I'm drawn to the novelty of the new. It's a strangely unsettled feeling being caught between these two worlds, but these days that's what my life's all about.

At the moment I'm reading an advert in a gym window. 'Lose inches with no effort. Let our machines do the work.' Why am I even bothering with this? I'm thinking absently. I don't need to lose weight; if anything I need to gain it. But I've always been interested in what machines do with the body. So with free time and little else to do, I walk in. When the receptionist looks up I tell her I'm curious about what they offer, and she invites me to tour the facilities. Standing in the doorway to a large windowless room filled with equipment, I watch several hefty women outfitted in designer gym clothes at work on a variety of machines. One is a table that you lie on while the bottom half moves from side to side, swinging the legs back and forth in unison. The receptionist tells me this is so you can have a small waist. I have other ideas.

Another one swings the legs open and closed like scissors to exercise the inner thighs. I do know someone who needs that sort of exercise. And there is one with independent sections that vibrate on either side of the upper back and move a little up and down. I later learn that it was designed some forty years ago for cystic fibrosis patients. But at this moment, I am thinking in terms of moving Scott's bad shoulder to loosen it up.

Then there is a table where the bottom half goes up and down to exercise the hips. And another that bends the knees. As I take it all in, I'm laughing to myself. The machines are doing all the work! What kind of exercise is that? Then the full realization dawns. This is exactly what Scott needs: mechanical volunteers. My real volunteers spend hours each week encouraging him to do exactly what these machines do in minutes. If Scott could have just twenty minutes on one of these, think of the progress we could make!

I'm so excited with my discovery I run all the way home and burst through the door gasping out my great find to three startled volunteers. 'We've got to go right now!' I tell them. 'Let's get Scott in a car and go to the gym. It's too rainy to push him across the common.'

Thirty minutes later the four of us are manoeuvring Scott's wheelchair down several steps and through the door into the gym. Before I darted off I'd made arrangements with the manager to return for a free demonstration. Of course I hadn't shared all the details with her, and now she stands open-mouthed as, in a swirl of commotion, we wheel Scott into the exercise room.

I can see from Scott's expression that he thinks this is another one of my fads but he is humouring me. Cautiously we try out every machine for a few minutes on the slowest setting. The most stressful part is getting Scott up onto each table. We strap his legs in place and the machine that opens like scissors pulls them apart and pushes them closed, stretching inner thigh muscles that have been beyond our manual manipulation. The vibrating machine runs up and down his back, focusing especially on the shoulder blades. The table with the elevating lower half gives Scott's lower back and abdominal muscles a workout. Then he's on the machine that bends his knees. I can see his enthusiasm growing as the machines move in a consistent and calibrated way to achieve smoothly in minutes what would take one or two people hours.

After thirty minutes of trials, Scott is back in his wheelchair and

I'm in the office with the manager. 'Can we arrange a membership for my son?'

Dazed, she says 'Yes' in a quiet voice, having no doubt guessed what I will say next.

'We'll need only one membership, as my volunteers and I will be along strictly to lift him on and off the machines.'

I see the wheels begin to turn in her mind. Handicapped people may well be a new source of membership. She agrees to a special introductory rate for Scott, which mysteriously is never increased.

I'm very proud of myself for recognizing the possibilities. Ever since the military base episode I've been searching for such a solution, yet for months I've walked by this gym oblivious to its potential. For some unknown reason, this time I listened to my inner voice and went inside to discover a whole new world.

With the help of volunteers the gym becomes part of our weekly routine. After several visits, Scott's progress confirms that I'm on to something. The next Friday afternoon I hurry off to share my secret with the physiotherapists at the rehab hospital. I corner two of Scott's former therapists.

'I've found the answer to a lot of your problems, and to my problems.' I quickly relate my story of discovery. 'The machines are just what I need. They're just what *you* need. You've got to come and see these things; they're miracle workers.'

As sympathetic as the therapists have been with me in the past, all I get for my trouble now are sceptical looks. I press them harder, a little annoyed at their reluctance. 'Look here,' I say, 'you know me well enough. I'm telling you these machines do the job. Come and see for yourselves. I'll even pay for the taxi.'

A taxi isn't necessary. Either they credit me or they want to get rid of me, and we soon pull up before the gym in the car of one of the therapists. After a short tour I can see they're impressed, though they say little directly. 'Let's go to my home and get Scott,' I insist, 'and come back here for a real demonstration.' That's what we do, and after watching Scott go through another thirty minutes on the tables, the therapists admit to the possibilities.

Over the next few weeks I continue to pester them for action. Finally, the physiotherapy unit agrees the machines are beneficial, and soon two other brain-injured patients become a common sight in the gym, working to regain use of their atrophied limbs alongside Scott and the large ladies eager to lose inches.

None of this interferes with our intense therapy programme at home. Even as we reach out to facilities in the community, the number of volunteers continues to increase. More of our neighbours become involved, not just from our street, but from several streets away. Some walk in as guests of others, while some just appear on our front step asking hesitantly and in a roundabout way if they might be of service. As in Sydney I turn no one away.

Dominique is one of the neighbours, who appears with her two boys Alexander and Nicholas in tow. She's suddenly in our living room asking if they can meet Scott. Tall and slender, with short blonde hair in a stylish cut, she's impeccably dressed in the latest fashion and seems out of place in my home-spun environment. Reserved at first, she quickly turns boisterous and chatty upon encountering my fabric art and the clothing I've designed and created over the months. At once she commissions me to knit her a black wool sweater with small red roses near the right shoulder. Soon I have been paid commissions for several others, and once again what I learned of fashion, style, design, weaving and dyeing at

Nanna's knee serves me well. In the months ahead, Dominique frequently brings the boys round for short visits, and I greatly enjoy her companionship.

Another new friend is Jean, the owner of Fielder's Bookstore in the village. I love books and look forward to her visits. Over tea we discuss the newest releases and debate their merit compared to the classics we've been raised on. Jean is a petite woman who loves to ride her big chestnut horse on the common. She gives us a call and a while later appears in her black riding habit. With a clicking noise she urges the horse forward through the gate to our doorstep where Scott is waiting to feed her a green apple. The horse knows what to expect, and if Scott isn't outside she puts her nose through the front door, but comes no further.

Sometimes entire families volunteer. Ingrid, brown-haired and sad-eyed, has an infectious laugh that reverberates through our cottage. She's also a lover of antiques and has an intimate knowledge of every secret shop in every flea market in London. Her husband Duncan is quite the opposite. A very proper and softly spoken English gentleman, he would rather read quietly than tramp through cobwebs after neglected treasures. Ingrid and Duncan never appear without their three daughters, aged ten to fifteen, and the five of them quickly fill our home with energy and laughter.

Leaving Duncan in charge of Scott, who is always delighted to have the girls around, Ingrid and I sometimes slip off to comb the back streets for antiques. We return from one hunt with a beautiful old cage once used for fowl, a cube about two feet each way of weathered wood, with dowel bars around the sides and a door on top. I paint the cage beige-white and hang it sideways on the wall in the conservatory, with dried hops surrounding it, herbs and spring flowers growing through the bars. Immediately several volunteers place orders and in gratitude for their services, I now crawl with Ingrid through the flea markets on their behalf.

We return from antiquing one day with a brass bell that has a hoop attached and I give it to Scott to ring for emergencies. I soon discover it has an annoyingly harsh ring and I'm sorry I ever gave it to him. Every five minutes he rings and I come running, fearing the house is on fire. He seems to enjoy testing how fast I can respond. Very soon I grow tired of being tortured and I take it away until he promises he'll ring the bell only for real need.

On one excursion Ingrid and I chance upon an old and very dusty piece of exercise equipment buried under an avalanche of junk. I purchase it for just a few pounds, as the owner is more than happy to see it go. It's an inversion table, and with Duncan's help we set it up in the living room, lift Scott onto it, and strap down his ankles and knees. Manually we tilt the table gradually backward until Scott's feet are in the air. The idea is to harness gravity to stretch Scott's spine and feed more blood to his brain, but I dare only tilt him about sixty degrees, as I fear the bad arm will not hang comfortably upside down. And so another contraption is transformed and added to our arsenal.

Volunteers continue to find us, to my amazement, and they all have such big hearts. They roll up their sleeves and plunge in. Some come often, some only occasionally. Some are quiet and some are chatty. Some bring food, some bring strong backs and great energy. They all join our family and make our home theirs.

In many ways it's Sydney all over again, but interestingly, in some ways it's not. Susan was right when she told me months ago that under the frost London's waters are as warm as Sydney's, the land of sand and surf. Friendship in Sydney is brash, gregarious and colourful, always infected with a sense of festival. In London, land of history and grey weather, friendship is more subdued and seasoned, like watching an old movie, Bogart and Bergman in *Casablanca*, where emotions lie deep under layers of subtlety and where glances say so much. While it's taken longer to gather volunteers in London, partly due to Scott's lengthier stay in rehab, my early fears of being rebuffed by reticent Londoners were misguided.

Our cottage becomes as disorganized and serendipitous as our apartment in Sydney, with people coming and going, candles glowing and music filling the air. Aromas of spices, hot breads and vegetable soups waft from the kitchen, mixing with the lingering fragrances of lemon oil and lavender. My friends say even among all the commotion they always feel peaceful in my house of light.

We're caught by surprise to awaken from our winter hibernation to the yellow-green glaze of spring leaves on the common. I can't account for the last few months; it's been so hectic with daily schedules and nightly routines. My small kitchen calendar again says the end of April, and the number of the year has advanced by one, so with little notice Scott and I pass our first anniversary in London. Spring also unleashes change. Siobhan has graduated, and with bags packed and tearful farewells she's off to rejoin her family and teach music in Ireland. A strange emptiness settles over the cottage with our Pan now departed.

Just as I've adjusted to her absence, another prospective boarder turns up at our door. Jason is in his early twenties, and studying at a school of art and design. Of course when I hear those magic words I welcome him with open arms. He has delicate features with intense brown eyes and a lock of hair that's always falling in his face. He's always brushing it aside, but never cuts it off. There's nothing neat and tidy about creativity and I wholeheartedly endorse his desire for individuality. I warm to Jason even more when I learn of his passion for costume design and, still better, for opera costumes, one of my loves. We waste no time setting up mannequins in the living room and in the evenings, surrounded by swirls of bright fabric, yards of material, we design and create ornate jackets and coats and exotic ball gowns that could be used for the opera, but of course are not.

Scott and I wait eagerly for Jason to come home in the evenings. He is perpetually late, but always arrives in a state of excitement and tells fascinating stories of the opera world and the costumes and sets he's working on as an apprentice. On Friday nights he never fails to rush in with a large bouquet of flowers. Sometimes we play charades, with Scott waving his arms and making faces when it's his turn. In the mornings Jason is often first into the kitchen, and makes us breakfast while I wash Scott. After a quick bite he's up and away, racing through the front door, calling, 'I'm late, I'm late, I'm going to miss my bus!' – like Siobhan, like my boys, like students everywhere.

After a few months Jason moves in with a friend and once again our upstairs lair is empty, but he returns often with news and to see how Scott is doing. On one visit Jason is positively over the moon. 'I've secured a position as a designer with the Royal Opera House in Covent Garden!' he announces, so excited he can barely sit. I'm very proud of him, and wonder secretly if one of the designs the two of us cooked up in our living room might one day grace the stage of a major production.

I consider once again renting the upstairs bedroom, but decide against it as, like our garden flowers, our lives are blooming and filling our space, and more than ever our evening privacy becomes a priority. Scott and I announce the warmer weather by rolling up the door of the garage so he can sit in his wheelchair looking out and stroking a curled-up Thumper in his lap. Once again he can view the expanse of the common and meet and greet passersby. Last summer he could carry on a broken conversation with those who stopped to chat, while this year he can do little more than acknowledge their greetings with a wave and a smile, remaining quiet.

Summer also brings more visits from Susan and her daughters Claire and Holly. Several of our friends from the rehab hospital, as well as some of the staff from St George's who live around Wimbledon, drop in on their way to and from work. Even a few of the doctors stop by sometimes, and I'm gratified, even a bit surprised, at their interest in my son's welfare. Arnold appears more often now with Justin, and we wheel our sons in formation, crisscrossing the village in search of new sights and adventures. The boys of King's College are on summer holiday so they no longer volunteer in an organized fashion, but I still receive notes in my letterbox from individual students asking if they might stop in to see Scott. I'm impressed and welcome them – such a sense of compassion from such young men.

I have eagerly resumed my solitary walks on the common, constantly entranced by the myriad shades of green, bright and dull, tinged with yellows or purples or blues, hues only nature could create. As I tramp the narrow brown paths, sometimes muddy and sodden from showers, my mind is freed to find creative ways to move Scott forward. Last season we managed the small miracle of getting him on his feet. This season we're pushing for the next miracle of getting him to walk. Supported by a pair of volunteers, he can already manage a few steps, but the effort required to get him onto his feet and hold him upright means he's not likely to have enough practice to achieve balance. That's the problem: how do we keep Scott on his feet long enough to develop his muscles and sense of balance?

Well, how do babies do it? My mind returns to when my boys were learning to walk. I remember putting them in a bouncer so their feet could touch the floor but they were still supported. As they bounced, they would work their leg muscles and feel the balls of their feet against the floor. Sometimes they'd stand for a few moments before toppling gently against the restraints. Once their brains linked their feet with balance, they could stand for longer, and of course that eventually led to walking. That's what Scott needs: a bouncer.

With a solution in mind I rush home and set to work. Scott's too big for a bouncer that stands on the floor, but maybe I could devise a hanging one. I call around to volunteers and soon have a large piece of grey canvas, which I trim and shape into an adult-sized nappy, with straps across the front where safety pins might go. I attach four ropes to the edges and tie them at the top to a spring I've bought at a hardware store, and that's attached to a metal eye hook. Feeling satisfied with my creation, I send a volunteer up a step ladder to screw the hook into the brown beam that separates the conservatory from the living room, and the nappy hangs ready at the end of the ropes. Ready for his maiden voyage, Scott is wheeled over and with the help of two volunteers I stand him up and strap him in. Then we all move back as Scott flexes his leg muscles and begins to bounce.

All is going perfectly and I'm smugly congratulating myself on my ingenuity when disaster strikes. With a loud crash and a chorus of screams, the beam tears loose from the ceiling and falls on Scott, who is collapsed in a heap on the floor. Pieces of plaster fly and the air quickly fills with dust. We rush to pull the debris off Scott, expecting the worst, but he peers up at us smiling, his brown eyes the only colour amid a layer of white dust, and out of a great sense of relief we all break into fits of hysterical laughter. Scott laughs with us, his tears forming dark lines on his white face.

'Why not hitch this thing to the tree outside?' one of the volunteers says. That's a grand idea, and so we move outside and screw the eye hook firmly into a branch of the flame tree. Soon Scott is bouncing slowly up and down and the tree seems not to mind at all. Success! But my thoughts quickly return to the disaster. I'm in big trouble. The beam was ornamental and the ceiling has a jagged tear. This house is still actually listed for sale. I'll have to get it repaired quickly before the estate agent hears about it. That problem too is taken care of in the next few days by volunteers with building skills. The ceiling looks new, and I feel fortunate that in the end no damage has been done.

But as our summer days roll on, my thoughts turn towards autumn and the cold, wet winter with its long nights, and increasingly I begin to consider Scott's medical future, what would be best for him. While I'm a native and can adjust to English winters, the last one was hard on Scott. As he cannot exercise like a normal person, the damp cold ate into his joints and settled into his chest, and we had to work even harder to keep him active and ward off congestion. His life in California was filled with bright skies, sunshine and ocean breezes, as it was in Sydney. I sense he's homesick. When I ask Scott if he'd like to return to California, he nods vigorously. Maybe it's time to get back to our other home in

America. There might be more advanced methods of rehab in the Golden State, though without insurance they will be expensive.

I've also been thinking of Scott's other futures, including one without me. I've no doubt he will outlive his mother, and who will take care of him then? I don't want to burden my other sons with that prospect, even though when I express my concerns to Jonathan he quickly dismisses them. 'Mom, you shouldn't worry about that; that's years away, and even if it were to happen, Scott would be more than welcome in our home.' I'm gratified at my children's love for each other. I don't even know at the time that Ulla has been looking into purchasing an insurance policy to provide security for him later on in life; when I do find out, I'm deeply moved by her thoughtfulness. Yet I feel that Scott is my responsibility, not theirs, and that it is I who must consider where he would be most comfortable in the long term and try to prepare for that.

As July turns to August, I broach my concerns to Dr Rhys. 'I'd like to take a few days to visit California and check out rehab facilities,' I tell him on an early morning visit to his office. 'It may be Scott's best hope if he's ever to walk again.' The doctor nods sadly. Despite the flurry of press coverage about the lack of options for the brain injured, and the spark of interest it generated in Parliament, there's talk now of even tighter budgets and further cuts in treatment.

'I do understand, Glenys,' he says quietly. 'We've done all we can for him. If you can find better treatment in America, you have my blessing. How much time will you need for the trip?'

'Two weeks.'

Dr Rhys leans forward over his desk and drops his forehead into his hands for a while. Finally looking up, he says, 'When you're ready to go, bring Scott back. We can keep him while you're on a respite leave. The rules allow for that. I'm grieved that we can't do more, but I know you understand.'

With Scott safely tucked into the rehab hospital, I board a direct flight from Heathrow to San Francisco. I haven't much of a plan except to contact old friends and visit hospitals in the Bay Area to determine options and costs. I also wish to look into opportunities for employment, and to find out what sort of day care would be available while I work, in case rehab proves too expensive, or Scott never learns to walk. Alternatively, I think of the volunteers I would need, of starting all over again, and as I gaze out the window into banks of muslin clouds, I find myself deflating into my seat. I'm so tired, mentally and physically, and I am not immune to feelings of discouragement. This will be our last move. It has to be. Neither of us can keep running.

My old friend Tony picks me up. It has been such a long time since we saw each other. The deep love is still there, but not to be ignited. He sees Scott as his youngest child as well as mine. At the thought that we may return to California, Tony is busy making suggestions. We drive an hour south to San Jose where I will stay with our oldest family friends from California and the East Coast, Phil and Sue and their son David. They rush out to meet me. It's been years now, and our hugs and small talk are joyful, but Scott is so obviously absent that there is also a sense of sadness among us all.

As soon as we settle down we are reminiscing about him. Sue reminds us of the period when I and all three of my teenage sons were working together at a restaurant in Connecticut. Scott was the dishwasher, Sammy and Jonathan were sous-chefs with Jonathan doubling as busboy, and I was the waitress. We would all run off to work together after the boys came home from school and I had finished my other job, and we worked the weekends as well. This lasted two years. Even though I was the parent, supposedly in charge of everything, at the restaurant we were colleagues and friends with no difference in status. I turned in the food orders, and sometimes I had to tell them if they were a little slow, but they likewise had to tell me if I was a little slow in picking up the prepared dishes. After closing time we'd all bundle into the car exhausted, but usually smiling or joking, and the boys would count up the tips I had collected, which we would pool. Those days were full of learning experiences and mistakes, laughter, joy, independence and approaching manhood. How lucky we were to have had that opportunity to work together.

Sue and Phil were regulars and they were constantly amused at our antics, and we can't stop laughing as we trade stories about it now. Sue claims the owner told them we were the best crew he'd ever had. David, who was Scott's best friend at the time, tells me how disappointed he was that he never came to work with us. Sue also recounts how she and Scott had set off driving together across the country, and only when they reached California did she learn that he only had his learner's permit. He was like the second son they never had.

The next morning I go through the phone book, calling the area's rehab facilities for information on rates and waiting lists and possibilities for financial assistance, government or otherwise. The Stanford Medical Center gives me further suggestions, and I doggedly make all the follow-up calls. Over the next week I tour a series of hospitals and rehab centres, and then fly south to Los Angeles to visit some facilities there. Back in San Jose I have one more night with Phil and Sue before we are hugging goodbye and I reluctantly head to the international airport. I long to go back to the comfort of old times, when all our children were young, but of course I can't, and I can't even waste my energy wishing for it or reminiscing further.

I board the flight to London with a sheaf of notes in my bag, and use the long hours to digest my trip. Care is available for Scott, and he would be eligible for some financial aid, but only in the short term. Australia, England, America, it's the same old story: a few weeks and then you're out, before the real healing can begin. Long-term care is also available, I found, but at costs beyond my reach. As for jobs, I could always return to waitressing and to selling clothes I've designed and made, and perhaps my art. All in all, I'm reasonably optimistic, and conclude that moving to California is doable. What price will we have to pay? There's one price to be paid if care is available, and another if it is not. But we'll have to give it a try.

Scott returns from rehab and once more we pick up our routine. I tell my volunteers of our long-term plans, of our need to return to a warmer climate and advanced treatment for Scott, that when I've raised sufficient money, we'll set off for California. I doubt it would be before the next summer, I caution, and their help will be needed more than ever until then.

My announcement galvanizes several neighbours and volunteers into fundraising schemes. I receive a series of phone calls with suggestions, some of them far-fetched. The ideas that worked in Sydney, the grand art auction and the blowout flea-market stall, seem out of place in London, but other ambitious ideas do seem quite possible. One of Scott's volunteers, an athletic young man named Rory, offers to raise money by bicycling from John O'Groats right through to Land's End a distance of almost 900 miles. Rory has a personal interest in Scott, as his younger brother was in a terrible car accident and lived brain-damaged for six months before he died. The Body Shop outlet in Wimbledon village hears of his plan, and the company agrees to sponsor the ride, placing jars for Scott's fund in all their stores along the length of the route. As Rory pedals down from the north, he calls in at each local Body Shop to prove he's riding. The spurt of publicity generated in these towns attracts business and helps fill the jars.

Dominique also joins the effort. She walks over to our cottage one morning to announce that she'll soon be running in the local marathon. 'The idea is that I get sponsors to pledge money to Scott,' she explains, 'so I'm running on their behalf but for Scott. I think it's a terrific idea, don't you?' I agree it's first rate, yet I have my doubts. As usual, Dominique is decked out with the latest in summer sportswear, but I can't quite picture her burning up the miles in actual athletic gear. I don't know everything about her, so it's unfair to judge.

Two weeks before the event, Dominique knocks on my door. She's wearing a designer jogging suit, her face is red with a sheen of perspiration, and she's huffing and puffing so hard I'm afraid she'll collapse on the spot. 'My God, this is difficult,' she wheezes.

'I thought you must be a runner,' I say. 'That's why you offered to run the marathon for Scott.'

'Lord knows,' she gasps, 'I've never run a race in my life. I don't even walk, and I'm a smoker!' After drinking some water and regaining her breath, she asks meekly, 'Would you mind terribly if I only run the half marathon?'

I can't keep from laughing. 'Dominique, if you just run around the block I'll be impressed.'

She bears down with fresh determination, giving up smoking and training every day. On the day of the marathon, I wheel Scott to our pavement to watch the runners stream by. Back towards the end is Dominique. She shouts out as she passes and blows us a kiss. She finishes fifth in the half-marathon and donates her purse to Scott's relocation fund, which I place in a special account along with what Rory's collected.

These are only two of the many small events in which our volunteers and neighbours raise money for Scott, but they are the first efforts and I remember them with great fondness. Others are to follow, and one in particular will live with me for ever.

On one warm August afternoon Scott asks me to take him out for a walk. He loves to feel the cool air on his bare feet, and as we're moving along the pavement he asks if I would remove his shoes and socks, which I do. Our spirits are high as we stop near the common to watch a family on horseback trot by towards the open meadows. As I manoeuvre the wheelchair over the kerb to cross the street, Scott stubs his big toe on the pavement. I wipe a little grit off the scratch and think nothing of it, and upon returning home I clean it more thoroughly with peroxide. We go about our daily business. A few days later, as I check on him in the middle of the night, I'm alarmed to discover his body is burning with fever. Dr Rhys has cautioned me that a fever might trigger a serious seizure, and I'm afraid he might be right, but there's little I can do now except try to control the damage.

I begin to wash his face with a cloth and bowl of cold water, and of course I throw off his covers. To my horror, his stubbed foot is swollen, so is his ankle, and it has begun to advance up his leg. By the next morning the leg is huge, twice its normal size. Fearfully I call Dr Rhys and explain the symptoms.

'Get him to the hospital. This minute,' he says curtly. 'I'll meet you there.'

I hug the side wall as doctors rush in and out of Scott's hospital room. His fever is a raging 105°, and his gown is soaked with perspiration. A nurse takes blood for tests, an orderly juggles ice packs to break the fever, a nasal tube is inserted for feeding, an IV is slid into a vein, and machines are hooked up to monitor vital signs. I'm on guard for the first signs of a seizure that everyone but me considers inevitable. Finally, after what seems hours, Dr Rhys enters the room with an open folder in his hands. 'I have the lab results, Glenys. It's not good, I'm afraid.'

Scott has contracted erysipelas – what used to be known as St Anthony's fire – a blood and skin infection brought on probably when he scraped his toe or maybe from something else, and left to rage by a weakened immune system. 'It's hard to know,' Dr Rhys continues. 'In the old days it was usually fatal. We have antibiotics now and normally they'd take care of the problem.' He pauses, and I'm silent too, as we both know Scott is allergic to antibiotics. Now what? What can we do?

The doctor clears his throat and adds quietly, 'Prepare yourself. This could turn very ugly.' He leads me to the bed, turns back the sheets and slides back the gown, revealing Scott's leg. With a finger he traces the faint red line on the inside of the left calf that has been working its way up from the toe, a few inches each day. 'If it gets past the thigh and on to the groin, it will soon work itself into the heart, and then you know what will happen. In the old days,' he continues, 'if the line reached the thigh, the only way to save the patient was to amputate.'

The word sends shockwaves through my body. I want to scream, You can't do that! But I bite my tongue and keep control. 'How much time do we have?' I ask slowly, fearing the answer. Dr Rhys studies Scott's leg. 'My best guess is a day, perhaps more or maybe less, one never really knows. With Scott I'm not sure. He's a fighter, but all the same, Glenys, you'd better be prepared.'

The next days are one long nightmare. I pace through the night and can't sleep when I try. During the day I sit by Scott's side, a solitary figure, silent amidst the flurry of doctors and nurses, and hold his hand. He's sedated and, for a while, I fool myself into believing that he's asleep, that it's almost time for school and he'd better get up. Then I pray and remember all the times Scott's come so close, and how at the very last moment, when all seemed lost, he'd reverse, rally and grow stronger. Will he be saved again, or is this time different? With my heart pounding, I suck in my breath and wait and watch.

The line advances, slowly creeping up his leg like a rising tide upon the beach, and there's nothing I can do. When it gets past his knee, I know I will soon hear from Dr Rhys. When I do, he points to a spot about halfway up the thigh. 'When it reaches here, we're running into trouble.'

I tell him firmly, 'Scott will win this, I know he will. Remember how everyone told me a high fever would trigger another grand mal seizure? Well, it hasn't happened, has it? In spite of his burning up he hasn't had a seizure, and in spite of everything I know he'll beat this red line.' Dr Rhys cannot look me in the eye. He's convinced I'm wrong, but what can he say?

Hold My Hand

For another day I watch the line continue its creep up his thigh. Inexplicably it stops a few inches short of his groin, and in the following days the line slowly fades away. I am triumphant for Scott.

The hustle into his room slows, and now when doctors and nurses enter they do so quietly, to stand at the foot of his bed and shake their heads in wonder. I also stand there in wonder.

What is it about Scott? He must have some special energy reserve that he is somehow able to draw upon as his body reaches its last thread, without the powerful medications that are so common today. He did it in Sydney and he's done it twice in England, with the septicaemia and now this. Not just the comas, but also the infections. What is it that he has – that we all must have – which can do the work of medicine and doctors all by itself? What does he tap into?

I know we're not supposed to know all the answers, but I don't think we've looked for this process in an organized way. There seems to be very little research into what we really draw upon within ourselves, aside from the drugs that may not really make the difference. Is it in the brain? In the spirit? Is it simply our trust that we can make it? And yet it doesn't always work, even with the most positive thinking and greatest love.

I ask myself these questions over and over. What's the miracle of survival? What's the universe telling me? What is this spirit telling me? I have no answers. Perhaps it's not mine to know.

Scott improves rapidly. The nasal feeding tube is removed, as are the wires to the monitoring machines, and finally the IV. I pack Scott's bag and we go home to resume our lives, as if he's had no more than a bad cold and those frightening days were simply a bad dream.

Hold My Hand

As we wheel through our front door, a dozen neighbours and volunteers meet us with cheers and hugs. Our cottage has been festively decorated with red and yellow ribbons and blue and green balloons and I smell hot food in the kitchen. 'Well done, Scott!' they're saying, even though he's still very weak and will require at least two weeks of recuperation. Hugging my dear friends, I can't keep back the tears. Life is one great, wonderful, joyous, magic blur.

Scott and I slip back into our old routine of the gym, the hospital rehab after working hours, and long, lazy wheeling strolls into the village, with Scott's shoes always tied on. Our volunteers return to their crazy schedules, popping in and out, and when Ingrid appears we leave Duncan on duty and run off antiquing.

The Olympic rowers pick Scott up on Fridays and take him to the gym, reappearing two or three hours later with the smell of beer on their breath. I corner the two and demand to know where they've been after the gym, though I already know the answer. They look at each other with devilish grins.

'We stop by the pub to sit on the grass,' Nicholas, the tall one, says innocently. 'Of course it gets a wee bit hot on the grass,' he adds with a shrug, 'so we order a pint or two. No harm's done.'

'There's beer on Scott's breath too,' I scold.

'Scott gets hot too,' Nicholas says with a kidding grin.

'You can't give head-injury patients alcohol,' I say sternly. 'You know that.'

'Just sips, mind you,' Justin answers. 'Just sips.' They're so good-natured, athletic and strong and Scott loves being with them; maybe they're right. What harm's done? What's in a few sips? I can't be so fearful that I push joy and happiness away. Life is for living.

Fifteen

I love to stroll through the autumn woods of the common to buy groceries and have my ritual coffee at Annabel's, even if they're only borrowed moments. One day, as I move deeper into the woods, a shaft of sunlight bathes the narrow path before me and I am swept away by a great sense of inner peace. I know now with finality that taking care of Scott is my life's work. I will have no other. How could I pay someone to care for him, when he's my own flesh and blood? I thought I'd already surrendered to my fate, but I was wrong. Perhaps I'd surrendered in my mind, but not in my soul. Now I know utterly what my destiny is to be, and acceptance flows through my body and calms my spirit.

From the window of the little coffee shop I watch the world churn by on brisk parade, very much at peace with myself. When I return to Scott and my volunteers, I see them in a new light. I'm more patient now, more willing to let life unfold, rather than press for quick miracles and rapid progress. After supper that night, no longer fearful of the future, I light a fire, and as Scott and I lie before the hearth I'm content to just hold his hand in silence and let it be.

Friday evening, as our Olympic rowers and their girlfriends are cleaning up after dinner, Nicholas says, 'I've been noticing how tired you are, Glenys. Why don't you take a little holiday? Go visit your son in Copenhagen? We can sort of move in here and take care of Scott. The girls will help too, won't you?' He throws the girlfriends a wide grin, and I can see this scene wasn't rehearsed in advance. But the girls are soon talking up the idea like it's theirs.

I'm caught totally off guard, but the idea takes root. I've never had an offer like this, but would it work? Scott would certainly be up for it. He loves spending time with the rowers. While they're having an adventure, I could be having one too. 'I've never been to Jonathan and Ulla's new home,' I say cautiously, not in answer, but more to test the idea on myself. After a while I find I still like it. 'Are you sure you can handle everything without me?'

The two young men give me mischievous grins. 'We've taken Scott pub-crawling and he survived,' Nicholas says. 'What could happen? Your doctor's close by and nurse Susan's down the road.'

All of that is true. Perhaps this is doable. 'Of course I'll have to call Jonathan first and arrange dates,' I tell them.

Nicholas tosses his head in dismissal. 'Details, Glenys, details. We're ready when you are.' Details, they say. This would be the first time I've left Scott when he wasn't staying at a rehab hospital, and that's quite a big detail for me.

It is late October when I finally fly out of Heathrow, having informed Dr Rhys and Susan and the Potts and a few other friends, and left many instructions with the rowers. I'm excited about my visit to Jonathan and Ulla, and gratified at my own ability to entrust Scott to others.

I have a marvellous little trip. I love their very Danish apartment with its modern, un-English furniture, and each day brings a new museum, a new market, a new restaurant. I spend hours looking at the sea with its crashing waves. My thoughts are carried back to our days in the Santa Cruz Mountains, and our frequent jaunts to the beach to watch the sunset. This isn't the warm Pacific of course, and these aren't California sunsets, and the sand is stonier, but the seagulls make the same squawks as they ride the air currents and swoop down to pluck some morsel, then up again. Walking on the water's edge feels the same, except the wind is frigid and I can't seem to get warm enough, but I'm loving every minute and I understand fully why Jonathan has chosen marine biology as his life's work. Ulla makes soups and baked potatoes, and we stay up late in the evenings, reminiscing and chatting on the phone with Scott and Sammy. So it is with some regret that I leave for home after five packed days, with last-minute hugs and a promise to see each other at Christmas.

On the plane I detect an itching soreness in the back of my throat. At first I think the aeroplane's dry air is playing games with my sinuses. Then I begin to wonder if I may have picked up a head cold. I make a mental note to take vitamin C and echinacea and some of my other medicinal herbs as soon as I'm home. With that promise, I move on to think about the next week, arranging volunteers and Scott's therapy. When I walk in my front door, I give my four surrogates warm hugs of thanks for their loving ways, then turn to Scott and give him a special hug and a kiss on the cheek. Dinner is already prepared, and the six of us sit cross-legged on the living room floor eating hot soup with bread and jam, swapping stories about our week apart. I drink herbal teas and take a massive dose of vitamin C, just in case I've caught something. I also give Scott several of the vitamin tablets, and move his mattress closer to the fire than usual.

I awake the next morning with a terrible head cold that quickly descends into my chest. As I drink pints of water and herbal teas and take plenty of vitamins, I wonder if I should give in and take some antibiotics. I'm becoming rather worried about Scott, but he has yet to show any symptoms, and I'm praying we'll squeak through. By the fourth day, my cold's at bay, though I'm coughing a lot, and with each hour I grow stronger. Scott continues to show no symptoms and I begin to relax. It's amazing how he seems to survive everything – infections, blood poisoning and raging fevers, conditions that strike down even the healthiest of people. Once again I have to wonder: what is the secret of his immune system?

The next morning I am feeling much better, thankful my cold hasn't been more severe, and that Scott has escaped. Dressing slowly, I descend the stairs from the bathroom and lean over my son on his mattress before the fire, ready for a long cuddle and a morning kiss. One look at him and I'm filled with terror. Scott's face is flushed red and radiates heat like an oven. He's perspiring and his pyjamas are soaked. I immediately call Dr Rhys. 'Get him to St George's without delay,' he instructs. 'I'll meet you there.'

'Of course,' I hear myself say. I know it's the right thing. It has to be done, but I'm frightened of large hospitals, and St George's is one of the biggest in London. Everyone's overworked in these places, in a hurry. People slip through the cracks. But within thirty minutes Scott is wheeled in, Dr Rhys is there, and I'm once again flat against the rear wall of the room while needles are inserted, blood is taken and he's wired to machines.

Dr Rhys is in the hall and I join him. 'Scott has pneumonia,' he says quietly, intent on the medical chart. My worst fear.

'I came back from Copenhagen with a head cold. I didn't have it long; I thought Scott had escaped.'

'I'm afraid your cold went right to his lungs. Lying down as much as he does, he's highly susceptible. You can get up and walk around – all that activity helps drain the lungs – but Scott . . .'

I stay with Scott through ten days while therapists do their work, feeding him oxygen and cough medicine to break the congestion, sitting him up, cupping his back and chest, and raising his arms until his lungs slowly drain. And he begins to recover. The worst is over. 'If all goes well,' Dr Rhys tells me while flipping through the chart, 'we'll be releasing him in a few days.'

Once again Scott's beaten the odds, and I'm over the moon with relief and joy. It's mid-November and instantly I'm knee-deep in planning our second English Christmas. Sammy will come from Westport, Jonathan and Ulla from Copenhagen, and Niall and Scott's other Irish friends from his days in hamburger heaven will be there, not to mention our larger family of neighbours and volunteers. Before Scott got sick I'd already begun working on decorations, food, and ideas for the gifts I will create.

I am given permission to bathe Scott the day before his release. At the end of the ward is a bathtub much larger and deeper than a home-size tub, with a door on the side so Scott can be slid in before the water is run. At home baths are relatively rare, as they require a volunteer strong enough to carry him up the stairs, so this will be a treat. Scott loves them, as they relax his muscles and ease his joints. 'Do you remember, Scott,' I ask quietly, 'when all of you were little, how I used to bathe you together and blow soap bubbles at you through my fingers?'

Scott is floating in his little paradise; I'm running my fingers through his hair, massaging shampoo into his thick curls. His head is back, his eyes are closed, and a serene smile unfolds upon his face. Playfully, I blow bubbles at him. Scott giggles and turns his head, and for a brief moment I'm back in those simple days so long ago they could be in another life.

I call a nurse for help lifting him out, wrap him in a huge, warm, white hospital towel, and put him back to bed. I read him a short story, and with his eyes nearly closed, kiss him goodnight and tiptoe from the room to prepare the cottage for his homecoming. On the way out I ask the doctor on duty if it might be possible during the night to feed Scott through the gastronasal tube, as he's lost weight and could use the added nourishment and energy for the trip home. The doctor agrees, and I continue blissfully on my way home.

My cottage, still heavy with the fragrance of lemon, lavender and eucalyptus, feels large and empty. I sit in the dark living room before the bay window with a cup of warm chocolate between my hands, staring out into a cold and blustery night towards the woods I know are there, thinking about my babies and what Christmas will be like. I fall into a comfortable sleep only to awaken at three a.m. with the urge to go to Scott. I get up and walk around, up and down the stairs. I put music on to quiet myself, but still I'm thinking, 'I have to get to the hospital.' But it's not time yet, so I potter around some more and finally return to bed about five, and lay there unable to shake the thought that Scott needs me.

At seven the phone rings. Half awake, I pick it up. 'Is this Mrs Carl?' It's a man's voice, deep and resonant and very English. My body freezes. I'm back in that apartment in Stuttgart nearly four years ago, penetrated by the formal, impersonal enquiry of a stranger. 'I'm calling about your son.'

I'm choking, unable to breathe.

'Mrs Carl?'

'Yes,' I finally say quietly, knowing, fearing what's to come. 'I'm Doctor Hanson at St George's. I suggest you come immediately. Your son's had a setback, I'm afraid.'

I rush headlong into the hospital, pushing past nurses and through swinging doors, running down long corridors, blind to everything and everyone but Scott. He is under a white sheet, surrounded by grim-looking medical staff, his face a mask of tormented pain. Each sucking gasp for breath comes with the horrible rasping sounds of a drowning man. He cannot speak but he clutches my hand, digging his nails deep into my palm, a silent message for me to do something, to help him.

I'm petrified. 'What's happened?' my mind screams, or is it my mouth? 'Somebody do something!' Soon a hand is on my shoulder and Dr Rhys is pulling me away. A team of physiotherapists descends upon Scott, sitting him up, administering oxygen, thumping on his back and chest, raising his arms in desperation to get him breathing.

In the hall, Dr Rhys's face is ashen, his voice quavering. 'There was a malfunction during the night, Glenys. The gastronasal tube. Instead of his stomach, the liquid went into his lung. By the time it was discovered, around three o'clock, the damage had been done. We're trying to get the liquid out.' The doctor stops talking and inhales deeply. His eyes are moist, and for the first time I see the shadow of fear in his face.

'It's not good, Glenys. His temperature is rising. I'm afraid infection's already set in. We're doing all we can, but after his pneumonia we can only pray.' His voice trails off as he turns his eyes towards the therapists who are making heroic efforts.

I rush down the hallway to be alone and staunch my own tears. I comprehend, but I don't understand. Last night he was ready to come home, ready to live again. How could this be? I feel so small and so powerless.

I find a phone. Jonathan answers, groggy. 'You must come, now. Scott's condition is very serious. Don't wait. And call Sammy, whatever time it is in Westport.'

I rush back to Scott's room to find a team of doctors around his bed. I grab hold of a hand, I don't remember whose, and look up into unknown eyes. 'Please, please do something, anything. He's suffering.'

The doctor shakes his head. 'The only thing we can do is give him morphine.'

'Yes, give him morphine!' I am frantic. 'Anything that will help.'

'Mrs Carl, you need to understand, if we give him enough morphine so he can breathe without pain, he'll probably die.'

I'm stunned. This can't be happening. Oh God, let me wake up. I look over at Scott. His face is contorted, he's gasping and clawing in pain. I can't do this, not to my son. My knees are weak, my strength is ebbing, my legs are turning to liquid.

I search the faces of the doctors. They look back expectantly. What will it be?

'Do something!' I scream. 'Anything! You can't let him suffer like this.'

The doctor springs into action. Scott is quickly moved to a room on a higher floor, with a window overlooking the grey winter city, and hooked up to a morphine pump. Soon his body relaxes, his breathing is less laboured, and his afflicted face softens and turns angelic. I sit by his side throughout the day holding his hand. Jonathan arrives in the evening. I throw myself into his strong arms and break down. 'This time I think Scott's going to die,' I say, my voice cracking with sobs.

Inhaling deeply and clutching his hands, I struggle to swallow my fears and gather strength. 'Did you call Sammy?'

Jonathan nods. 'He's coming as soon as he can.'

'I told them to give him morphine. I couldn't help it.'

Jon nods. 'It was the right thing to do, Mom.'

Sitting on either side of Scott's bed, we maintain our vigil throughout the night. At four in the morning, Margie, a pretty young therapist from the rehab hospital who has been very devoted to Scott, slips quietly into the room. 'I heard about it last night,' she says in a quavering voice. 'I thought I might be able to help.' Distraught, she's ridden her bicycle for miles to be by Scott's side.

Margie, Jonathan and I work for two hours, sitting Scott up, raising his arms, thumping his chest with the heels of our hands, anything to break the fluid loose from the lining of his lungs. But Scott, in a drugged haze, has trouble holding himself up and it's difficult to work with him. 'I'm sorry,' Margie says finally with tears in her eyes, 'but I can't stay any longer; I'm on duty in two hours.' And she slips out into the dawn light to ride back home.

During the morning the organ donation coordinator, a gentle, compassionate woman, comes to see me. When Scott was first admitted to St George's after the fishing trip, I'd indicated his organs would be donated if they could be used. She sits beside me, a sheaf of forms in her hands.

'Are you aware, Mrs Carl, that his organs, if they're to be used, have to be harvested within twenty minutes?' I nod a slight yes. 'We can use the heart valves and kidneys, but if we're to use his heart, he'd have to be put on a respirator and then it would be turned off.'

I shake my head no to this idea. I can't do that, just turn him off like an unwanted light.

'We will use the heart valves and kidneys then.' I begin signing several papers, wherever she points my hand. 'And I believe at one time you had mentioned his eyes.'

I finish scribbling. 'I can't agree to his eyes at this time,' I tell her. 'I have to think about it.'

Jonathan and I gently turn Scott throughout the night, loving him as much as we know how. We rarely speak; our hearts are too heavy. To everyone's surprise, he lives through the night and into the next day. As the word spreads, many people come to say their goodbyes, though Scott is now unconscious. Neighbours and volunteers, nurses, doctors and therapists come. Luther is there, the Potts, Susan with her two daughters, Ingrid and Duncan with their children, Dominique, Wendy, and Constable Riggs. Howard sits by Scott's bed for an hour in silence, his eyes far away. People I love dearly stream in and out, and some I barely know. I'm deeply touched and for ever grateful for their outpouring of compassion and love.

Nicholas and Justin arrive in late afternoon, this time without girlfriends. They sit with me, then shift to Scott's bed, and after a while return to my side. 'You know, Glenys,' Nicholas says quietly, 'tomorrow morning is our rowing competition.'

I turn to meet his eyes. Rowing competition? Through these weeks of crisis, a warp of time, I have forgotten completely. Long planned, with much publicity, it is to be a big affair. Everyone has been invited to watch and cheer. I'd planned to be there along with Scott. Everything's so different now, so jumbled. What should we do? I wonder.

'We've got other teams lined up. King's College School is one of them, and some of our old teammates have pulled together two more shells. Eight in the morning on the Thames. We've all got sponsors.' Nicholas takes my small hand in his and gives it a gentle squeeze. 'When your son pulls through this we'll get him home to America where he belongs.'

I play Scott's favourite music during the night, and Jonathan reads. I crawl into bed with Scott and hold him as I did when he was a little boy, wondering if he knows he's safely in his mother's arms. It is a long night. At seven in the morning, I bolt upright in the bed and immediately start speaking firmly to Jonathan, who is half asleep in a bedside chair. 'When it's ten to eight, I'm going out to wash my face in cold water, then I'll make a phone call and go to the canteen for coffee, and when I come back here, then I want you to do the same.'

At the appointed time, precisely ten to eight, I walk to the bathroom. Slowly, ritualistically, I wash my face in cold water. Then I phone Wendy with an update on Scott's condition, as I promised her I would, and go on to the canteen for coffee. I sit by myself in a corner, numbly thinking of little except to ask myself, Why am I here? What made me leave the room?

I return at ten after eight and tell Jonathan to go get his coffee. He looks at me oddly, in silence, then does as I ask. The donation coordinator comes into the room, asks how I am, and says something about the long night. It is about 8.15 now. I look over at Scott, then back at her, and tell her resolutely: 'Quickly! Find Jonathan and bring him back. Tell him Scott is dying.' I don't know how I know, I just do. I know.

The coordinator leaves and I crawl into bed, wrap my arms

around Scott and lay my face on his head. I hug him close and turn to look out the window into the morning mist. As the cadence of Scott's pulse weakens, I envision ghostly rowing shells on the river Thames, and the boys with their backs bent to the oars, their muted blades rising and falling as they pull, and in my mind, the silent beat of the oars melds with Scott's faint heart until they become one. Jonathan enters and pushes the music on. In her ethereal voice, Enya sings, 'Sail away, sail away, sail away,' and I whisper into Scott's ear, 'Go into the light, my darling,' and he does.

At 8.20 in the morning, at exactly the same minute he was born, a little more than twenty-five years earlier, Scott dies. On the river the oars cease their toil as the shells cross the finish line and silently evaporate.

Unnoticed, a dozen medical staff have gathered against the back wall, some of them obviously crying. Calmly, I lay Scott down, and after kissing him on the forehead I rise to make way for the medical donation team. Tears are streaming down Jonathan's face, though he is quiet, being as brave as he can. I straighten Scott's white gown, then fold back the white sheet. I remove two photographs of him from the wall above his head and pin them to the gown.

When the donation team rushes in with their trolley, I say calmly, 'You'll be gentle with him, won't you?' I point to the photos. 'Tell the surgeon, this is who Scott is.' They let Jonathan and me wheel the trolley from the room and into a lift, and then directly into the operating theatre. I tell the surgeon, 'This is my son; be gentle.'

Scott is returned to us in the little chapel attached to the hospital. He's dressed in a choirboy gown of royal purple with a ruffled Elizabethan-style white collar. His agony has gone now. He's serene, with a warm smile. I sit with him, outside time, until he is collected by the mortician. Jonathan's face is white and strained as we depart for home.

The fire is burning softly and quiet music is playing as we enter the front door. The aroma of hot baked bread drifts from the empty kitchen, and a jar of homemade strawberry jam sits on a china plate next to a dish of butter and a knife. Our neighbours have prepared for our return, then left us to our private thoughts and feelings. Soon an enormous bouquet of flowers is delivered from a young nurse at the rehab hospital. I wonder at first why she is sending flowers when Scott is gone, and then it sinks in that they are for me. It touches and surprises me that everyone is thinking of me, rather than Scott.

I stand before the bay window staring numbly into the shadows of the common with tears rolling down my cheeks. Never again will I push Scott through those trees, never again will I push him into the village for hot chocolate or hear him laugh or enjoy his gentle teasing. I stand there for what must be an hour before turning to Jonathan to tell him I need to go out in nature and just walk.

I disappear into the woods on a long, aimless meander. I think of my childhood in Wales, the birth of my boys, our move to a new world, Detroit, Berkeley, our little house in the redwoods, Los Angeles, Westport, Sydney. I see little Scotty fishing in the reservoir. I see the puppies. I see the broken rowing boat mired in the sands of Carmel. I see Scott so full of life and dreams. Where is he now? I wonder. I picture him running across a field of clouds, pulling a kite with his laughing face turned to the sky, shouting with glee as it takes flight. Wherever he is, I am sure he is joyful and happy. I think of Jonathan back in the cottage by himself and what he might be thinking. He too needs this time alone. Pushing into a clearing,

I find myself before the old cemetery, its ancient mossy trees on guard, and I make a mental note. This is where Scott will be buried.

In the afternoon our mood lightens. The King's College School rowing team comes by, along with Nicholas and Justin, their girlfriends and some of the other rowers. I laugh as they relate their antics during the race. A neighbour drops in with a pot of lentil soup big enough to feed an army. The phone rings with condolences, and I manage to keep my mood light. Maybe Scott is helping me. 'Mom, let's not get too serious now,' he's saying. 'I'm just around the corner. Remember how you used to hold my hand? Well, now I'm holding yours and watching how you're doing. So far maybe a plus two. You've got plenty of room for improvement.' And I smile inwardly.

The hospital donation team calls to let me know that the kidney recipients are doing fine. And they are both women – what a surprise. It was hard for me to let strangers touch him – the surgeon and now I suppose the morticians. Strangers who haven't loved him. And now part of what was Scott is part of the life of strangers.

In bed that night I stare into the dark ceiling and replay the scene in the hospital. What drove me to leave Scott's room? I could have washed my face at the basin in the room. There was coffee there too, and a phone. I wasn't hungry. Why leave? There's a deeper meaning. Scott and I had always been so close, almost like a pair of children, laughing and playing with one another, becoming angry and frustrated, but always laughing again. Perhaps the instinct in me that had sensed his death had also forced me out of the room to break the bond.

The next day Jonathan and I go to pick out a coffin. The lady is very kind but matter-of-fact. 'What sort would you like?'

'Just a simple one,' I say. The lady pushes the catalogue across the desk. 'Just a simple one,' I repeat, without looking down. 'It's not about the box, it's about the person that's in the box.' The lady says nothing. Patiently she awaits our decision. Jonathan and I look at each other, thinking the same thing. I ask, 'Can we make our own?'

'No. You need a permit, and have to obtain it before the person dies.'

My usual stubborn self presses on. 'Can my son here carve on the coffin?'

'No.'

We pick a simple design and rise to leave. 'There's a flower shop next door. Would you like to order flowers?'

'No,' I answer quickly, jumping up in protest. 'I hate those chopped-off flower heads stuck together. Flowers. We'll find our own.'

We return home in a turbulent sea of emotion, one moment laughing at all the craziness of the past, the next sombre under the weight of the present. I'm yearning to touch Scott one more time. We go to meet Sammy at Heathrow and bring him home. I'm sad that he missed seeing his brother alive. He looks pale and frail, and I worry about him. Ulla also arrives. I make the arrangements for a funeral service the following Wednesday afternoon at a beautiful old church in Wimbledon, St Mary's. Robin, the headmaster, will conduct the service.

On Wednesday morning we go to the funeral home to ready Scott. I cut a lock from his thick curly hair and ask that he be dressed in his favourite 'Save the Rainforest' T-shirt. I slip his brown teddy bear, from the flea market in Sydney, into the coffin. I hug him and touch his face. It is cold and I feel empty. Then Jonathan and Ulla arrive to say their goodbyes. When Sammy arrives, he produces a book of old coins that he and Scott collected together as boys, and places it inside the coffin. As we depart for the church, Sammy decides to stay while they seal the coffin, and he even rides in the hearse to the church. There I cover Scott's coffin with nature's art: holly branches and blackberry brambles from the common interwoven with other wild plants, baby's breath and other fresh flowers collected from my neighbours' gardens. Amazingly, even in November, each garden yielded some blooms; red, yellow or white. We go home.

As we pull up before St Mary's for the service we are met by hundreds of people, even a few who have flown in from Sydney. Richard, one of our volunteers there, is originally a Londoner and has brought forward his visit to his mother so he can attend the funeral. I am astounded. Colin, my costume design partner, and Howard, the international lawyer, officiate as we gather, and Siobhan plays her flute. Robin conducts the service, which is positive, uplifting and suffused with music.

Some of the boys from King's College School read from Corinthians: 'We are nothing without love,' I remember one of them saying.

Many people – volunteers and old friends – stand to speak of how being part of Scott's life has changed their own lives in some way. Some tell of becoming more open and accepting of strangers, others say they came to understand the meaning of unreserved love. A childhood friend from California says, 'It's hard to measure one man's influence on another, but I like to think that the very moral fibre of which I'm made was in part shaped by the influence and guidance of Scott.'

Howard reads: 'Never did you seek pity or patronage. Fighting to the last, with your one-armed hugs, was more than I can describe. Mine was but one of many lives enriched by getting to know you. You died as you lived, with a smile.'

And Jonathan, at the close of the service, says, 'Is his work done? Has mine just begun? Who was the teacher, and who was the student? Who was the healer and who the healed? If we've been helped, let us move on to help the next.'

Parts of the soundtrack from *The Mission* have been playing in the background, just as they were when Scott was in his comas, and I can't help but feel his presence. I have not lost a son, I've been given a gift of boundless love, happiness and joy. Scott lit up my world and brought out my best. He enriched my life, as he did for so many his spirit touched, and I find no sorrow or grief in that gift.

I stand at the church door hugging all who file out. The boys of King's College School, nurses and therapists from the rehab hospital and St George's, Wendy and Susan and Dr Rhys, many dear friends, many volunteers, and many others I meet for the first time.

We bury Scott in the common, in Putney Heath Cemetery near a corner of the wrought iron fence. It is here, after the short graveside service, as I watch my sons, Scott's brothers, bear the coffin and help lower it into the earth, that my heart almost breaks. Sammy plants a sapling at Scott's feet and we drive home through the cold afternoon, silent and stricken, the truth of loss etched in our hearts.

We are a grieving family that night, but also a family ready to go into the future. Ulla stays up late embroidering a piece of linen with Scott's name and dates of birth and death, with a tree in the corner, that I later have framed. In the morning Sammy and Jonathan purchase a slab of oak for a headstone. They carve Scott's name and dates on it, and a row of falling leaves along one edge.

The day after the funeral I spend curled up on my bed, left alone by my friends to grieve. But that afternoon the phone rings; it is an unfamiliar voice, the estate agent who rented us the cottage. He has had some people who are interested in looking at the house – three different parties in fact.

Hanging up, I walk to the bay window and look out at the common. How very strange. I've lived here for a year and a half, and not once was our cottage shown to a prospective buyer. I'd almost forgotten it was for sale.

Two days later, after we place the oak slab at Scott's grave, Sammy, Jonathan and Ulla leave for home, and after nearly four years I am utterly alone. There is nothing I need to do, nowhere to go, and I spend a few days curled in my own cocoon, not even going out for walks.

As I sit looking into the fir trees one morning, I decide that since Christmas is coming I should go out. I wrap up warmly and walk to the bus stop, but when I arrive I don't know which bus to get on. It's a strange and disorienting feeling to be free. Do I want to go to a movie? To the Victoria and Albert Museum? Covent Garden? I haven't a clue. It's as if I don't know what to do with this empty time. I turn about and walk through the common, passing Scott's grave, and let myself into the empty house. I can't begin to decide where to go, so home is the answer. I put on music and make hot chocolate and sit in front of the fire once again, staring into the gas flame.

That night brings my first heavy sleep in what feels like ages. When I awake, Thumper is standing on his rear legs with his front paws on the covers, looking up at me. I reach over and scruff his neck. 'Such a funny little rabbit. I know what you're thinking,' I whisper to him. 'You're wondering where Scott is, aren't you? He's in a wonderful place full of laughter and he's doing just fine. You don't need to worry, little bunny, Scott's doing just fine.'

Sixteen

One week after Scott's death the cottage is almost sold. I had been looking forward to staying here by the common, near Scott's grave. But perhaps it is time to move on. Miraculously, the very next day I hear from my old friend Bob in Los Angeles, whom I had last seen when I was there to investigate rehab facilities. He told me then that he was building a second house, where he would live in five years or so. It is in Santa Fe, in the state of New Mexico, about a thousand miles from California. I've heard that Santa Fe is a good place to live, but I don't really know anything about it. The house is finished now, Bob says, and he needs someone to live in it, and he wonders if I'm ready for a change now that Scott has passed away.

Ready for a change? I have no alternative. In a few weeks I will have to leave my home. Santa Fe is in the desert, not what I've ever imagined for myself. But fate seems to have intervened, to be sweeping me off in an unknown direction. My tentative yes to Bob's offer instantly becomes a firm plan, and once again I am turning into a gypsy, preparing my mind and spirit to fly off to a strange place in another land.

Five weeks later Thumper has been taken in by Susan and the cottage is nearly empty. The night before my departure, I put music on and lie down on the bed, the last remaining piece of furniture.

As I sleep fitfully, my mind is full of memories, trying to reach some better understanding of all that has happened over the past few years. I feel torn in two. One part of me wants nothing more than to remain right here where I can visit Scott's grave often, to hold still and not do anything in particular. The other part of me knows that Scott would surely want me to go on with my life, and he has left me such a legacy that I owe it to his memory, and to all the people who have helped us, to go forth in the world. In any case the wheels have been set in motion and I am indeed leaving this nest, my community, the common, England, and all the friends who have been so important to Scott's life and mine.

Several neighbours drop by in the morning to say goodbye. I love them all, and I also feel a numbness which must be covering my sadness, for now. The weather fits my mood, a dull, cloudy, January day. Sue drives me to Heathrow airport and I watch the city through the window. We go from laughing at some of the memories to the pain of losing Scott and my now being on my own on my journey. When I reach the check-in counter, alone, and actually see my bags placed on the conveyor belt, it hits me. I am really going. Where, I don't really know. But I do know that it is a land that embraced me once before, when I arrived two decades earlier with my little children, and this brings a measure of comfort. I spend the time before my flight wandering through the gift shops, just looking and, I suppose, saying a farewell to Britain as represented by the symbols and souvenirs, those toy double-decker buses and Royal Family tea-towels.

I settle into my window seat for the twelve-hour flight to Los Angeles, where I will pick up a shorter flight to Albuquerque. As the hours pass I look out at the clouds or the sea and take a few naps.

I am weighed down with an exhausting sadness, and yet part of me manages to sift through the happy times. For the first time I start to feel some excitement about my future. I've heard that Santa Fe has a lot of art and culture, and that it is a place of healing. How appropriate. Again I marvel at how destiny always seems to serve me.

At the Albuquerque airport, clutching the sheet with Bob's directions and an envelope containing a key, I ask a taxi driver if he can take me where the map points. It is sixty-five miles, he tells me, more than an hour's drive, and he will need the return fare as well, but I have no energy to deal with public transport. I have the presence of mind to stop at a grocery store in Santa Fe, which is fortunate because I soon learn that my new home is ten miles out of town, the last five miles on a dusty, unpaved mountain road. The driver grows dubious, for there are no signs at all as we advance further and further along the road, raising a moving cloud of dust that hovers behind the car. All we can do is follow Bob's map, go so many miles and turn, another mile and turn. With half a mile to go, I see a house on top of a hill that looks like an old Spanish colonial mission. There is no other building in sight. 'Well, that looks much too big for a house,' I say to the driver. 'But it seems to be where the map is pointing.' And it is.

The taxi drives off and I look up at the imposing two-storey house, which is unlike any building I have seen before. It has very thick walls, coated with tan stucco and somehow not perfectly flat, the corners not quite sharp. Beneath the flat roof, where an English house would have eaves, are rows of projecting beams that are really just stripped logs. There is a large balcony on the upper floor and some unfinished brick patios below. The soil is sandy and dry, a slightly reddish tan, with unfamiliar wild plants and no garden, as the builders have just left. Around the lot runs a stuccoed wall a few feet high, and there is nothing else in sight but trees and hills and sky. It is a typical winter afternoon in the high desert: the sky deep and cloudless, intensely blue and bright, the sharp heat of the sunshine tempered by the coldness of a faint, shifting breeze.

The house looks bare yet somehow inviting, its adobe bricks of mud and straw at one with the environment. As I stand before this vacant house in the middle of empty desert hills, I realize that my roots, my world, are entirely within myself.

I carry my suitcases and groceries to the door and let myself into a large two-storey hall. I have one overpowering impression: This is a house of light! Sun is streaming through the skylights and the windows, even though it is the middle of winter, casting shadows on the tile floor and stark white walls. The high ceiling is supported by log beams, with hundreds of sticks filling the spaces between them in a herringbone pattern.

The first thing is to make myself some toast and a cup of hot chocolate, but in order to do so I have to climb up on the blue-and-white tiled counter so I can reach the dishes in the cupboard. I laugh to myself, wondering if everybody in this part of the world is a full foot taller than my five foot two. The snack leaves me weary, but I can't resist the impulse to investigate my new world. The house is surrounded by piñon trees and a few junipers, which are smaller than the trees I'm used to. The starkness and vastness of the landscape are impressive and inspiring.

I find myself wondering, where are the Indians I've heard so much about? Santa Fe is within a few miles of several reservations, and there are some twenty of them within a couple of hours' drive. I have heard some of these groups are the descendants of the vanished Anasazi civilization that left the famous cliff ruins. I stare out all around, half expecting an Indian to suddenly appear on a horse, but no such luck: that is the stuff of childhood games.

I put my head on the pillow of the brand new bed and take a nap. Then I wander through my new house of light with nothing to do, marvelling at the handcrafted walls that sometimes undulate into a rounded bench or a corner fireplace. Though the house is mostly just full of space, it has all I need: a bed, a kitchen with fine dishes and appliances (but no table), a working phone with several extensions, and a music system with speakers in every room. There are fireplaces everywhere, though I have no wood. Every window has a view that is nothing short of spectacular, towards mountains in the middle or far distance, or the evening lights of a faraway town, or the gorgeous sunset. I can see the whole world, 360 degrees. The temperature is dropping quickly. I rummage for scarf, sweater and hat; I want to go outside.

When night falls I walk out the French doors onto the patio and gaze in wonder at the coal-black sky. I am carrying the lock of Scott's hair, all I have left of him to touch. I clutch it to my heart and find myself screaming into the night.

'They don't even know my name! Nobody in this place knows me!'

Tears run down my face as I stand on the bricks. I look up at the stars, crisper and brighter than I've ever known, so numerous they paint a twinkling white swath from rim to rim, so close I feel I could scoop them from the sky and fill a basket. Somewhere up there I know Scott is looking down with a smile.

'You are gone,' I cry inwardly. 'Where are you? Will we ever meet again?'

'I'm watching you, Mom,' I can almost hear him say with a teasing voice. 'You're not doing badly at all. Full marks, I'd say.'

I feel as if there's a string attached to my heart, tugging me . . . and yet at the other end there is no one there. My pain is immense but still I understand I must go forward, alone now but ready to carry on, to work, to love, to live. I play Scott's favourite song, 'What a Wonderful World' by Louis Armstrong and my mind goes back to what I would be doing if I were still in London, then switches to now. I know no one within a thousand miles and yet I know I am going to be all right. How could I have been given this wonderful gift of a house on top of a hill and not be all right? I don't know how I am going to pull it off, but then I never have.

Epilogue

I made my first friend in Santa Fe at the flea market. A woman
stopped me and asked where the coat I was wearing had been
purchased. It was a knee-length coat of Scottish wool with Celtic
symbols, which I had woven myself. She introduced herself as
Pamela and said she'd like to buy it, and the six more I had at home.
She asked me if they could be delivered and I told her I had recently
arrived in Santa Fe and had no car. 'Then how,' she asked, 'are you
going to carry the wooden table that I've just seen you purchase?'
Telling her I didn't know yet, but that maybe a taxi would be called,
I explained that I had walked and hitchhiked to reach the market.
She took me home and wrote me a cheque on the spot that was
sufficient to buy a second-hand car.

Everything in its time. I'd been wondering why I had decided at
the last minute to bring the coats in their heavy extra suitcase to
America. Pamela was especially drawn to the coats because of the
symbols that adorned them, wanting to wear them at the various
ceremonies she was involved in for the solstice and the equinox. We
are special friends to this day.

A few days later while sitting in the coffee shop a woman sitting
near me heard me speak to the waitress. She asked about my accent

and whether I was a visitor. I told her I lived here though I had been born and brought up in Great Britain.

'I thought so,' she said. 'We're opening a hospice centre here based on the British method. Do you know about hospices?'

'Oh yes,' I answered. 'It is a much-needed programme.' Then becoming very quiet, she asked what my occupation was, to which I replied that I was not working at the moment.

'Oh, you're a lucky one,' she said.

Deciding I'd better clarify this I said, 'I'm looking for a job, but I haven't worked for almost four years.' After I had told her a little of my story she stopped me and asked if I wanted a job – would I be prepared to take the state examination for a hospice nurse certification? It turned out that Julie was the nursing director for the programme.

My time with Scott had of course been perfect training, both medical and psychological, and the state officials took it into account when awarding my certification. I started working two weeks later.

During my time as a hospice nurse I have worked with AIDS patients, cancer patients and others, elderly, middle-aged, and young adults, always caring for them in their homes. I firmly believe that people should be able to die with dignity in their own abode, with the comfort of familiar surroundings and close to their loved ones.

Caring for the dying has brought me great rewards. I enjoy the intimacy created between the patient and myself – in one's last weeks of life there is no time for anything but honesty. Often we become confidants. As I began to work I found that while I was focusing my attention on patients, my memories of Scott were not so constantly present. Even though there was much sadness again, usually there was also the balance of laughter. Hospice care helps patients to surrender and not be afraid of the unknown, to be at peace with themselves and live every day to its fullest.

My continuing hospice work took me into the homes of Spanish families that had been here for centuries, first- and second-generation Mexican immigrants, Native Americans who had spent part of their lives on the reservation, and people from other places who had come here to live or to die because it is known as a place of healing and spiritual power.

I was rapidly forming close friendships and loving so much about this little city. Santa Fe is eclectic, artistic, brimming with alternative therapies and schools, and with culture – opera, theatre, music, plenty of good art, artists and writers. So many of the people in Santa Fe are open and accepting of each other. I think part of the reason is that many choose to live here for the community, not because of industry.

Treasuring my solitary time at the house, I fell further and further in love with the powerful clarity and beauty of the desert and was in awe of the bright skies and sunsets. As summer came I felt alive again, sometimes dancing by myself on the patio, even singing out loud to the mountains. I slowly planted a garden, learning about plants that do well in the desert: Russian blue sage, lavender, hollyhocks, geraniums, Russian olive trees. At the top of the hill I made a circle of stones and dead branches and in the centre placed a small statue of the Chinese goddess of compassion. Looking out across the mountains I spent many hours there feeling at peace with the world. At times during my six years in the house I placed in this circle the ashes of several of my patients who had no one else to tend to them.

One evening at an art opening a woman approached me and

insisted that she knew me. I was sure she was wrong as I have a good memory for faces, but her Australian accent was quite recognizable and I told her I had lived in Sydney. 'That's it!' she said. 'You're the woman from the television programme! Watching what you were doing with your son I went and took my own son out of a nursing home. He had brain injuries, too. I brought him home and had the happiest year of my life with him before he died. Thank you so much.' It was very moving to know that my message had actually helped her get back in touch with her son and given her the confidence to look after him herself.

That year my first grandchildren were born. Sammy's daughter Meghan arrived on 14 March. Sammy was overjoyed with his sweet little daughter, but mixed with his happiness was a little sadness that Scott was not there to see her. We had many long conversations about Scott, as I knew Sammy had so much wanted to visit Scott more often but the expense of the journey, and the fact that his job did not allow him much time off, made it impossible. He felt guilty, although I told him that his phone conversations and letters were an ever-present reminder to Scott that he was loved. I also reminded him that the times he did come were very special. When he looked into Meghan's eyes, I told him, 'Remember, in a way she is a gift from Scott.' He is still healing to this day.

Jonathan and Ulla's first child, Louise, was born one year to the minute after Scott's death, at 8.20 on the morning of 20 November. Such a little being! As I held her, my heart felt full. Another gift from Scott. Their second child, Oscar Scott, entered the world four years later.

I didn't have anywhere to go for my first Christmas in Santa Fe, and neither did my good friend Melissa. We were sitting in a coffee shop called Downtown Subscription on Christmas Eve when she said, 'Well, you like to cook, Glenys. Let's have a big Christmas dinner. You have the house for it.' So we decided to mill through the morning crowd and sure enough a lot of our friends were available for Christmas dinner. I told them I would roast a turkey and try my hand at South-western cuisine then gave everyone a map to the house. Laughing as we left, I quickly had to find a store open that had a turkey available as the shops were soon to close. I rushed around like a mad lady, throwing things into my shopping basket, all kinds of fruits, vegetables, candles, stuffing, Spanish spices, green chilli and ingredients for my all-time favourite Christmas desert – Welsh Trifle with lots and lots of cream. I quickly put everything in the car and said goodbye to Melissa.

Driving home I saw a few remaining Christmas trees in a parking lot soon to be closing. Though the tree I picked had all the branches on one side, I took it home, set it up and made a cardboard placard saying: 'This tree whispered, "Take me home, Take me home" and I did.' I didn't have any decorations so if anyone turned up I planned to put them to work making decorations using old twigs and what-not. I stayed up half the night cooking and baking muslin bows as Scott and I had done two Christmas Eves before.

Thirty-five people showed up! People had told their friends and they all found their way up the icy road, many with food in hand. Of course most of us didn't know each other very well if at all, but as will happen in Santa Fe, our impromptu festivities turned into a bonding for almost everyone. The ones who got the most out of making the Christmas decorations were the men. We put the decorations all over the house, then we shared poems and music. I had asked each person to bring a poem or a piece of music to play, either on my new piano or on the stereo.

My life after all these years is very full. After Bob returned to his house it was time for me to move to the hustle and bustle of the town. I still work as a hospice nurse, dance in a free-movement dance group twice a week, do my art and designs. Sammy, who now works as a fireman, moved with his family to Santa Fe a few years after I arrived and I see my granddaughter often. I have a wonderful man in my life.

I know the universe has blessed me, filling up my heart and life with so much richness and warmth. I know that somewhere out there, near the end of the string that runs from my heart, Scott, my greatest blessing, who has taught me so much of what I know of life and love and compassion, is giving us all full marks.